S0-AAE-609

Computer Accounting Essentials Using QuickBooks Online Edition

Third Edition

Carol Yacht, MA
Software Consultant

Susan V. Crosson, MS
Professor of Accounting
Santa Fe Community College

Gibbs College Farmington, CT

Boston Burr Ridge, IL Dubuque, IA Madison, WI New York San Francisco St. Louis
Bangkok Bogotá Caracas Kuala Lumpur Lisbon London Madrid Mexico City
Milan Montreal New Delhi Santiago Seoul Singapore Sydney Taipei Toronto

The McGraw-Hill Companies

About the Authors

Carol Yacht is a textbook author and accounting educator. Carol contributes regularly to professional journals and is the author of Great Plains, Peachtree, QuickBooks, and Excel textbooks and Carol Yacht's General Ledger and Peachtree CD-ROMs (www.mhhe.com/yacht). In 1978, Carol started using accounting software in her classes at institutions including California State University, Los Angeles; West Los Angeles College; Yavapai College; and Beverly Hills High School.

Carol Yacht is the 2005-2006 Chair of the American Accounting Association's Two-Year College section and recipient of its Lifetime Achievement Award. She has worked for IBM Corporation as an education instruction specialist, and served on the Computer Education Task Force for the National Business Education Association. Carol is a frequent speaker at state, regional, and national conventions. Carol earned her MA degree from California State University, Los Angeles; BS degree from the University of New Mexico, and AS degree from Temple University.

Susan V. Crosson is Coordinator and Professor of Accounting at Santa Fe Community College in Gainesville, FL. She previously taught on the faculties of University of Florida, Washington University in St. Louis, University of Oklahoma, Johnson County Community College, and Kansas City Kansas Community College. Susan teaches financial and managerial accounting courses and speaks and writes on the effective use of pedagogy and technology in accounting courses. Susan is co-author of several accounting textbooks and the Computer Accounting Essentials series.

Susan has received the Florida Association of Community Colleges Professor of the Year Award for Instructional Excellence and University of Oklahoma's Halliburton Education Award for Excellence as well as the Two-Year College Educator Award from the American Accounting Association. Susan received her Master of Science in Accounting from Texas Tech University and her undergraduate degree in accounting and economics from Southern Methodist University. She is a CPA and serves on AICPA's Pre-certification Education Executive Committee. Susan also has served as the American Accounting Association's Vice President of Sections and Regions and as Chair of the Accounting Careers and Members in Education committee for the Florida Institute of CPAs.

COMPUTER ACCOUNTING ESSENTIALS USING QUICKBOOKS®
Carol Yacht, M.A. and Susan V. Crosson, M.S.

Published by McGraw-Hill/Irwin, a business unit of The McGraw-Hill Companies, Inc., 1221 Avenue of the Americas, New York, NY 10020. Copyright © 2007 by The McGraw-Hill Companies, Inc. All rights reserved.

No part of this publication may be reproduced or distributed in any form or by any means, or stored in a database or retrieval system, without the prior written consent of The McGraw-Hill Companies, Inc., including, but not limited to, in any network or other electronic storage or transmission, or broadcast for distance learning.

1 2 3 4 5 6 7 8 9 0 QPD/QPD 0 9 8 7 6
ISBN-13: 978-0-07-313112-2
ISBN-10: 0-07-313112-1

Editorial director: *Stewart Mattson*
Senior sponsoring editor: *Steve Schuetz*
Editorial assistant: *Megan McFarlane*
Lead project manager: *Pat Frederickson*
Production supervisor: *Debra R. Sylvester*
Designer: *Cara David*
Executive marketing manager: *Rhonda Seelinger*
Senior media producer: *Victor Chiu*
Lead media project manager: *Cathy L. Tepper*

www.mhhe.com

Preface

Computer Accounting Essentials Using QuickBooks Online Edition teaches you how to use the Internet-based accounting program QuickBooks Online Edition. In this book, you will sign up for a free trial of QuickBooks Online Edition. Then, you will start a service business from scratch and enter all the business transactions for the service business. The activities will take about 25 hours to complete. Try to set aside those 25 hours within the free trial period. If you decide to extend QuickBooks Online Edition beyond the free trial, there is a monthly subscription fee (at time of printing, $19.95/month).

QuickBooks Online Edition is designed for straightforward service-based businesses with broadband connections. Up to 3 users plus your accountant can use it. Add-on packages can be purchased separately for payroll, business, or sales or you can subscribe to an enhanced version, Online Edition PLUS that includes these additional packages for a higher monthly subscription fee (at time of printing $39.95/month).

Browser Requirements

If you can access QuickBooks Online Edition's website at http://oe.quickbooks.com you already have what is needed – a computer, a browser, and a modem. QuickBooks Online Edition is an operating system that works with Windows 98, XP. or 2000. Mac OS is not supported. Continuous high-speed Internet access using DSL, cable modem, or T1 is recommended. QuickBooks Online Edition does work using any Internet access, although processing time can be slow. It prefers the browser version 6 or higher of Internet Explorer® on Windows.[1]

[1] For more system requirement details, access the link to QuickBooks Online Edition's home page at oe.quickbooks.com

Computer Accounting Essentials Using QuickBooks Online Edition has six chapters:

1. Accessing QuickBooks Online Edition
2. New Company Setup
3. Setting Accounting Defaults
4. Fourth-Quarter Transactions
5. End-of-Year & Beginning-of-Year Transactions
6. Advanced Features

Each Chapter of *Computer Accounting Essentials Using QuickBooks Online Edition* includes:

- Software objectives
- Web objectives
- Step-by-step instructions with screen captures
- Transactions and reports
- Check your progress
- Flashcard review
- Internet homework
- Multiple-choice
- True/false
- Exercises

In *Computer Accounting Essentials Using QuickBooks Online Edition* you learn how to set up a service business. When you finish this book, you will have a working familiarity with QuickBooks Online Edition, a web-based accounting program.

Chapter 1: Accessing QuickBooks Online Edition

In Chapter 1, you will access QuickBooks Online Edition software from the Internet. The step-by-step interview shows you how to do that.

Chapter 2: New Company Setup

In Chapter 2, you will learn how to use the software to set up a service business. New Company Setup includes selecting a chart of accounts, entering opening balances, and printing a beginning balance sheet.

Chapter 3: Setting Accounting Defaults

In Chapter 3, you learn how to set defaults for accounts payable, accounts receivable, and cash transactions that follow in Chapter 4. Defaults are information or commands that the software automatically uses. You also learn how to change default settings.

Chapter 4: Fourth-Quarter Transactions

In Chapter 4, you record transactions for the fourth quarter of the year: October, November and December. You will record accounts payable, accounts receivable, and cash transactions. At the end of each month's transactions, you will reconcile the bank statement.

Chapter 5: End-of-Year & Beginning-of-Year Transactions

In Chapter 5, you will complete end-of-year adjusting entries, print financial statements, and make closing entries. Chapter 5 also includes transactions for the start of the new year – January 1 - 31, 20XX.

Chapter 6: Advanced Features

In Chapter 6, you learn how to memorize forms, customize forms, copy data to Microsoft Excel and create graphs, and print your activity log.

Case Problem 1

Case Problem 1 includes two more months of transactions for your service business – February and March. You will complete the accounting cycle for the first quarter and print reports.

Case Problem 2

Case Problem 2 includes the end-of-quarter transactions for the first quarter. You will complete the accounting cycle for the first quarter and print reports.

Case Problem 3

Case Problem 3 is a student-designed project. You are instructed to write transactions for the next month and complete the accounting cycle showing a net loss for your business.

Glossary: Terms that are boldfaced and italicized through the book appear here.

Index: The introduction and each Chapter of the book ends with an index. The index at the end of the book is an alphabetic listing of these individual indexes.

Table of Contents

Preface iii

Introduction 1

Introduction Index 3

Chapter 1: Accessing QuickBooks Online Edition 5

Software Objectives 5
Web Objectives 5
Computer Accounting Essentials Website 5
Getting Started 6
QuickBooks Online Edition Log Out and Log In 12
Explore QuickBooks Online Edition Website 13
Logging in 13
Check Your Progress 14
Flashcard Review 14
Internet Homework 15
Multiple-Choice 15
True/False 17
Exercise 1-1 18
Chapter 1 Index 19

Chapter 2: New Company Setup 21

Software Objectives 21
Web Objectives 21
Computer Accounting Essentials Website 21
Logging in to QuickBooks Online Edition 22
Getting Started 24
Setting up the Cash Account 28
Revising the Chart of Accounts 31
Deleting an Account 31
Adding an Account 33
Changing an Account Name 36
Beginning Balance Sheet 37

Help Screens 40
Displaying the Balance Sheet 40
Copying Report Data to Excel 42
Logging out of QuickBooks Online Edition 44
Check Your Progress 45
Flashcard Review 45
Internet Homework 45
Multiple-Choice 46
True/False 48
Exercise 2-1 49
Exercise 2-2 49
Chapter 2 Index 50

Chapter 3: Setting Accounting Defaults 51

Software Objectives 51
Web Objectives 51
Computer Accounting Essentials Website 51
Getting Started 52
Customer Overview 53
Set Preferences for Customer Charges 53
Set Preferences for Customer Statements 55
Set Preferences for Entering Transactions 55
Set up Customers 56
Set up Products & Services 59
Vendor Overview 61
Set Preferences for Entering Transactions 62
Set up Vendors 63
Displaying the Balance Sheet 65
Check Your Progress 67
Flashcard Review 67
Internet Homework 67
Multiple-Choice 68
True/False 70
Exercise 3-1 71
Exercise 3-2 71
Exercise 3-3 71
Exercise 3-4 72
Chapter 3 Index 73

Chapter 4: Fourth-Quarter Transactions 75

Software Objectives 75
Web Objectives 75
Computer Accounting Essentials Website 75
Getting Started 76
Vendor Transactions: Enter Bills 77
Purchases of Supplies: Enter Bills 78
Purchase Returns: Enter Vendor Credits 81
Vendor Payments: Pay Bills 83
Customer Transactions: Create Invoice 86
Sales Returns and Allowances: Give Credit or Refund 90
Displaying the Accounts Receivable Register 92
Receipts from Customers: Receive Customer Payments 93
Cash Transactions 96
Cash Sales: Enter Sales Receipts 96
Cash Payments: Write Checks 98
Reconcile the Bank Statement: October 100
Printing October's Reconciliation Report 103
Printing Transaction List by Day: October 103
Printing October's Trial Balance 105
Editing October 31 Trial Balance 106
Printing October's Income Statement 107
Printing October's Balance Sheet 108
November Transactions 110
Reconcile the Bank Statement: November 111
November's Reconcile Screen 113
Printing November Reports 113
November Transaction List by Day 114
November Trial Balance 115
November Income Statement 116
November Balance Sheet 117
December Transactions 118
Reconcile the Bank Statement: December 120
December's Reconcile Screen 121
Printing December Reports 122
December's Transaction List by Day 123
December's Trial Balance 124
October 1 through December 31, 20XX Income Statement 125
December's Balance Sheet 126
Check Your Progress 127

Flashcard Review ... 127
Internet Homework ... 127
Multiple-Choice ... 128
True/False ... 131
Exercise 4-1 ... 132
Exercise 4-2 ... 132
Chapter 4 Index ... 133

Chapter 5: End-of-Year & Beginning-of-Year Transactions ... 135

Software Objectives ... 135
Web Objectives ... 135
Computer Accounting Essentials Website ... 135
Getting Started ... 136
End-of-Year Adjusting Entries ... 137
Printing the Adjusted Trial Balance ... 140
Printing End-of-Year Financial Statements ... 141
Income Statement ... 141
Balance Sheet ... 142
End-of-Year Closing Entries ... 143
Transaction List by Day Report ... 144
Post-Closing Trial Balance ... 145
Beginning-of-Year Transactions ... 146
Reconcile the Bank Statement: January ... 148
January's Reconcile Screen ... 149
Printing January Reports ... 150
January's Transaction List ... 151
January's Trial Balance ... 152
January's Income Statement ... 153
January's Balance Sheet ... 154
Check Your Progress ... 155
Flashcard Review ... 155
Internet Homework ... 155
Multiple-Choice ... 156
True/False ... 158
Exercise 5-1 ... 159
Exercise 5-2 ... 159
Chapter 5 Index ... 160

Chapter 6: Advanced Features 161

Software Objectives 161
Web Objectives 161
Computer Accounting Essentials Website 161
Getting Started 162
Memorizing Reports 163
Customizing Reports 163
Customizing Options: Display and Date 164
Customizing Options: Filters 166
Copying Report Text to a Spreadsheet Program 167
Customizing Graphs 168
Customization 171
Activity Log 171
Check Your Progress 172
Flashcard Review 172
Internet Homework 172
Multiple-Choice 174
True/False 177
Exercise 6-1 178
Exercise 6-2 178
Exercise 6-3 179
Chapter 6 Index 180

Case Problem 1: Complete First Quarter Transactions 181

Case Problem 2: End-of-Quarter Adjusting Entries and Reports 189

Case Problem 3: Student-Designed Project 193

Glossary 195

Index 199

TIMETABLE FOR COMPLETION		Hours
Chapter 1	Accessing QuickBooks: Online Edition	1.0
Chapter 2	New Company Setup	1.5
Chapter 3	Setting Accounting Defaults	3.0
Chapter 4	Fourth-Quarter Transactions	6.0
Chapter 5	End-of-Year & Beginning-of-Year Transactions	4.0
Chapter 6	Advanced Features	2.0
Case Problem 1	Complete First Quarter Transactions	2.5
Case Problem 2	End-of-Quarter Adjusting Entries and Reports	1.5
Case Problem 3	Student-Designed Project	2.0
Final Exam		1.5
	TOTAL HOURS	25.0

Text and screen variations may occur since web-based software products backup and upgrade automatically.

Introduction

Computer Accounting Essentials Using QuickBooks Online Edition teaches you how to use QuickBooks Online Edition, a popular online accounting package for small business. From any computer connected to the ***Internet*** QuickBooks Online Edition users can work on their business's finances anytime, anywhere. Owners, employees, financial advisors, and accountants can work simultaneously in different locations.

To use QuickBooks Online Edition, you need a connection to the Internet and a ***browser***. A browser is the software used on a computer to connect and display information from a Web site called a server. Commonly used web browsers are Internet Explorer® and Mozilla Firefox®.

The Internet is the worldwide electronic communication network that allows for the sharing of information. The Internet is also called the World Wide Web (WWW) or Web.

QuickBooks Online Edition works on computers with Windows 98, XP, or 2000. An IBM-compatible 1GHz computer with 256MB RAM is recommended. Mac OS is not supported. It uses the browser version 6 or above of Internet Explorer® for an Internet connection to QuickBooks Online Edition and a high-speed Internet connection is recommended. Screen resolution minimum is 800x600 and Adobe Reader 4.0 or higher is required for printing forms (free download available). Exporting to Excel requires Excel 97 or later. Active X component is also required (free download available).

To make an Internet connection, your computer must be equipped with a ***modem***. The word modem is an abbreviation of **Mo**dulator/**Dem**odulator. A modem is a device that allows you to connect to an ***Internet Service Provider*** (ISP). ISPs can be companies such as America OnLine™ (AOL), Earthlink™, or local providers. If telephone lines are used to make this connection (not recommended), your connection will be very slow since most telephone lines were designed for voice communication not electronic data from a computer.

Faster connections to the Internet are possible using *an* ***Integrated Services Digital Network*** (ISDN) or leased lines. An ISDN line is a digital network that provides faster transmission of voice, video, and text. Leased lines, referred to as T-1 and T-3, are available for faster connections, too. The backbone of the Internet consists of T-3 lines. Leased lines are expensive and used by companies that need to transfer massive amounts of data.

Faster Internet connections are also offered via cable, wireless radio modems, and satellite TV. A digital subscriber line (DSL) is another way to access the Internet faster. DSL lines are always connected to the Internet (are always *on*) so there is no need to dial up. Continuous high-speed Internet access using DSL, cable modem, or T1 is recommended when using QuickBooks Online Edition.

In the next section, Accessing QuickBooks Online Edition, you will learn how to go to QuickBooks Online Edition's website at oe.quickbooks.com. You will also start using QuickBooks Online Edition to record business transactions.

INDEX

browser 1
Integrated Services Digital Network..2
Internet...1, 2
Internet Service Provider...1
modem..1, 2

1 Accessing QuickBooks Online Edition

In Chapter 1 of *Computer Accounting Essentials Using QuickBooks Online Edition*, you will set up the QuickBooks Online Edition software on the Internet. The step-by-step instructions that follow show you how to do this.

SOFTWARE OBJECTIVES: In Chapter 1, you use the software to:

1. Start QuickBooks Online Edition.
2. Sign up for free 30-day trial version of QuickBooks Online Edition.
3. Name your company after yourself.
4. Select "Miscellaneous services" as the company type.
5. Assign a password.
6. Confirm signup information.
7. Complete activities for Chapter 1, Accessing QuickBooks Online Edition.

WEB OBJECTIVES: In Chapter 1, you use the Internet to:

1. Access the Computer Accounting Essentials website at www.mhhe.com/yachtessentials3e to check for updates.
2. Access QuickBooks Online Edition's website at http://oe.quickbooks.com.
3. Access QuickBooks Online Edition's 30-day free trial version.
4. Log in to your QuickBooks Online Edition account.
5. Receive an email from QuickBooks.
6. Log off from QuickBooks Online Edition.
7. Complete Flashcard review.
8. Complete Internet homework.

COMPUTER ACCOUNTING ESSENTIALS WEBSITE

Before you begin your work in Chapter 1, Accessing QuickBooks Online Edition, check the Computer Accounting Essentials website at www.mhhe.com/yachtessentials3e. Select the QuickBooks link, and then link to Text Updates. Check this website regularly for reference and study.

GETTING STARTED

Follow these steps to access QuickBooks Online Edition.

1. Start your Internet browser. You need Version 6 or higher of Microsoft Internet Explorer for an Internet connection to QuickBooks Online Edition.

> **Comment:**
> Internet Explorer, Version 6 was used for the screen illustrations shown in *Computer Accounting Essentials using QuickBooks Online Edition.*

2. Type http://oe.quickbooks.com in the "Address" box of your browser, then click on "Go." The "QuickBooks Online Edition" screen appears.

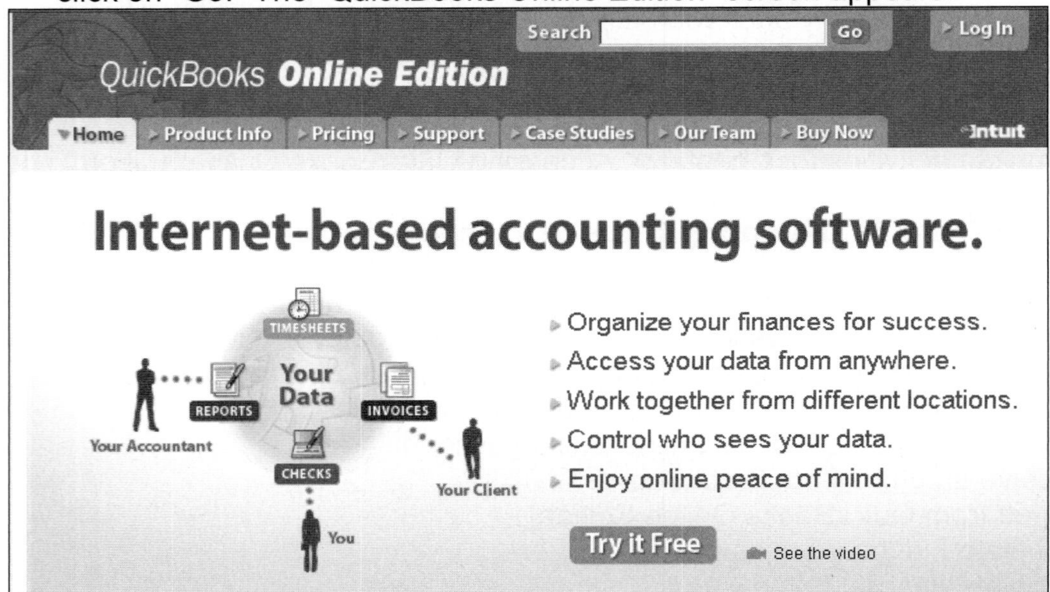

3. Set up the 30-day Free Trial Version of QuickBooks Online Edition.

   a. The "QuickBooks Online Edition" home page should be displayed. If not, go to http://oe.quickbooks.com.

   b. Click on Try it Free.

   c. Link to Start your free trial

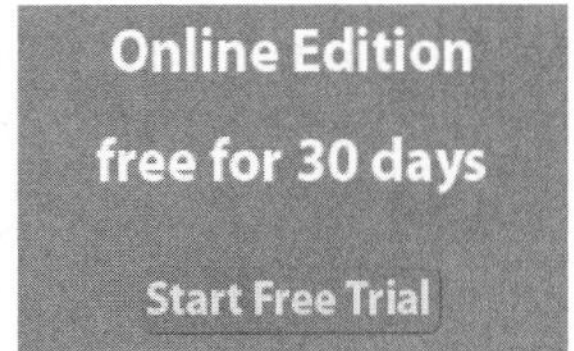

d. Select the "Start Free Trial" link for the Online Edition.

e. The "QuickBooks Online Edition Startup Interview" screen appears. Instructions for completing this form are shown on the next page.

1. **What is your name?**
   First Name Last Name
2. **What is your email address?**
   Please enter the address where you want to receive email from us about your QuickBooks Online company.
   Privacy Options
3. **What would you like your login name to be?**
   You must have a unique login name. It should be at least four characters long. Case doesn't matter (for example: AB=ab).
4. **What would you like your password to be?**
   Passwords must be between 6-32 characters.
   Please verify your password by entering it again.

   I want to add extra password protection

> **Comment**
> Some interview question variation may exist between this text and the interview you complete since QuickBooks continuously upgrades its software to better serve its users.

f. Follow the directions to answer the following questions. (Press the <Tab> key between fields.)

1. **What is your name?** Type your first and last name.

2. **Enter an email address to receive your password confirmation.** Type your email address; type your email address again. *Write your email address on the line below.*

   ____

3. **What would you like your login name to be?** (*Your email address shows up in this box. It is okay to use your email address as your login name.* If necessary, type your 6-32 character name.

   Write your Login Name here:

   ____

4. **What would you like your password to be?** Type a 6-32 character password that contains letters or numbers but no spaces.

Write your password here:

Type *exactly* the same password again.

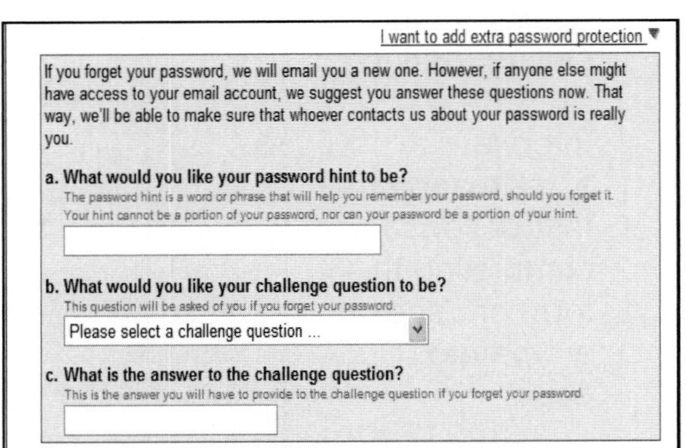

5. **Click on "I want to add extra password protection."**

   a. A screen appears asking, **What would you like your password hint to be?**

   Type a password hint that will be asked if you forget your password.

   Write your password hint here:

   b. **What would you like your challenge question to be?** Select a challenge question that will be asked if you forget your password.

   Write your challenge question here:

   c. **What is the answer to the challenge question?** Type the answer to your challenge question.

   Write your answer here:

   g. In the next section, you will use the following information to complete the New Company Setup Interview.

   Company name: Your first and last name Service Corporation
   Business address and phone: Your address and phone
   Business email: Your email
   Type of business: Miscellaneous, All Other Miscellaneous Services

Role you play: Owner/Partner/CEO
People who give you money: Customers
Start from another version of QuickBooks: No
Create accounts based on industry: Yes

Follow these directions carefully because your responses will be used in other parts of setting up your company.

1. **What type of business do you have? Please select an industry:** In the menu scroll to **"Miscellaneous services"** and then select "**All Other Miscellaneous Services**."

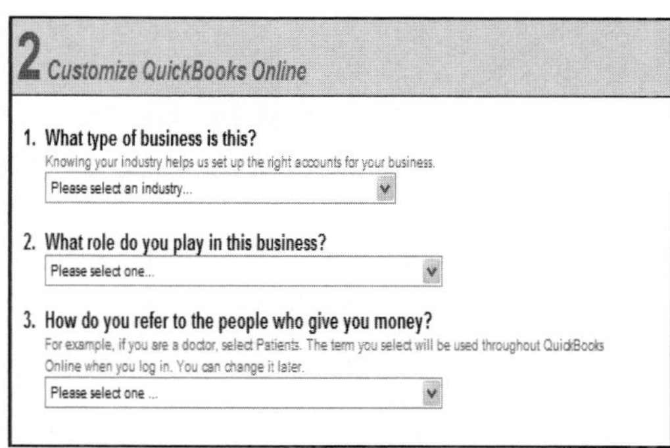

2. **Please select the role you play in the business:** From the menu, select "**Owner/Partner/CEO**."

3. **What does your business call the people who give you money?** Select "**Customers**."

h. In the section 3, you will complete information on the "Import Data" form. Follow these directions carefully.

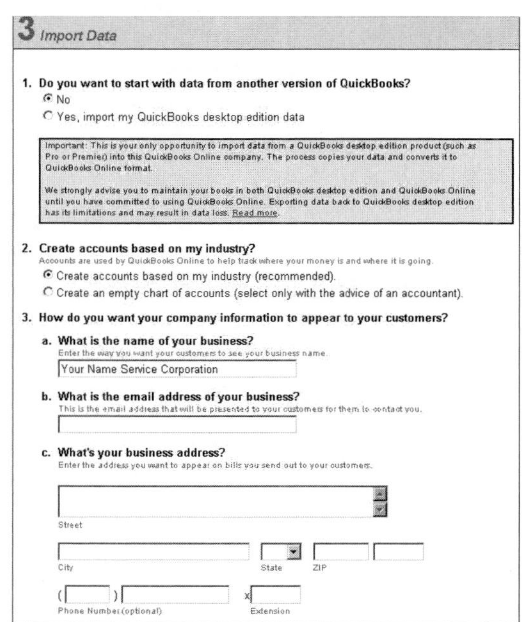

1. **Do you want to start with data from another version of QuickBooks?** Select "**No**."

2. **Create accounts based on my industry?** Select "**Create accounts based on my industry (recommended)**."

3. How do you want your company information to appear to your customers?

   a. **What is the name of your business?** Type **Your first and last name Service Corporation**; for example, Susan Crosson Service Corporation (use your first and last name). In this book Your Name Service Corporation will be used for the company name. ***You should use your first and last name so that report printouts have your name on them.***

   b. **What is the email address of your business?** If necessary, type your email address again.

   c. **What's your business address?** Type your address; type your city; select your state; type your Zip code; type your phone number [optional].

i. In the section 4, you will complete information on the "Finish Setup" form. Follow these directions carefully.

1. **Do you accept the terms of service?** After reading the "User Agreement", select "**I accept**."

2. **Privacy Statement:** View "Intuit's Privacy Statement."

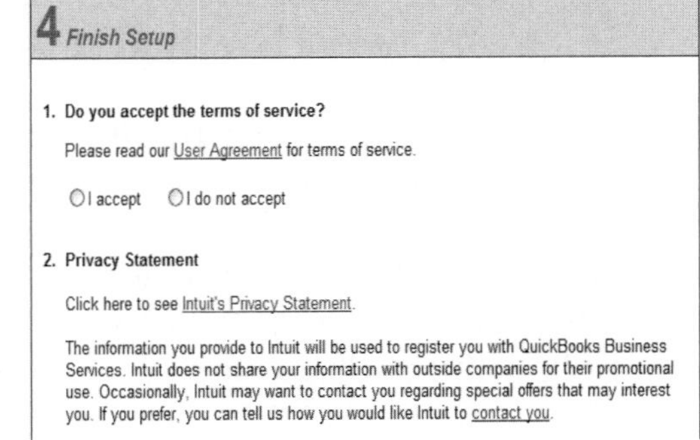

3. Close "Intuit's Privacy Statement" and click on "contact you."

4. The "Intuit Privacy Settings –Web Page Dialog" opens. After reading contact preferences, make your selection and then click "OK."

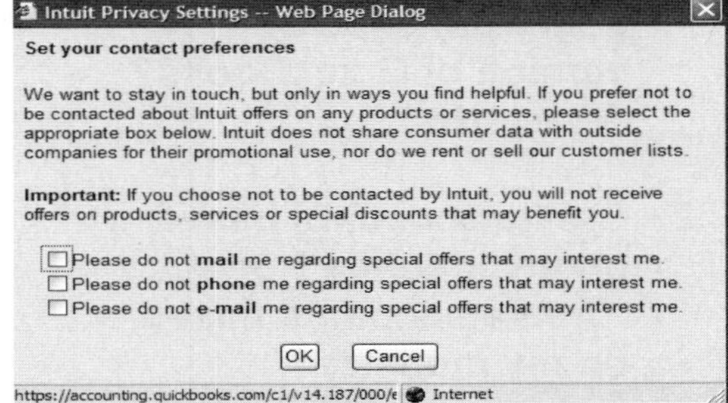

5. **Optional: Where did you hear about QuickBooks Online Edition?**
   Select "**Other**." Leave "Referral Code" blank.

j. Click on Create Company. Click on Start Free Trial... . Click on "Continue."

> **Comment**
> The information you have entered will not be saved until you click the "Start Free Trial..." button.

> **Comment**
> If an "ActiveX Description—Web Page Dialog" box pops up, click on "Continue." Then, when the "Security Warning" screen pops up, click on "Yes." (You may need to install ActiveX.) Continue with step 4.

4. The "QuickBooks Financial Software Online Edition" home screen appears. Your business "Welcome" screen is shown. You can log back on to QB Online Edition from any Internet connection, which means you can continue your work anytime and anywhere.[1]

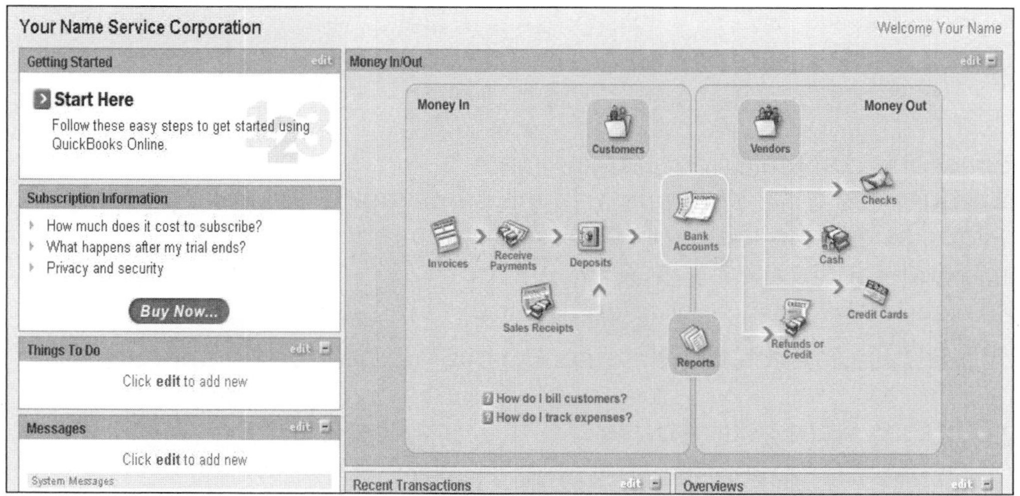

[1]You will receive an email from the QuickBooks Online Edition Team confirming your account information. When you check your email, you can read this message. Additional information about how to log in, adding users, startup checklist, and getting help is included in this email.

LOGGING OUT OF QUICKBOOKS ONLINE EDITION

To log out of QuickBooks Online Edition, proceed with the following steps.

1. To log off, click on the logout button on the top right of your screen.

2. You could exit at this point or continue. Since the instructions that follow assume you are logging back in, do not close your browser at this time.

LOGGING IN TO QUICKBOOKS ONLINE EDITION: If you did *not* exit your browser

A screen similar to the one shown below should be displayed.

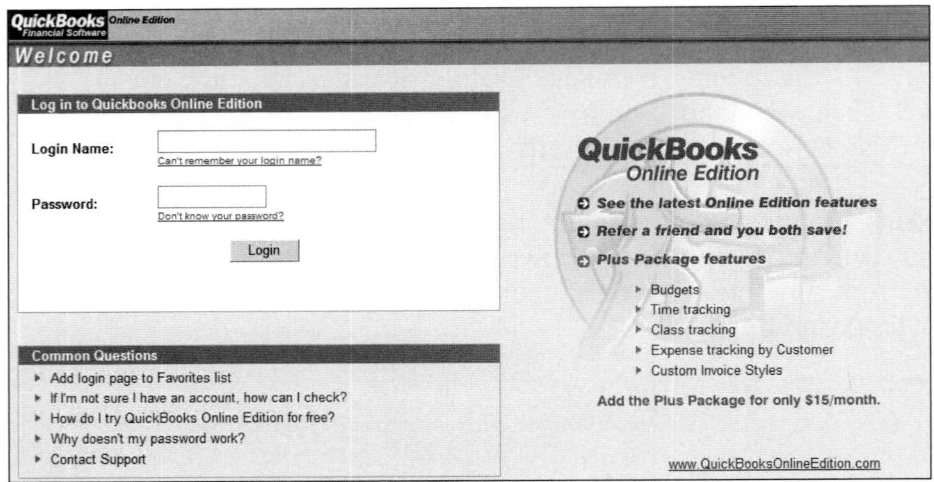

1. If necessary, complete your "Login Name."
2. Type your password. You *must* use the same login name and password that you assigned in the QuickBooks Online Interview, steps **3** (login name) and **4** (password), page 7.
3. Click Login. After a few moments your "Home" screen appears.
4. Log out, then close your browser.

EXPLORE QUICKBOOKS ONLINE EDITION'S WEBSITE

1. Go to http://oe.quickbooks.com. The "QuickBooks Online Edition" screen appears.
2. Click on the Pricing link. The "Pricing" screen appears. Read the information on this screen. Compare the information about QuickBooks Online and QuickBooks Online Plus.
3. Click on the Product Info link. The "Product Info" screen appears.
   a. From the left-side menu, click on the Features link. Scroll down the screen to review QuickBooks Online Edition features.
   b. If necessary, scroll up the screen. Then, click on the Compare link. The "Compare" screen appears. Scroll down the chart to see a comparison with other QuickBooks products.
   c. If necessary, scroll up the screen. Click on the Security link. The "Security You Can Trust" screen appears. Read the information on this screen.
   d. If necessary, scroll up the screen. Click on the For Your Business link. The "For Your Business" screen appears. Read the information on this screen.
4. From the top toolbar, click on the Support link. The "Support" screen appears. Read the information on this screen. ***This option is not available to students using this text.***

> **IMPORTANT!** Student use of the 30 day free trial DOES NOT include support. **DO NOT contact QuickBooks with questions!**

5. Return to the "Home page" by clicking on the Home link.

LOGGING IN TO QUICKBOOKS ONLINE EDITION: If you logged out completely and closed your browser, follow these steps.

1. Check your email. You should have an email from serviceconsulting@quickbooks.com. Read the email.

2. The subject of your email from QuickBooks is "Log in Now to QuickBooks Online Edition!" In the How to Log in section of the email there is a link to your account. Your login name is also shown.

3. Using Internet Explorer, link to the website shown in the email. As of this writing, it was https://accounting.quickbooks.com. That takes you to the QuickBooks Online Edition Welcome page. Your Login name is shown.
4. Type in your password, then click Login. You business's Home page appears.

CHECK YOUR PROGRESS

Flashcard Review

Based on what you learned in this chapter prepare step-by-step instructions on flashcards for the following tasks. Flashcard templates are available on the text website:

1. Logging out of QuickBooks Online Edition.
2. Logging in to QuickBooks Online Edition.

Flashcard Example: Completing the Startup Interview.

> **Completing the QuickBooks: Online Edition Startup Interview**
>
> Using Internet Explorer, go to http://oe.quickbooks.com and select 30 day free trial.
>
> Step 1: Enter your name, email address, login name, and password. Click on extra password protection and complete password hint and challenge question.
>
> Step 2: Customize QuickBooks Online-complete
>
> Step 3: Import Data-complete
>
> Step 4: Finish Setup-complete
>
> Start Free Trial. Your company's "QuickBooks Financial Software Online Edition" home screen appears. Begin using QuickBooks from any Internet connection in the world.

Internet Homework

1. If you are already logged in, you do not have to start QuickBooks Online Edition again. If necessary, go to http://oe.quickbooks.com. The "QuickBooks Online Edition" screen appears.

   a. Click on the ▸ Product Info link. The "Product Info" screen appears. Scroll down the screen to review QuickBooks Online Edition features.

   b. If necessary, scroll up the screen. Then, click on the Compare link. The "Compare" screen appears. Scroll down the chart to see a comparison with other QuickBooks products.

2. For QuickBooks Online Edition and one other QuickBooks product, write a 50 to 75-word essay describing each of the product's' features and compare the two products to each other. Include the web address of each of the products. Use a word-processing program to type your reports. *Hint:* Spell check your report before turning it in.

Multiple-Choice: In the space provided, write the letter that best answers each question.

_____1. To use QuickBooks Online Edition, you need to use the following browser:

a. Version 6 or higher of Microsoft Internet Explorer.
b. Mozilla Firefox.
c. Microsoft Office.
d. None of the above.
e. All of the above.

_____2. To start QuickBooks Online Edition, you type the following web address.

a. www.microsoft.com
b. www.yahoo.com
c. www.QuickBooks.net
d. www.peachtree.com
e. None of the above.

______3. From QuickBooks Online Edition's home page, you can do the following:

a. Sign up.
b. Log in.
c. Select links.
d. Learn more about QuickBooks Online Edition.
e. All of the above.

______4. The software that you accessed is called:

a. QuickBooks Online Edition.
b. QuickBooks Online Edition Business.
c. QuickBooks Online Edition Personal.
d. QuickBooks Online Edition Checking.
e. None of the above.

______5. When QuickBooks Online Edition is accessed, the following icon appears on your screen.

a. Hourglass.
b. Hand.
c. Arrow.
d. I-bar.
e. None of the above.

______6. How long can you use QuickBooks Online Edition for free:

a. 10 days.
b. 20 days.
c. 30 days.
d. 40 days.
e. None of the above.

_____7. You set up the following type of business with QuickBooks Online Edition:

a. General.
b. Manufacturing.
c. Service.
d. Retail.
e. None of the above.

_____8. In order to make changes to your startup interview, you use:

a. Submit.
b. Back.
c. Basic.
d. Log off.
e. None of the above.

_____9. After signing up for QuickBooks Online Edition, you receive:

a. Instructions displayed on your screen.
b. An email from QuickBooks Online Edition.
c. An Authentication code from QuickBooks.
d. Both a. and b. are true.
e. None of the above.

_____10. After signing up for QuickBooks Online Edition, you need to use the following to log in:

a. Login name and password.
b. Authentication code.
c. Email address.
d. Name and address.
e. None of the above.

True/False: Write T for True and F for false in the space provided.

_____11. You access QuickBooks Online Edition software from the Internet.

____12. You use Outlook Express to access QuickBooks Online Edition.

____13. The web address for QuickBooks Online Edition is http://oe.quickbooks.com

____14. The software that you access is called QuickBooks Online Edition Household.

____15. When signing up for QuickBooks Online Edition you identify a challenge question and answer.

____16. The trial version of QuickBooks Online Edition will last for two months.

____17. When assigning a name for your business, use the same name as everyone else.

____18. You must use your login name and password each time you start QuickBooks Online Edition.

____19. A browser is the software used on a computer to connect to the Internet.

____20. Any internet browser can be used to access QuickBooks.

Exercise 1-1. QuickBooks Online Edition keeps a log of your activities while using the software. To print your "Activity Log," complete the following steps:

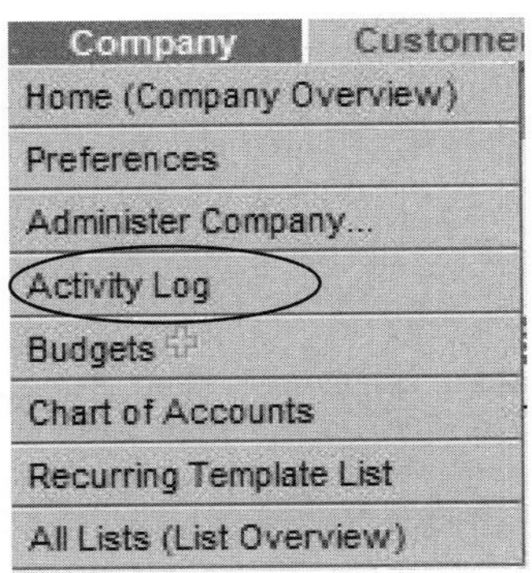

1. On your Company home page, move your mouse over "Company" on the QuickBooks Online Edition menu bar. When the drop-down menu appears, click on "Activity Log."
2. When the activity log appears, notice it displays the date, time, user, and activity while on your company site.
3. Click on the Print... to print your "Activity Log."
4. Click on logout to exit QuickBooks Online Edition.
5. Exit your browser.

CHAPTER 1 INDEX

Check your progress 14
Computer accounting essentials website 5
Flashcard review 14
Getting started.. 6
Internet homework.. 15
Log in 12, 13
Log out 12
oe.quickbooks.com.. 5
Software objectives 5
Web objectives.. 5

2 New Company Setup

In Chapter 2 of *Computer Accounting Essentials Using QuickBooks Online Edition,* you will learn how to use the software to set up your business. New Company Setup includes selecting preferences, a chart of accounts, entering opening balances for your business, and printing a beginning balance sheet.

SOFTWARE OBJECTIVES: In Chapter 2, you use the software to:

1. Set company preferences.
2. Enter October as the first fiscal month for your business.
3. Revise the chart of accounts for your business.
4. Enter beginning balances from the October 1, 20XX balance sheet.
5. Use QuickBooks Online Edition's help screens.
6. Copy a QuickBooks Online Edition report into Microsoft Excel.
7. Use external media to back up report data.
8. Complete activities for Chapter 2, New Company Setup.

WEB OBJECTIVES: In Chapter 2, you use the Internet to:

1. Access the Computer Accounting Essentials website at www.mhhe.com/yachtessentials3e to check for updates.
2. Log in to your QuickBooks Online Edition account.
3. Enter your login name and password.
4. Navigate the software.
5. Complete Flashcard Review.
6. Complete Internet activities.

COMPUTER ACCOUNTING ESSENTIALS WEBSITE

Before you begin your work in Chapter 2, New Company Setup, access the Computer Accounting Essentials web site at www.mhhe.com/yachtessentials3e. Select the QuickBooks link, and then link to Text Updates. Check this web site regularly for reference and study.

LOGGING IN TO QUICKBOOKS ONLINE EDITION

Follow these steps to log in. You must have completed Chapter 1, Accessing QuickBooks Online Edition before starting Chapter 2, New Company Setup.

1. If necessary, start your Internet browser.

2. There are two ways to go to QuickBooks Online Edition's home page:

   a. Type http://oe.quickbooks.com in the "Address" box of your browser, then click on "Go."

   b. Click on the down arrow in the Address field. Select http://oe.quickbooks.com from the drop-down list.

3. Click on "Log In."

4. The "Welcome" screen appears.

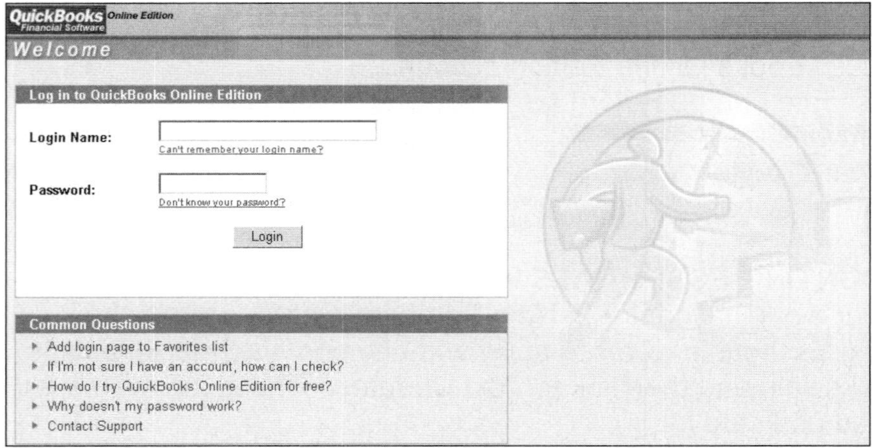

Complete the "Login Name" and "Password" fields. You *must* use the same login name and password that you assigned on page 7 in the QuickBooks Online interview, steps **3** and **4**.

5. Click on Login. After a few moments your "Home" screen appears. Read the "Comment" box below, then continue with the next section, "Getting Started."

Comment
When I log in, I get a "Security Warning" screen. What should I do?

QuickBooks Online Edition updates the software on a regular basis. Each time you log on you are using the current version of the software. If you try to log on and a screen similar to the one shown below appears, follow these steps.

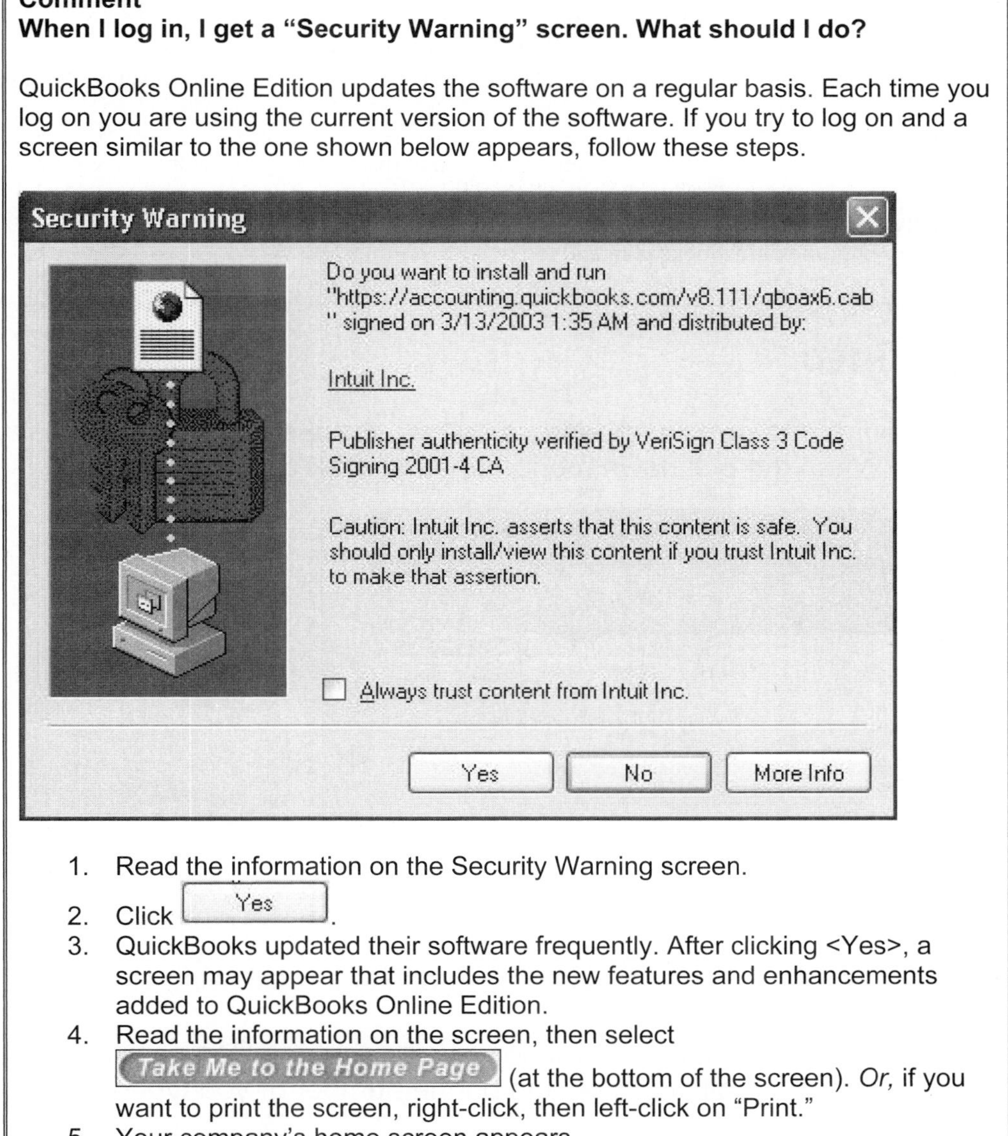

1. Read the information on the Security Warning screen.
2. Click Yes.
3. QuickBooks updated their software frequently. After clicking <Yes>, a screen may appear that includes the new features and enhancements added to QuickBooks Online Edition.
4. Read the information on the screen, then select Take Me to the Home Page (at the bottom of the screen). *Or,* if you want to print the screen, right-click, then left-click on "Print."
5. Your company's home screen appears.

If a Security Warning pops up, you should check the Text Updates link on the book's website to see if there are recent changes to the book or software.

READ ME
I can't remember my password. What should I do?

1. Log in to QuickBooks Online Edition (http://oe.quickbooks.com).
2. If necessary, enter your Login Name.
3. To reset your password, click on the link that says <u>Don't know your password?</u>
4. Answer the security question. Then, choose a new password and retype it. When through, click OK.
5. Now go to your email inbox and retrieve the email that QuickBooks sent to you. Link to QuickBooks Online Edition from the link within this email. The new password is activated.
6. Go to http://oe.quickbooks.com and log in with your new password.

GETTING STARTED

1. When your home screen appears, move your mouse over the Company toolbar. When the pull down menu appears, click on "Preferences."

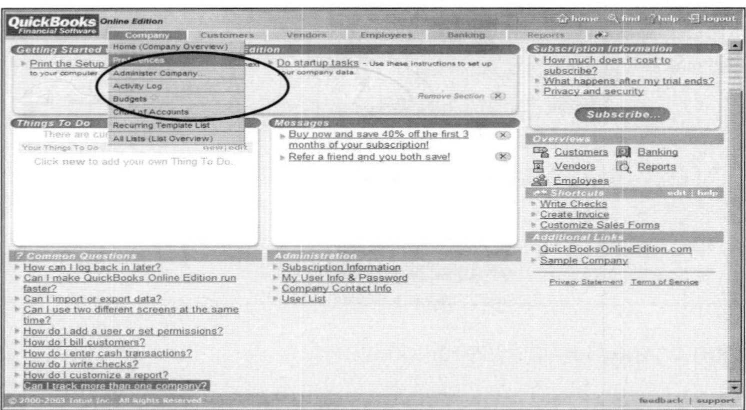

When the "Preferences" screen appears, complete the following steps:

- Company Contact Information: Verify that the Company name, address, email address, and phone number (if you typed a phone number) are correct.
- Company:
    i. Employee identification number (EIN). Leave this box blank.

ii. First month of fiscal year: Use pull down arrow to select "October" as the first month of fiscal year.

iii. First month of income tax year: Click on the radio button next to "January" as the first month of your income tax year. Compare your screen to the one shown below.

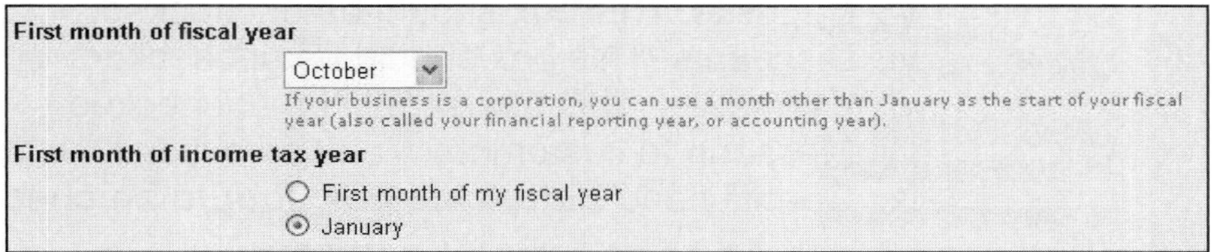

iv. Tax form: Verify that the radio button next to "One or more shareholders. A corporation filing Tax Form 1120." is selected.

v. Closing the books: Leave this box blank.

vi. Account numbers. This box should be unchecked.

vii. Terminology for Customer: Verify that "Customers" is selected.

viii. Email alerts. Leave this box blank.

ix. Automatically apply credits. **Box must be unchecked.**

x. Enable auto recall: Verify that the box is checked.

xi. Read Restart setup interviews. Take no action.

- Categories

  i. Read income and expense accounts. Take no action.

  ii. Read Expense accounts. Take no action.

  iii. Products and services (for income accounts): This box should be checked.

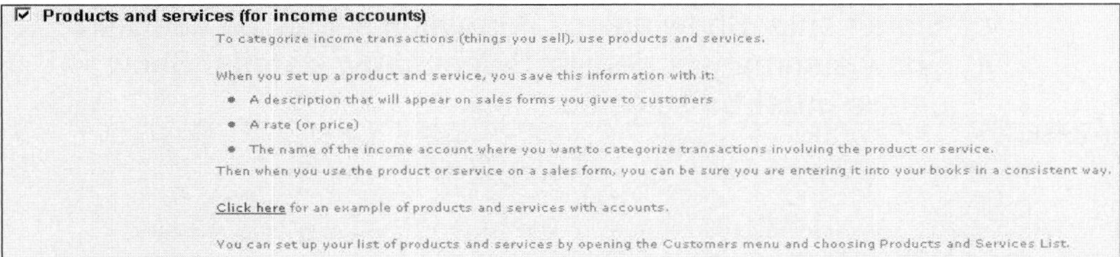

  iv. Location tracking. This box should be unchecked.

  v. Read Class tracking. Take no action.

- Sales Form Entry

i. Custom Fields. Take no action.
ii. Custom transaction numbers. Take no action.
iii. Delayed charges. Take no action.
iv. Read Custom fields. Take no action.
v. Deposits. This box should be unchecked.
vi. Discounts. This box should be unchecked.
vii. Estimates. This box should be unchecked.
viii. Message to customers. Take no action.
ix. Quantity and Rate. **This box should be checked.**

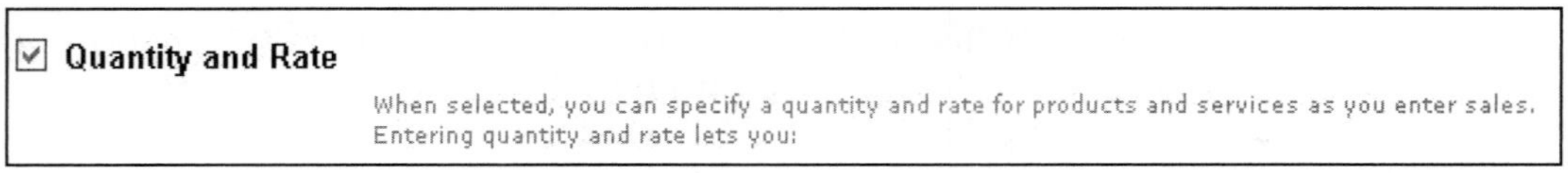

☑ **Quantity and Rate**

When selected, you can specify a quantity and rate for products and services as you enter sales. Entering quantity and rate lets you:

x. Sales Tax. This box should be unchecked.
xi. Service Dates. This box should be unchecked.
xii. Shipping. This box should be unchecked.
xiii. Terms. Verify that the "Default Invoice Terms" field shows "Net 30." If not, select it.

- Sales Form Delivery

i. Read Customize sales forms. Take no action.
ii. Delivery method default. Make sure that "Print" is selected.
iii. Read the Email message. Make no changes. All boxes must be unchecked.
iv. Email sales forms as attachments. Read the information. **This box must be unchecked.**
v. Statements. Show aging information should be checked.
vi. Show summary or details. Select **show details**. Show details **must be** selected.

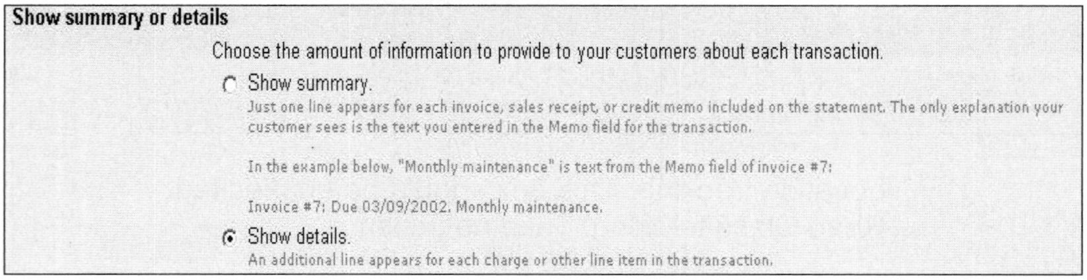

Show summary or details

Choose the amount of information to provide to your customers about each transaction.

○ Show summary.
Just one line appears for each invoice, sales receipt, or credit memo included on the statement. The only explanation your customer sees is the text you entered in the Memo field for the transaction.

In the example below, "Monthly maintenance" is text from the Memo field of invoice #7:

Invoice #7: Due 03/09/2002. Monthly maintenance.

◉ Show details.
An additional line appears for each charge or other line item in the transaction.

- Invoice Automation:
    i. Read Automation information. Take no action.

- Accept Credit Cards: Read information: Take no Action.

- Vendors & Purchases
    i. Manage bills to pay later **should be checked.**

    ii. Read the Expense tracking by customer information. Take no action.
    iii. Multiple split lines. This box should be unchecked.
    iv. Duplicate check warning. This box should be checked.
    v. Duplicate bill warning. **This box should be checked.**

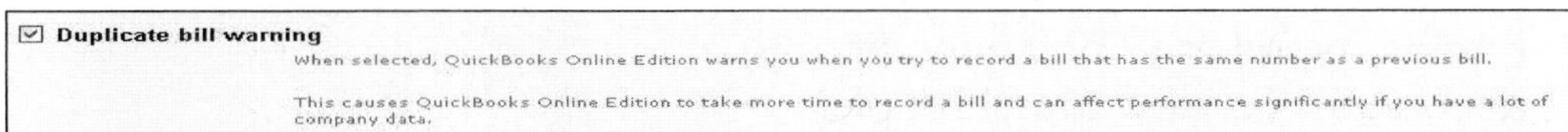

    vi. Terms. Read information. Take no action.

- Time tracking. Read information. Take no action.

- Payroll. Take no action.

- Reports:
    i. Default accounting method for summary reports. Verify that the radio button next to "Accrual" is selected.
    ii. Numbers format. Verify that the radio button next to "Normally" is selected and that the box next to "Except zero amounts" is checked.

To complete the company interview, click on the Save button at the bottom of your screen to save all of your preferences. In a few moments, your home screen will appear.

2. In the “Get Started with QuickBooks Online Edition” area, click on Start here link.

Getting Started

Start Here

Follow these easy steps to get started using QuickBooks Online.

3. Learn about QuickBooks Online Edition by taking interactive tours, experiment with a sample company, and get oriented by using the links located on your Welcome page.

4. When you are ready to proceed, click on home to return to your company’s homepage.

5. As you know from your study of accounting, a ***chart of* accounts** is a list of all the accounts used by a company to conduct its business. The Chart of Accounts set up by QuickBooks Online Edition for your company lists the names, types, and balances (if any) of accounts. To view the chart of accounts, move your mouse over “Company” on the QuickBooks Online toolbar. Notice all accounts have “0.00” balances and no cash account is listed. Before deleting or editing the names of these accounts, you need to set up your cash account.

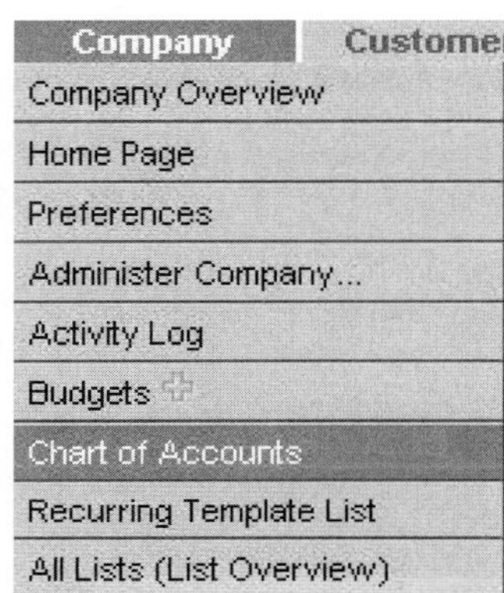

SETTING UP THE CASH ACCOUNT

Follow these steps to set up your cash account.

1. To set up your Cash account, move your mouse over “Banking” on the QuickBooks Online Edition toolbar. When the drop-down menu appears, click on “Banking Overview.”

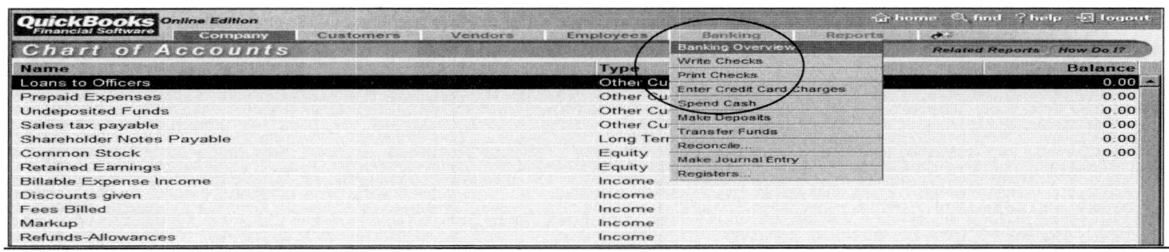

2. In a few moments, the “Banking Overview” appears. In the “Setup Tasks” list, move your mouse over “Set up a checking account” and click.

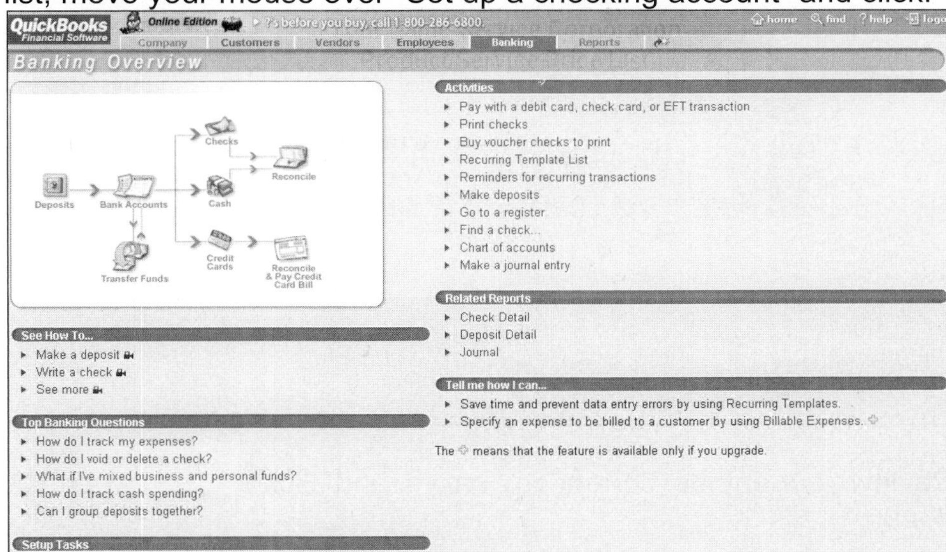

3. A QuickBooks Online Edition - Mini Interview–Web Page Dialog box appears. Type **Your Name** Service Corporation (your first and last name). Leave the subaccount box blank. Type **Primary Checking Account** in the “Description” field. Type **3000.00** in the “Balance” field. Type **10/01/20XX (use the current year, i.e., 2007 or 2008)** in the “as of” field. Compare your screen to the one shown on the next page.

Comment
When using this text, fill in **all dates.** If you do not fill in the date and year, QuickBooks will automatically assume your data is for today!
This is a common error when students make mistakes.

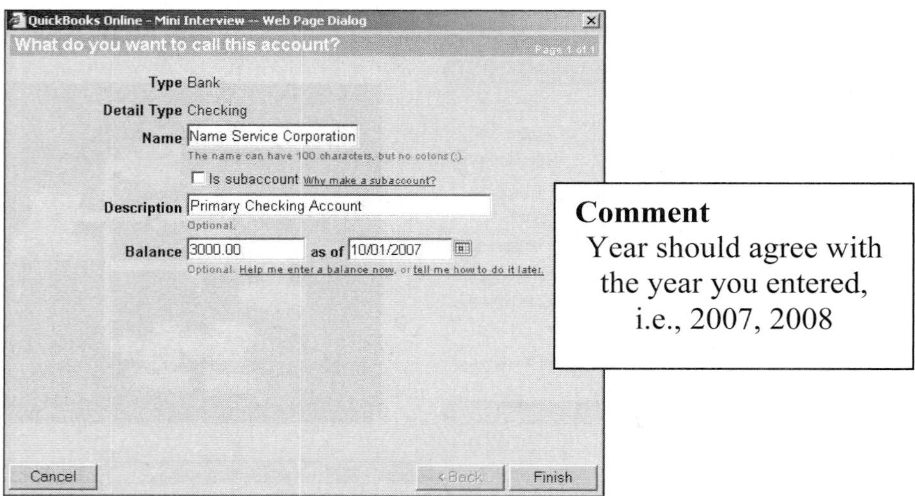

4. Review your entries, correct any errors, and click Finish when you are done.

Comment:
The business first started operations in a previous year. You are going to start recording transactions using QuickBooks Online Edition as of October 1, 20XX (your current year).

5. Return to your chart of accounts by accessing the chart of accounts from the Company drop-down list. Move your mouse over "Company" on the QuickBooks Online Edition toolbar. When the drop-down menu appears, click on "Chart of Accounts."

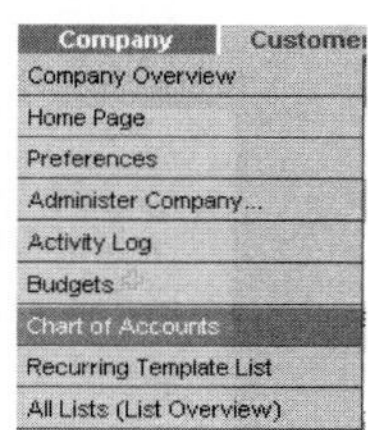

6. Now your chart of accounts contains a bank type of account called "Your Name Service Corporation" with a $3,000.00 balance. QuickBooks Online Edition bank types of accounts are the cash accounts of the business. Notice the account requires a name more descriptive than just "cash."

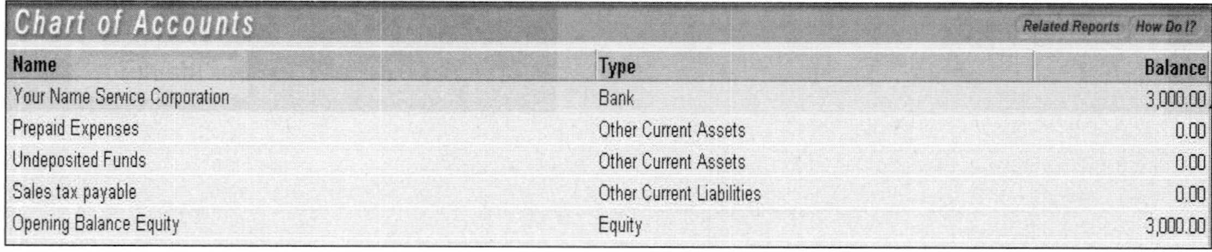
Chart of Accounts

Name	Type	Balance
Your Name Service Corporation	Bank	3,000.00
Prepaid Expenses	Other Current Assets	0.00
Undeposited Funds	Other Current Assets	0.00
Sales tax payable	Other Current Liabilities	0.00
Opening Balance Equity	Equity	3,000.00

REVISING THE CHART OF ACCOUNTS

Follow these steps to revise the chart of accounts.

1. If necessary, access your chart of accounts by moving your mouse over "Company" on the QuickBooks Online Edition toolbar. When the drop-down menu appears, click on "Chart of Accounts."

2. When the QuickBooks Online Edition constructed chart of accounts (based on your start up and preference interview answers) appears, you may want to scroll down this screen to see the entire chart of accounts. Since you will not be using all these accounts, let's revise some of these accounts.

Deleting an Account

These instructions show you how to delete an account from the chart of accounts.

1. To delete an account you will not use, move your mouse over the account, clicking on it to select.

2. For example, to delete the account "Refunds-Allowances" highlight the account.

3. Click on Delete. *(Hint: The "Delete" button is at the bottom right of your screen.)*

4. A "Please Confirm—Web Page Dialog" pops up asking, "Are you sure you want to delete?"

5. Click on Yes.

6. In a few moments a revised chart of accounts will appear without the deleted account.

7. Delete the following accounts:

Sales Tax Payable
Discounts Given
Shipping Income
Promotional
Miscellaneous
Meals and Entertainment
Legal & Professional Fees
Dues & Subscriptions
Commissions & Fees
Travel Meals
Travel
Taxes & Licenses
Stationery & Printing
Penalties & Settlements
Interest Earned

There may be one or two additional accounts that QuickBooks Online Edition will *not* allow you to delete. When you are finished with your chart of accounts, it will look similar to the one shown below.

Chart of Accounts — Related Reports | How Do I?

Name	Type	Balance
Your Name Service Corporation	Bank	3,000.00
Prepaid Expenses	Other Current Assets	0.00
Undeposited Funds	Other Current Assets	0.00
Opening Balance Equity	Equity	3,000.00
Retained Earnings	Equity	
Billable Expense Income	Income	
Fees Billed	Income	
Markup	Income	
Services	Income	
Advertising	Expenses	
Bank Charges	Expenses	
Insurance	Expenses	
Office Expenses	Expenses	
Rent or Lease	Expenses	
Repair & Maintenance	Expenses	
Supplies	Expenses	
Utilities	Expenses	
Other Income	Other Income	

Comment
What if my Chart of Accounts list looks different?
Your chart of accounts may differ somewhat. Depending on which version of QuickBooks Online Edition you are using, some accounts may not be deleted. These differences are insignificant. Along with the accounts you add in the next section, you will also learn how to add accounts "on the fly" later in the book.

Adding an Account

Follow these steps to add an account to the chart of accounts.

1. The chart of accounts list should be displayed on your screen. Click on the New button at the bottom of your screen.

2. A "QuickBooks Online Edition-Mini Interview—Web Page Dialog" pops up asking what type of account would you like to set up. Since you will be setting up a fixed asset account, select the radio button next to "Choose from all account types." This is shown below.

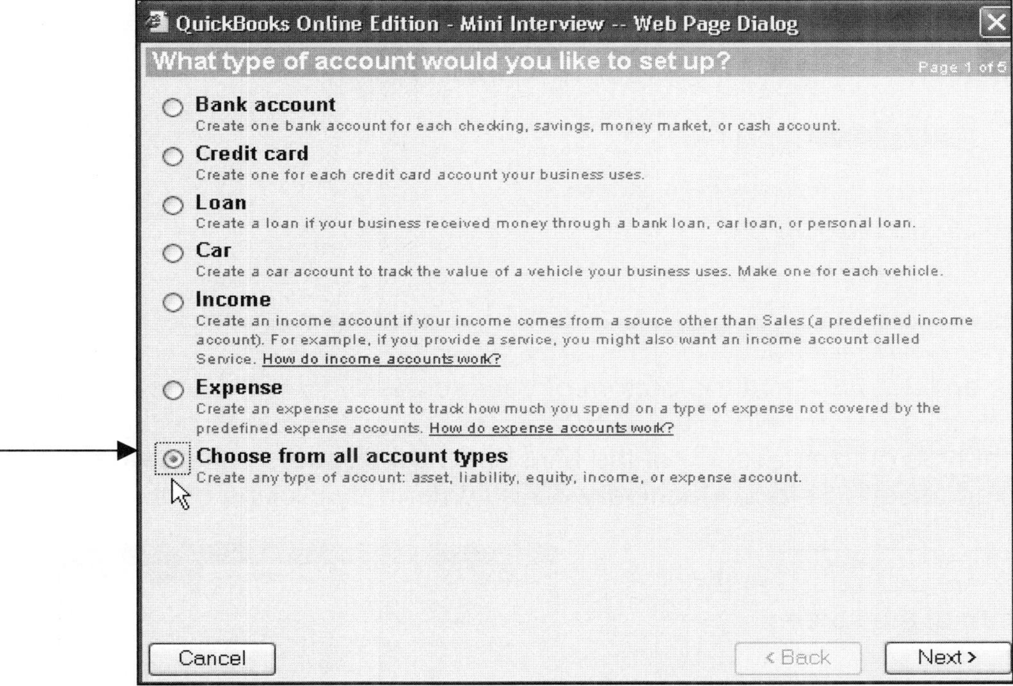

3. Click on Next > at the bottom of your screen.

4. Another screen, "What type of account would you like to set up?" of the Mini Interview asks what type of account you would like to set up. Click on "Fixed assets" to select it and to see a description. Compare your screen to the one shown on the next page.

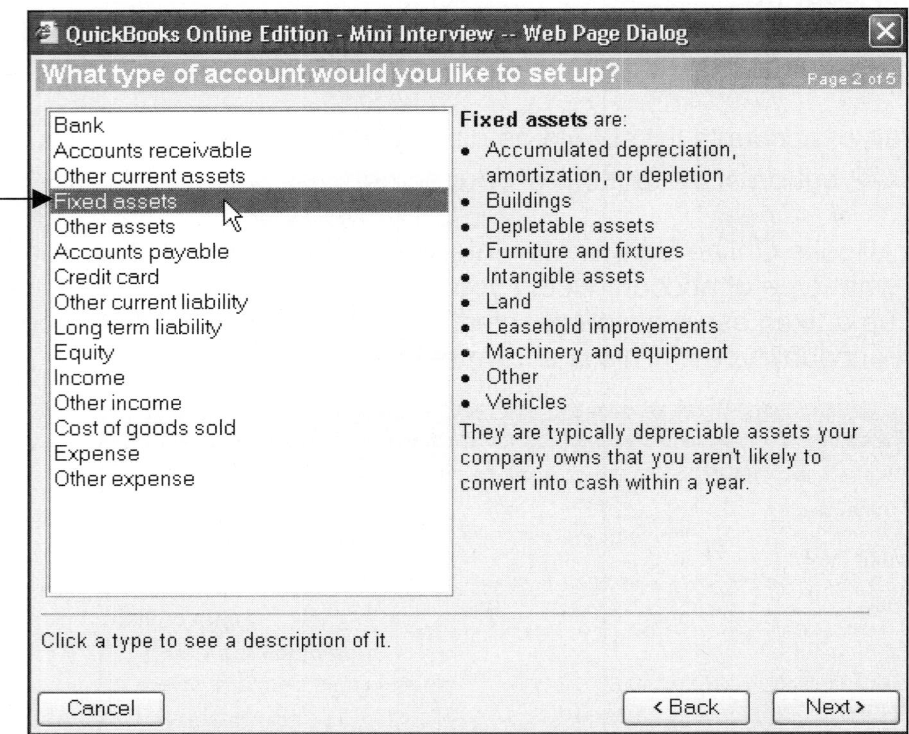

5. Click on [Next >] at the bottom of your screen.

6. "What type of fixed asset?" of the Mini Interview appears asking what type of fixed asset? Select "Machinery & Equipment" by clicking on it.

7. Click on [Next >] at the bottom of the screen.

8. "What do you want to call this account?" of the Mini Interview pops up asking several questions.

   a. Type **Computer Equipment** in the "Name" field.
   b. Leave the subaccount and Description boxes blank.

c. To the question, "Do you want to track depreciation of this asset?" Select the "Yes" radio button.
d. Review and revise your entries until you are satisfied.
e. Click on Next >.

9. The Mini Interview concludes with "What's the cost and amount depreciated?" Since the computer equipment was originally purchased for $6,000 on October 1, 2005, enter the following for the opening balances.

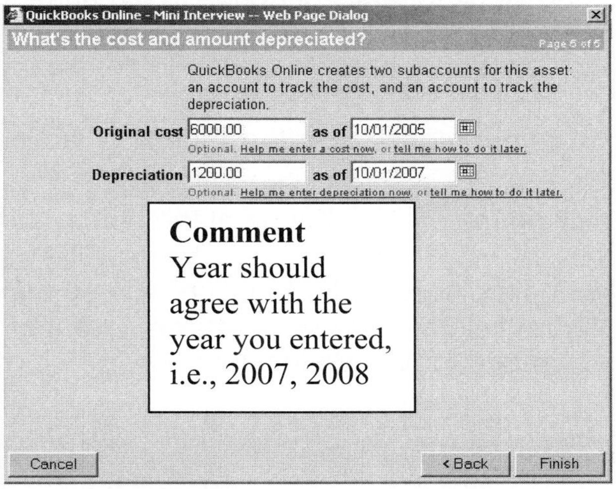

   a. Type **6000** for "Original cost." Type **10/01/2005** for "as of."
   b. Type **1200** for "Depreciation." Type **10/01/20XX (your current year)** for "as of."

QuickBooks Online - Mini Interview -- Web Page Dialog

What's the cost and amount depreciated? Page 5 of 5

QuickBooks Online creates two subaccounts for this asset: an account to track the cost, and an account to track the depreciation.

Original cost 6000.00 **as of** 10/01/2005

Optional. Help me enter a cost now, or tell me how to do it later.

Depreciation 1200.00 **as of** 10/01/2007

Optional. Help me enter depreciation now, or tell me how to do it later.

Comment
Year should agree with the year you entered, i.e., 2007, 2008

Cancel < Back Finish

   c. Use the < Back and Next > buttons at the bottom of your screen to review and revise all your responses to the Mini interview. When you are satisfied, click on Finish at the bottom of your screen.

10. Your chart of accounts will now contain the following accounts and balances for " Computer Equipment"

Computer Equipment	Fixed Assets	4,800.00
Depreciation	Fixed Assets	-1,200.00
Original Cost	Fixed Assets	6,000.00

11. Add an Accounts Receivable account.

   a. From the chart of accounts screen, click on New.
   b. What type of account: Select "Choose from all account types."

c. Type of account: Select "Accounts Receivable."

d. Account name: **Accounts Receivable** (leave Description blank). When you are satisfied, click on Finish at the bottom of your screen.

Changing an Account Name

Follow these steps to make changes to the name of an account.

1. The Chart of Accounts list should be displayed on your screen.

2. Move your mouse over the "Supplies" account and click to select it.

3. Click on the Edit button at the bottom of your screen.

4. When the "Account Information" screen appears, place your cursor in the "Name" field and type **Computer** in front of "Supplies" so the "Name" field is changed to "Computer Supplies."

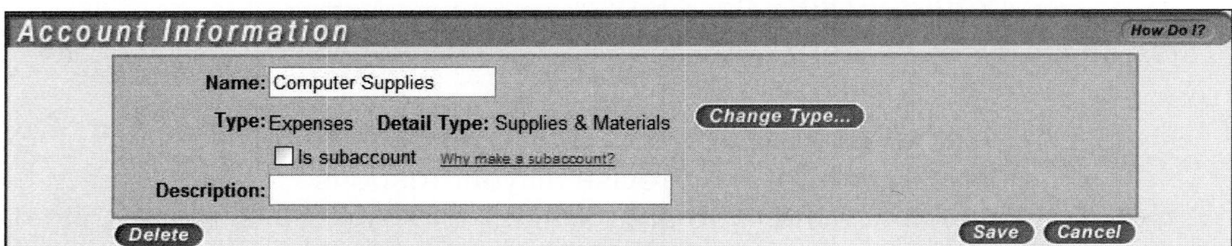

5. Click on Save.

6. Your chart of accounts list will now show the account "Computer Supplies."

7. Use steps 2-6 to edit each of the following account names and descriptions:

Name of Account	*Change to*	*Description*
Prepaid expenses	**Prepaid Insurance**	**Insurance paid in advance of use**
Depreciation (Fixed Assets)	**Accumulated Depreciation**	

Depreciation (Other Expense)	**Depreciation Expense**	
Opening balance-equity	**Paid in Capital**	**Opening balance**

8. To check that your revisions were made, compare chart of accounts to the one shown. (You may also have one or two additional accounts that QuickBooks Online Edition will not allow you to delete.)

Chart of Accounts — Related Reports | How Do I?

Name	Type	Balance
Your Name Service Corporation	Bank	3,000.00
Accounts Receivable	Accounts Receivable	0.00
Prepaid Insurance	Other Current Assets	0.00
Undeposited Funds	Other Current Assets	0.00
Computer Equipment	Fixed Assets	4,800.00
Accumulated Depreciation	Fixed Assets	-1,200.00
Original Cost	Fixed Assets	6,000.00
Paid in Capital	Equity	7,800.00
Retained Earnings	Equity	
Billable Expense Income	Income	
Fees Billed	Income	
Markup	Income	
Services	Income	
Advertising	Expenses	
Bank Charges	Expenses	
Computer Supplies	Expenses	
Insurance	Expenses	
Office Expenses	Expenses	
Rent or Lease	Expenses	
Repair & Maintenance	Expenses	
Utilities	Expenses	
Other Income	Other Income	
Depreciation Expense	Other Expense	

BEGINNING BALANCE SHEET

On page 28-30 you recorded the opening balance for your business' checking account; and on page 35 you recorded the opening balance for your equipment and depreciation accounts. Before you start recording transactions for your business, you need to record an additional beginning balance from the October 1, 20XX ***balance sheet***. As you know from your study of accounting, a balance sheet is a list of assets, liabilities, and stockholders' equity of a business as of a specific date.

The information in the Balance Sheet shown on the next page will be the basis for recording opening account balances for your business.

Your first and last name Service Corporation Balance Sheet October 1, 20XX (Your current year)		
ASSETS		
Current Assets		
Checking	$ 3,000.00	
Prepaid Insurance	200.00	
Total Current Assets		$ 3,200.00
Fixed Assets		
Computer Equipment	$ 6,000.00	
Accumulated Depreciation	(1,200.00)	
Total Fixed Assets		4,800.00
Total Assets		**$ 8,000.00**
LIABILITIES & STOCKHOLDERS' EQUITY		
Stockholders' Equity		
Common Stock	$ 1,000.00	
Paid in Capital	7,000.00	
Retained Earnings	0.00	
Total Liabilities & Equity		**$ 8,000.00**

Follow these steps to enter an opening account balance

1. The chart of accounts list should be displayed on your screen. All the opening account balances on the balance sheet have been entered *except for Prepaid Insurance and Common Stock*. Let's enter the opening account balance for "Prepaid Insurance" now.

2. Move your mouse over the "Prepaid Insurance" account and click the account.

3. Click the Edit button on the bottom of your screen.

4. The Prepaid Insurance "Account Information" screen appears. Type **200** for the "Opening Balance." Type **10/01/20XX (your current year)** in the "as of" date field.

(*Hint:* If you do not see "Opening Balance" and "as of" fields, you can enter an opening balance by using ?help on the QuickBooks Online Edition toolbar.)

5. Click on Save.

6. Add a Common Stock account.

   a. From the chart of accounts screen, click on New.
   b. What type of account: Select "Choose from all account types."
   c. Type of account: Select "Equity" then select "Common Stock."
   d. Account name: **Common Stock** (leave Description blank).
   e. Now enter the opening balance by typing **1000** for the "Opening Balance" and type **10/01/20XX (your current year)** in the "as of" date field.

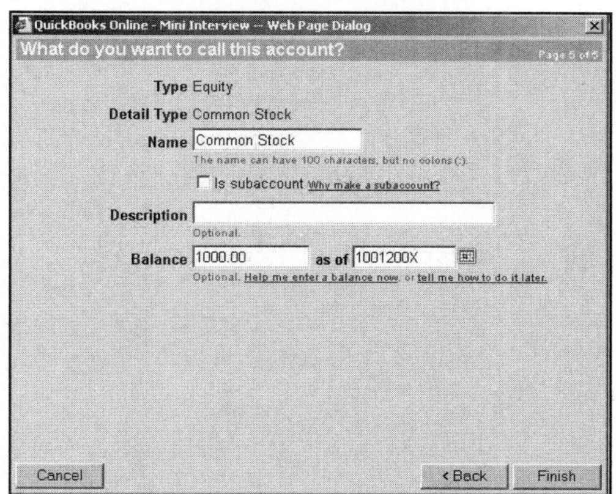

7. The chart of accounts now lists the "Prepaid Insurance" balance as $200 and the "Common Stock" balance as $1,000. Compare your chart of accounts with the one shown below. (This is a partial chart of accounts.)

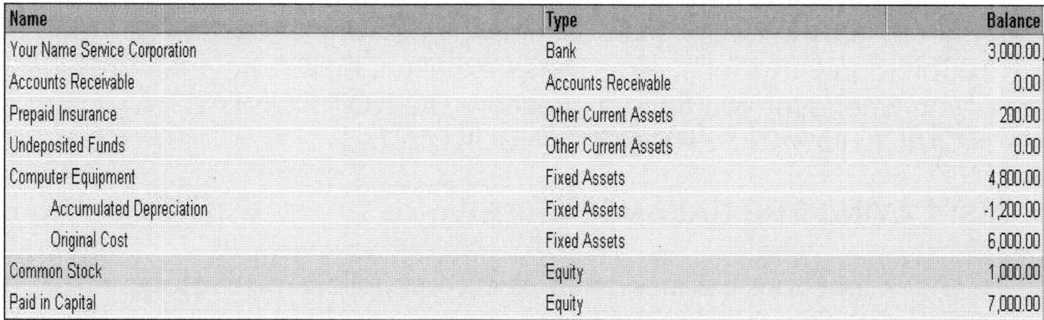

Name	Type	Balance
Your Name Service Corporation	Bank	3,000.00
Accounts Receivable	Accounts Receivable	0.00
Prepaid Insurance	Other Current Assets	200.00
Undeposited Funds	Other Current Assets	0.00
Computer Equipment	Fixed Assets	4,800.00
Accumulated Depreciation	Fixed Assets	-1,200.00
Original Cost	Fixed Assets	6,000.00
Common Stock	Equity	1,000.00
Paid in Capital	Equity	7,000.00

The balances shown should agree with the October 1, 20XX (your current year) balance sheet shown on page 38.

HELP SCREENS

Notice that every screen has a Help link on the QuickBooks Online Edition toolbar.

1. Click on help to see how the help screens work. Compare your screen to the one shown.

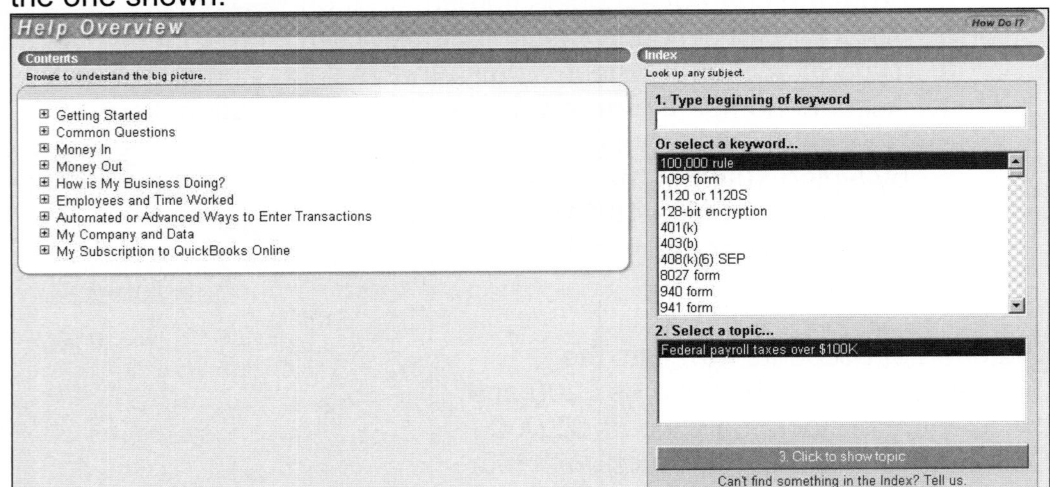

2. Read the information on the "Help Overview" screen to learn more. Notice that you can search by keyword or topic, seek help by screen, or get help by accessing various links; for example, Getting Started, Common Questions, etc. These excellent built-in help features will help you whenever you have a question. DO NOT CONTACT A QUICKBOOKS SERVICE CONSULTANT.

DISPLAYING THE BALANCE SHEET

To check that your balance sheet is correct, follow these steps.

1. Move your mouse over "Reports" on the QuickBooks Online Edition toolbar. When the drop-down menu appears, click on "Balance Sheet." When the screen pops up that asks, "Which do you want as a default basis for accounting reports?" accept the default for "Accrual" by clicking on Finish.
2. When the "Balance Sheet" appears it will be as of today's date. To change the date to October 1, 20XX (your current year), click on the Customize... button.

3. A “Customize Report: Balance Sheet—Web Page Dialog” pops up.

    a. For “Transaction Date” select “Custom” from the drop-down menu for dates. (*Hint: You may need to scroll up.*)
    b. Type **10/01/20XX (your current year)** in the “From” field.
    c. Type **10/01/20XX (your current year)** in the “To” field since this is the date of your company’s opening balances.
    d. For “Accounting Method,” make sure that “Accrual” is selected.
    e. For “Rows/Columns” if necessary, select “Total Only” from the drop-down menu.
    f. Review “Add Subcolumns for Comparison,” “Lists,” and “Numbers,” but do not change.

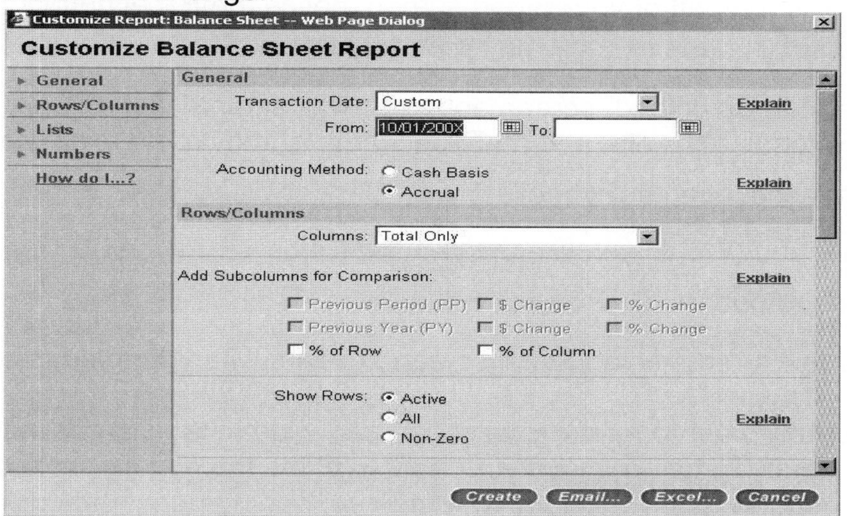

    g. Click the Create button.

4. The October 1, 20XX balance sheet for your business displays. Compare it to the one on page 38. Observe that at the bottom of your Balance Sheet screen, there are a number of links; for example, “See detail behind the numbers?,” “What does “Split” mean?.” You may want to explore some of these links to learn more about your report.

To see how to save your balance sheet to Excel, continue with the next section, "Copying Report Data to Excel."

COPYING REPORT DATA TO EXCEL

Copying and saving a report provides you with flexibility for reviewing and analyzing your business' data. You can easily copy QuickBooks Online Edition reports into a spreadsheet program like Excel and then save them to external media. You may want to use these features of QuickBooks Online Edition and Excel to back up your reports at periodic intervals.

To copy a report to Excel, follow these steps:

1. The balance sheet should be displayed on your screen.
2. In the upper left of your report screen, notice the Excel button. Click on the Excel... button to copy the report into Excel.
3. The "File Download" screen appears. This screen confirms that you are downloading the file, and an Excel name is shown; for example, "report1.xls from accounting.quickbooks.com." Click on Open.
4. When the "Would you like to open the file or save it to your computer?" screen appears, click on Open.
5. In a few moments, an Excel screen appears with your balance sheet.
6. You may want to format your report and widen the columns in the report to fit the data. To do so, move your mouse at the top of your spreadsheet to the line that divides two columns. When your pointer changes to a cross-bar, double click. The columns should automatically widen to fit the data in them. Or, you can move the cross-bar to the right or left to widen or narrow the spreadsheet's columns.

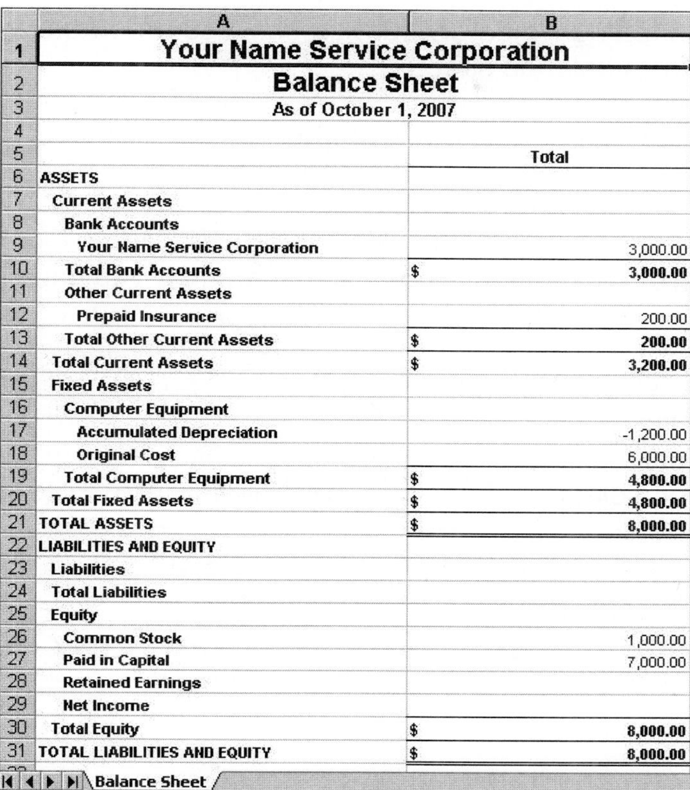

	A	B
1	**Your Name Service Corporation**	
2	**Balance Sheet**	
3	As of October 1, 2007	
4		
5		Total
6	ASSETS	
7	Current Assets	
8	Bank Accounts	
9	Your Name Service Corporation	3,000.00
10	Total Bank Accounts	$ **3,000.00**
11	Other Current Assets	
12	Prepaid Insurance	200.00
13	Total Other Current Assets	$ **200.00**
14	Total Current Assets	$ **3,200.00**
15	Fixed Assets	
16	Computer Equipment	
17	Accumulated Depreciation	-1,200.00
18	Original Cost	6,000.00
19	Total Computer Equipment	$ **4,800.00**
20	Total Fixed Assets	$ **4,800.00**
21	TOTAL ASSETS	$ **8,000.00**
22	LIABILITIES AND EQUITY	
23	Liabilities	
24	Total Liabilities	
25	Equity	
26	Common Stock	1,000.00
27	Paid in Capital	7,000.00
28	Retained Earnings	
29	Net Income	
30	Total Equity	$ **8,000.00**
31	TOTAL LIABILITIES AND EQUITY	$ **8,000.00**

Balance Sheet

If you want to save your spreadsheet to external media, complete the following steps.

1. Insert external media (USB drive, cd, dvd).

2. From the "File" menu choose Save As.

3. The "Save As" screen appears. Click on the down-arrow in the "Save in" box. Select the drive where your external media is located. Or, if you prefer, save to your hard drive on your computer.

4. Type **opening balance sheet** in the "File name" box.

5. Click on the Save button. You can now open this file using Excel.

6. After saving this file, you are returned to the balance sheet screen in your spreadsheet program. To close the spreadsheet program, click on the "X"

button in the top right side of your screen. You are returned to QuickBooks Online Edition's balance sheet.

To open this file in Excel, follow these steps:

1. Go to your desktop and start Excel.

2. From Excel's menu bar, click on File, Open. (Or, you can click on the "Open folder" icon.)

3. The "Open" screen appears. In the "Look in" box, select the drive where you saved file.

4. If necessary, select "All Microsoft Excel files" in the "Files of type" box.

5. Click on the file named "opening balance sheet."

6. Click on the Open button. Your October 1, 20XX (your current year) balance sheet displays as an Excel spreadsheet.

7. Exit Excel.

Remember to use the Excel button feature of QuickBooks Online Edition to back up (save) your reports at periodic intervals. For purposes of this exercise, the October 1, 20XX balance sheet was saved as "opening balance sheet." You could use a different filename; for example, "October 1 20XX balance sheet."

LOGGING OUT OF QUICKBOOKS ONLINE EDITION

To log out of QuickBooks Online Edition, proceed with the following steps.

1. To log off, click on the logout button on the top right of your screen.

2. The "Welcome" screen appears. You can log in again; or from the menu bar, click on "File" then "Close" to close your browser.

CHECK YOUR PROGRESS

Flashcard Review: Based on what you learned this chapter, prepare step-by-step instructions on flashcards for the following tasks:

1. Setting preferences
2. Setting up cash account
3. Deleting an account
4. Adding an account
5. Changing an account name
6. Displaying balance sheet
7. Copying report data to excel

Internet Homework: To learn more about QuickBooks Online Edition, follow these steps:

1. If necessary, start QuickBooks Online Edition, and then log in to your account. (*Hint:* If you are already logged on, click home.)

2. When your "Home" screen appears, observe that the "Administration" area includes a link to Subscription Information. Link to it. Observe the date in the "Status" field.

   Write the date of when your free trial ends:

   ___

3. Click Back. You are returned to your Home page. In the "Common Questions" list, link to How can I log back in later?

4. Read the information on the screen, if you want--add a desktop icon link or to your favorites list, and then close the window.

Multiple-Choice. In the space provided, write the letter that best answers each question.

_____1. The two ways to log on to QuickBooks Online Edition are:

a. Type http://oe.quickbooks.com in the "Address" box.
b. Click on the down arrow in the Address field and select the QuickBooks Online Edition's web address.
c. Both a. and b.
d. There is only one way to log on.
e. None of the above.

_____2. The first month for entering transactions is:

a. September.
b. October.
c. November.
d. December.
e. None of the above.

_____3. The opening balance in the checking account is:

a. $2,000.00.
b. $3,000.00.
c. $25,000.00.
d. $8,000.00.
e. None of the above.

_____4. The opening balance in the prepaid insurance account is:

a. $200.00.
b. $10,000.00.
c. $25,000.00.
d. $8,000.00.
a. None of the above.

______5. The default basis for accounting reports for your business is:

a. Cash.
b. Accrual.
c. Hybrid.
d. IRS.
e. None of the above.

______6. To change one of the accounts listed on the chart of accounts, you need to select which one of the following links?

a. Company Preferences.
b. Edit.
c. Number.
d. Account.
e. None of the above.

______7. The October 1, 20XX balance sheet for your business shows the following balance for Computer Equipment:

a. $6,000.00.
b. $8,000.00.
c. $4,800.00.
d. $7,500.00.
e. None of the above.

______8. The October 1, 20XX balance sheet for your business shows the following balance in your Paid in Capital account:

a. $7,000.00.
b. $10,000.00.
c. $6,000.00.
d. $2,000.00.
e. None of the above.

_____9. To change the date on a QuickBooks Online Edition report, you should select which of the following icons?

a. Preferences tab.
b. Calendar.
c. Customize.
d. Login.
e. None of the above.

_____10. To obtain assistance about QuickBooks Online Edition, you should select which of the following links?

a. Startup.
b. Reporting.
c. Other.
d. Help.
e. None of the above.

True/False. Write T for True and F for false in the space provided.

_____11. In Chapter 2 of *Computer Accounting Essentials Using QuickBooks Online Edition*, you enter customers and vendors.

_____12. The first month of the fiscal year for your business is December.

_____13. You use the four links on the "Company" screen to set up a new company.

_____14. There are five actions that can be taken from the chart of accounts screen: new, edit, delete, register, and report.

_____15. A chart of accounts is a list of all the accounts used by a company.

_____16. In QuickBooks Online Edition, the company menu includes the chart of accounts.

_____17. The balance sheet is a list of income and expenses on a specific date.

_____18. In QuickBooks Online Edition, the company menu includes the balance sheet.

_____19. The balance sheet is reported as of today's date unless it is customized.

_____20. To go back to the company preferences, you go to the company drop-down menu.

Exercise 2-1. Follow these steps to print a chart of accounts.

1. Start your browser and login to QuickBooks Online Edition in the usual way.
2. When your home screen appears, select the "Reports" menu. Choose All Reports (Reports Overview).
3. In the "Company" section, link to Account Listing.
4. Click on the Print... button, and then make the selections to print in landscape orientation.
5. *Optional: From the "Account Listing" report screen, click on the* Email... *button. Email the report to your instructor. Type* **Your Name** *and* **Exercise 2-1** *as the Subject.*
6. Continue with Exercise 2-2.

Exercise 2-2. Follow these steps to print a balance sheet

1. Click on the "Reports" menu.
2. Link to the "Balance Sheet" on the drop-down menu.
3. On the "Balance Sheet" screen, click on "Customize" to change the "Custom" dates from 10/01/20XX to 10/01/20XX (your current year).
4. Generate the customized report, then make the selections to print in portrait orientation.
5. *Optional: Click on the* Email... *button to email the report to your instructor. Type* **Your Name** *and* **Exercise 2-2** *as the Subject.*
6. Click on logout to exit QuickBooks Online Edition.

CHAPTER 2 INDEX

Adding an account 33
Balance sheet 38, 40, 41, 42, 43, 44, 48, 49
Bank type of account 30
Changing an account name 36
Chart of accounts 21, 28, 30, 31, 32, 33, 36, 37, 39, 49
Check your progress 45
Computer accounting essentials website 21
Copying report data to excel 42
Deleting an account 31
Displaying the balance sheet 40
Flashcard review 45
Getting started 24
Help screens 40
Internet homework 45
Mini interview –web page dialog 29
opening balance 21, 29, 35, 38, 39, 41, 44, 47, 48
QuickBooks online edition toolbar 28, 30, 31, 40, 41
Revising the chart of accounts 31
Setting up the cash account 28
Software objectives 21
Web objectives 21

3 Setting Accounting Defaults

In Chapter 3 of *Computer Accounting Essentials Using QuickBooks Online Edition,* you will learn how to set ***defaults***. Defaults are information or commands that the software or operating system automatically uses. QuickBooks Online Edition refers to the setting of defaults as setting preferences.

SOFTWARE OBJECTIVES: In Chapter 3, you use the software to:

1. Set preferences for customer charges.
2. Set preferences for customer statements.
3. Set preferences for entering customer transactions.
4. Set up customers.
5. Set up products and services list.
6. Set preferences for entering vendor transactions.
7. Set up vendors.
8. Display the October 1, 20XX balance sheet.
9. Copy report data to Excel.
10. Complete activities for Chapter 3, Setting Accounting Preferences.

WEB OBJECTIVES: In Chapter 3, you use the Internet to:

1. Access the Computer Accounting Essentials website at www.mhhe.com/yachtessentials3e to check for updates.
2. Log in to your QuickBooks Online Edition account.
3. Save the accounting preferences that you set with QuickBooks Online Edition.
4. Complete Flashcard review.
5. Complete Internet activities.

COMPUTER ACCOUNTING ESSENTIALS WEBSITE

Before you begin your work in Chapter 3, Setting Accounting Defaults, access the Computer Accounting Essentials website at www.mhhe.com/yachtessentials3e. Select the QuickBooks link, and then link to Text Updates. Check this website regularly for reference and study.

GETTING STARTED

Follow these steps to start QuickBooks Online Edition. You *must* complete Chapters 1 and 2, pages 3 – 50 before starting Chapter 3, Setting Accounting Defaults. *The exercises at the end of each Chapter must be completed, too.*

1. Start your Internet browser and login to QuickBooks Online Edition in the usual way.

> **Comment:**
> QuickBooks Online Edition regularly updates their software. For this reason, you may see some differences between screen illustrations in the book and your screen display. Once you log on to QuickBooks Online Edition, you will be using the latest software version. *Remember, websites are time and date sensitive and inevitably there will be some minor adjustments to the software.*

2. Your "home page" screen displays. (*Hint: Your business name will differ from the one shown below. In Chapter 1 on page 7, the Company Information should include your name.*)

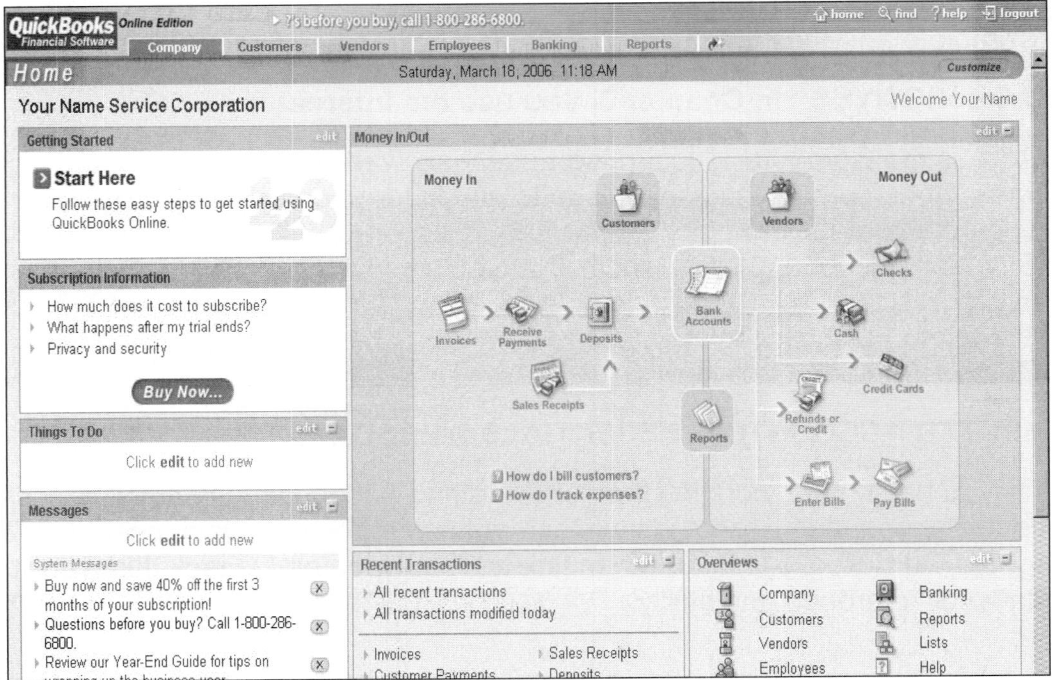

CUSTOMER OVERVIEW

Before you can enter sales transactions, you need to set up information about customers. ***Accounts receivable*** are what customers owe a business. Credit transactions from customers are called ***accounts receivable transactions***. In the next section, you will learn how to set up customer preferences and add credit customers for your business.
Follow these steps to set up customer preferences for your business.

From the "Home" screen, move your mouse over Customers on the QuickBooks Online Edition menu bar. When the drop-down menu appears, click on Customer Overview. The "Customer Overview" screen appears. In the next few steps you will be completing the tasks in the section called "Setup Tasks."

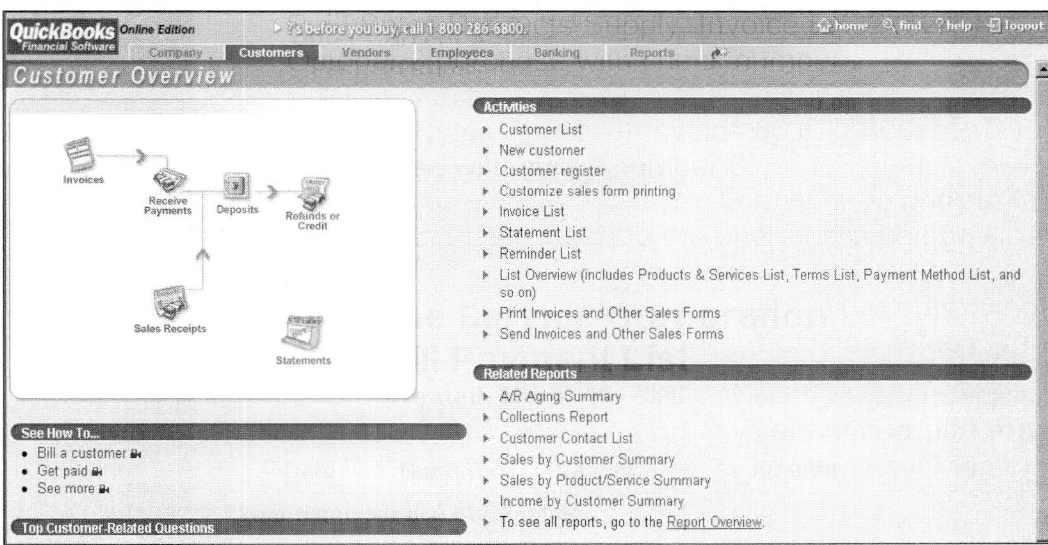

Set Preferences for Customer Charges

1. Scroll down to the Setup Tasks list, click on the link, Set preferences for charges. The "Mini Interview-Web Page Dialog" screen appears. Continue with step 2 on the next page.

Setup Tasks

- Set preferences for charges
- Set preferences for invoices
- Set preference for entering transactions
- Set up customers
- Set up products & services
- Enter historical customer transactions

2. The "Charges Setup" dialog box asks about standard products and services. Read the information on this screen.

3. If necessary, click on the radio button next to "Yes," then click on Next >. This selection will carry over to how QB Online creates invoices. So make sure "Yes" is selected.

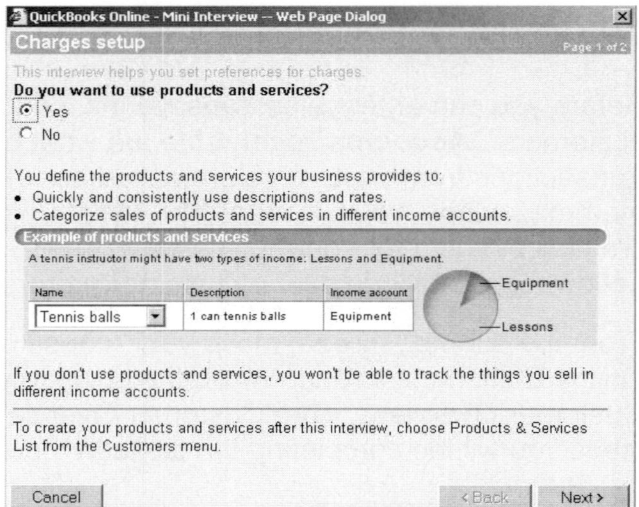

4. The "Tracking quantity and rate" dialog box appears.

5. Make sure the radio button next to "Yes" is selected, then click on Finish. You are returned to the "Customer Overview" screen.

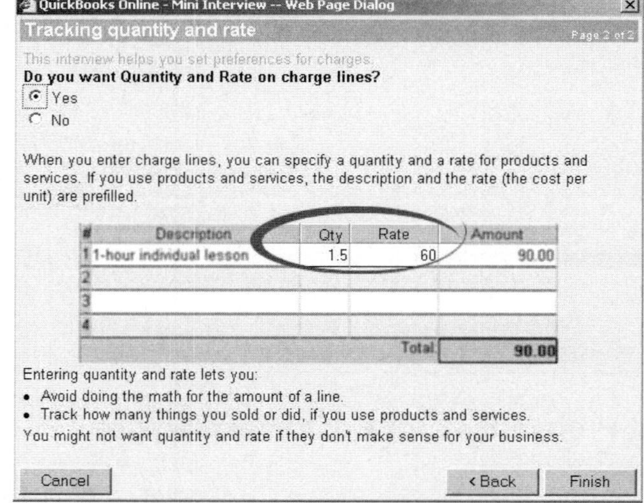

Set Preferences for Customer Statements

1. From the "Customer Overview" screen scroll down to the Setup Tasks list and click on the link Set preferences for invoices.

2. The "Due Date calculation" screen appears. Make sure that the "Default Invoice Terms" field shows Net 30.

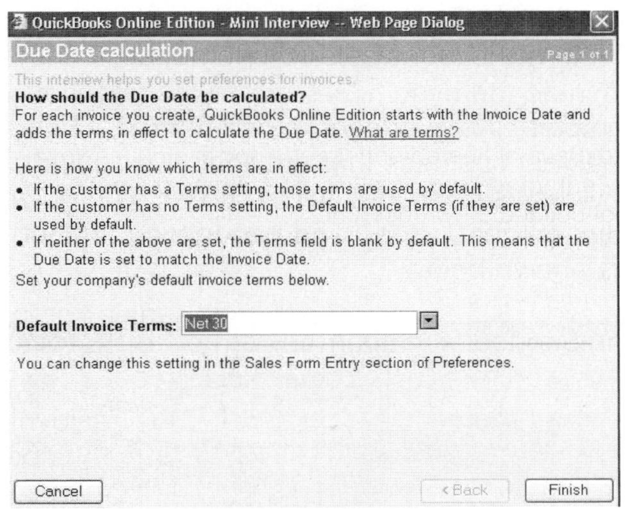

3. Click Finish.

> **Comment:**
> Net 30 means the bill is to be paid within 30 days of invoice.

Set Preferences for Entering Transactions

1. From the "Customer Overview" screen scroll down to the Setup Tasks list and click on the link Set Preferences for entering transactions.

2. The "Do you want autorecall transactions?" dialog box appears. Accept the default for "Yes" by clicking on Finish.

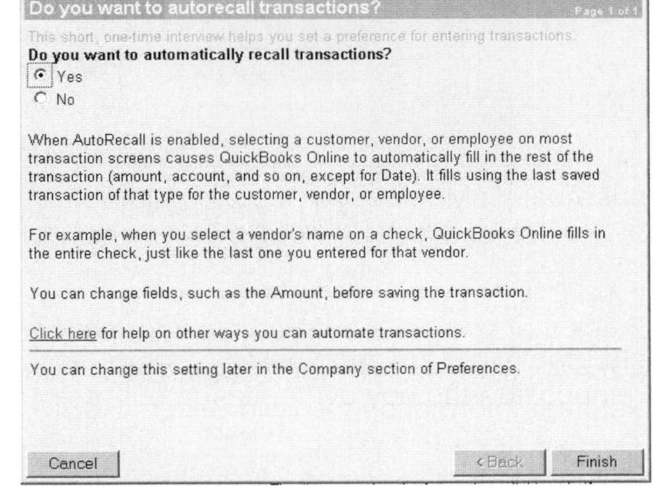

3. You are returned to the "Customer Overview" screen.

Set up Customers:

To enter a customer record, complete the following steps.

1. From the "Customer Overview" screen scroll down to the Setup Tasks list and click on the link Set up customers. After a few moments a blank "Customer Information" screen appears.

2. Complete the customer information for "Twin Sisters B&B," a bed and breakfast business that provides their guests with wireless Internet services using the following screen as a guide. Use your tab key to move between data fields. The information that will record for Twin Sisters B & B is shown below.

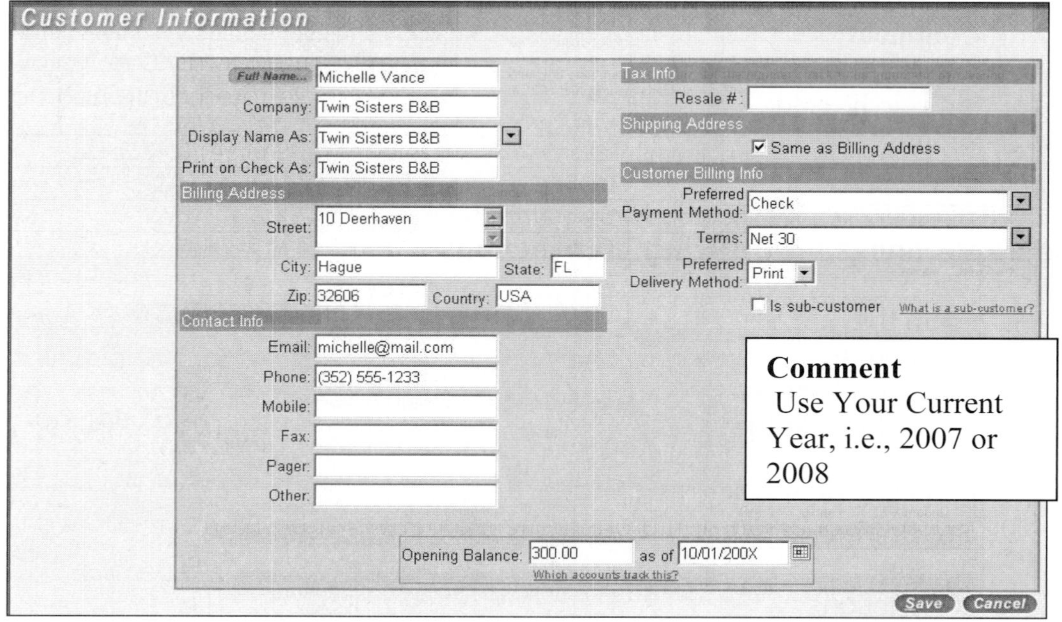

3. Check that you have entered the information correctly. *Hint: In the Display Name As field, select Twin Sisters B&B.* Then click on Save to save the customer information for Twin Sisters B&B.

4. Another blank "Customer Information" screen appears. Complete the customer information for "Cyberconnect Cafe," an Internet cafe business using the screen shown on the next page as a guide. Use your tab key to move between data fields. Check that you have entered the information correctly, (remember to select the company name in the Display Name As

field), then click on Save to save the customer information for Cyberconnect Cafe.

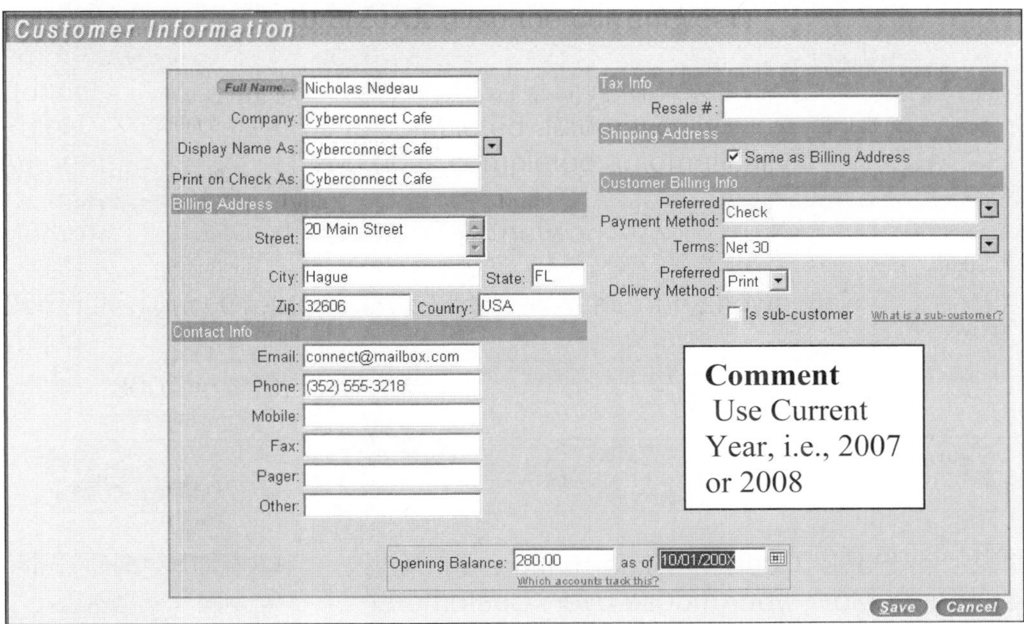

5. Another blank “Customer Information” screen appears. Complete the customer information for “NFP Access” a facility that provides Internet services for nonprofit organizations using the following screen as a guide. Use your tab key to move between data fields. Check that you have entered the information correctly, (remember to select the company name in the Display Name As field), then click on Save to save the customer information for NFP Access. The customer information is shown on the next page.

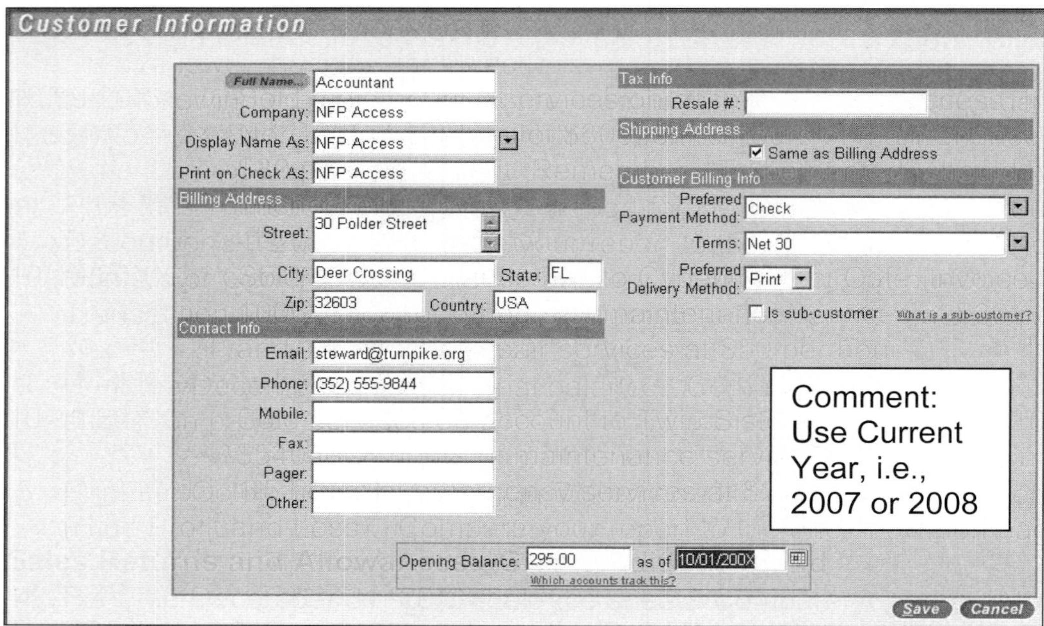

6. Another blank "Customer Information" screen appears. Move your mouse over "Customers" on the QuickBooks Online Edition menu bar. When the drop-down menu appears, click on "Customer List."

7. In a few moments the "Customer List" screen appears. Compare your customer list against the list of information about your three customer accounts below.

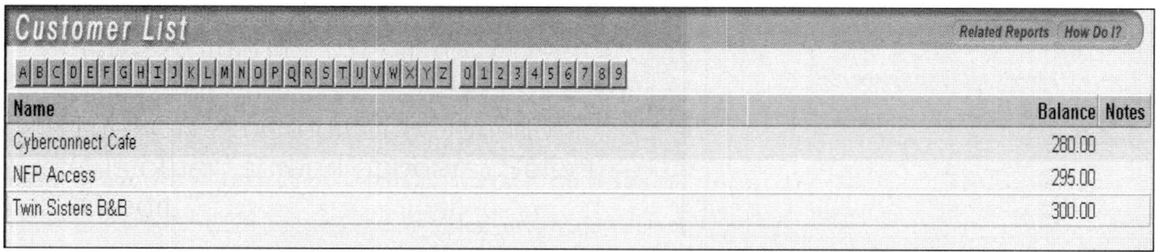

Customer List

Name	Balance	Notes
Cyberconnect Cafe	280.00	
NFP Access	295.00	
Twin Sisters B&B	300.00	

Observe that the balance for each customer is shown on this screen. When you check the balance sheet on page 66, you will see that the accounts receivable account has a balance of $875.

If necessary, you can edit the customer accounts by double clicking on the account, then selecting the Edit button.

8. Move your mouse over "Customers" on the QuickBooks Online Edition menu bar. When the drop-down menu appears, click on "Customer Overview."

9. The "Customer Overview" screen appears. From the "Setup Tasks" list you have set preferences for customer charges, invoices, entering transactions, and set up customers. Next you will set up products and services.

SET UP PRODUCTS & SERVICES

To set up your products and services proceed with the following steps.

1. From the "Customer Overview" screen scroll down to the Setup Tasks list and click on the link Set up products & services. After a few moments a blank "Product or Service Information" screen appears. Compare your screen with the one shown below.

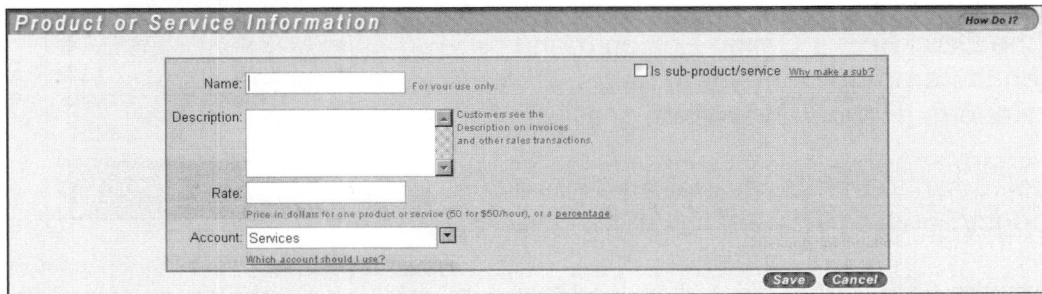

2. Complete the product or service information for "Maintenance service" using the following screen as a guide. Use your tab key to move between the "Name," "Description," "Rate," and "Account" fields. Check that you have entered the information correctly for maintenance service and then click Save to save the information on "Maintenance service."

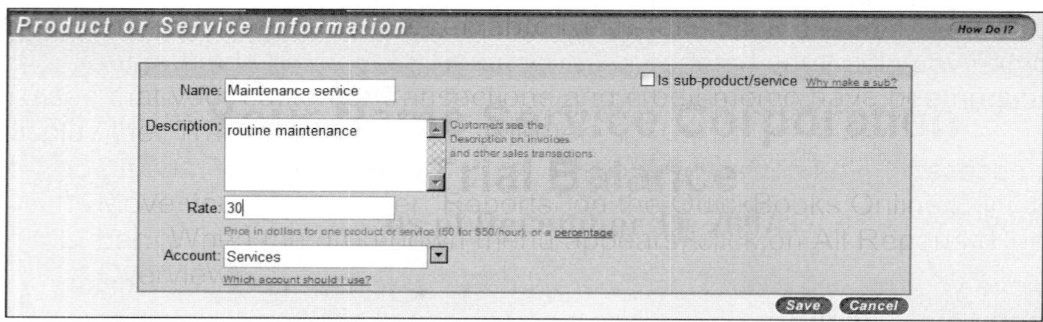

3. Another blank "Product or Service Information" screen will appear. For each of the items listed below, complete a product or service information screen. Check to verify the information is correct and then click Save. Each time a product or service is saved, a blank "Product or Service Information" screen will appear so that you can enter the next item.

Name and Description	Rate per Hour	Account
New service	$100	Services
Repair service	$ 50	Services
Emergency service	$200	Services

4. After completing and saving the "Product or Service Information" "Emergency service," another blank "Product or Information" screen will appear. Move your mouse over "Reports" on the QuickBooks Online Edition menu bar, when the drop-down menu appears, click on All Reports (Report Overview).

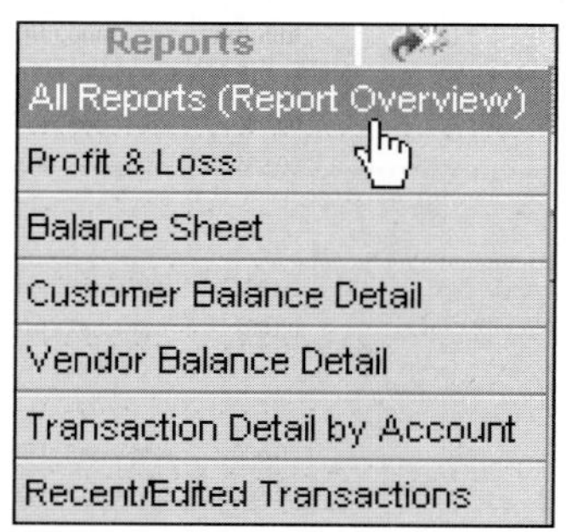

5. Scroll down to the "Sales" list and link to Product/Service Price List.

6. Compare your "Products & Service Price List" to the one shown on the next page. Correct any differences by clicking on the item needing correction to link to that item's Product or Service Information screen. Make the necessary corrections, then Save. You are returned to the Product/Service Price List.

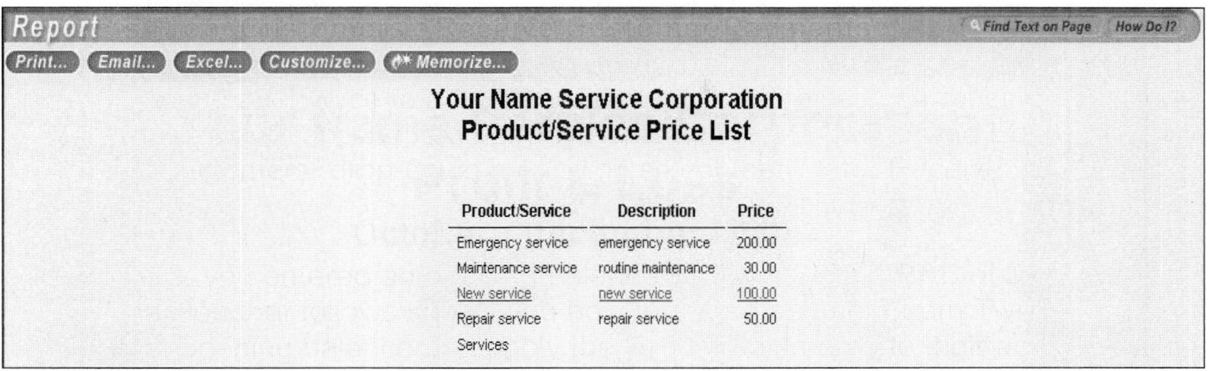

Your Name Service Corporation
Product/Service Price List

Product/Service	Description	Price
Emergency service	emergency service	200.00
Maintenance service	routine maintenance	30.00
New service	new service	100.00
Repair service	repair service	50.00
Services		

Observe that you can print, email, convert to Excel, customize or memorize this report.

9. Click on home to return to the "Home" screen.

VENDOR OVERVIEW

Service businesses purchase the supplies they use from suppliers known as ***vendors***. Vendors are the businesses that offer your business credit to buy service and/or assets, or credit for expenses incurred. When your business makes purchases on account from these vendors, the transactions are known as ***accounts payable transactions. Accounts Payable*** is the amount of money the business owes to suppliers or vendors.

From your "Home" screen, move your mouse over "Vendors" on the QuickBooks Online Edition menu bar, when the drop-down menu appears click on Vendor Overview to see an overview of the vendor process. In the next few steps you will be completing the tasks in the section called "Setup Tasks."

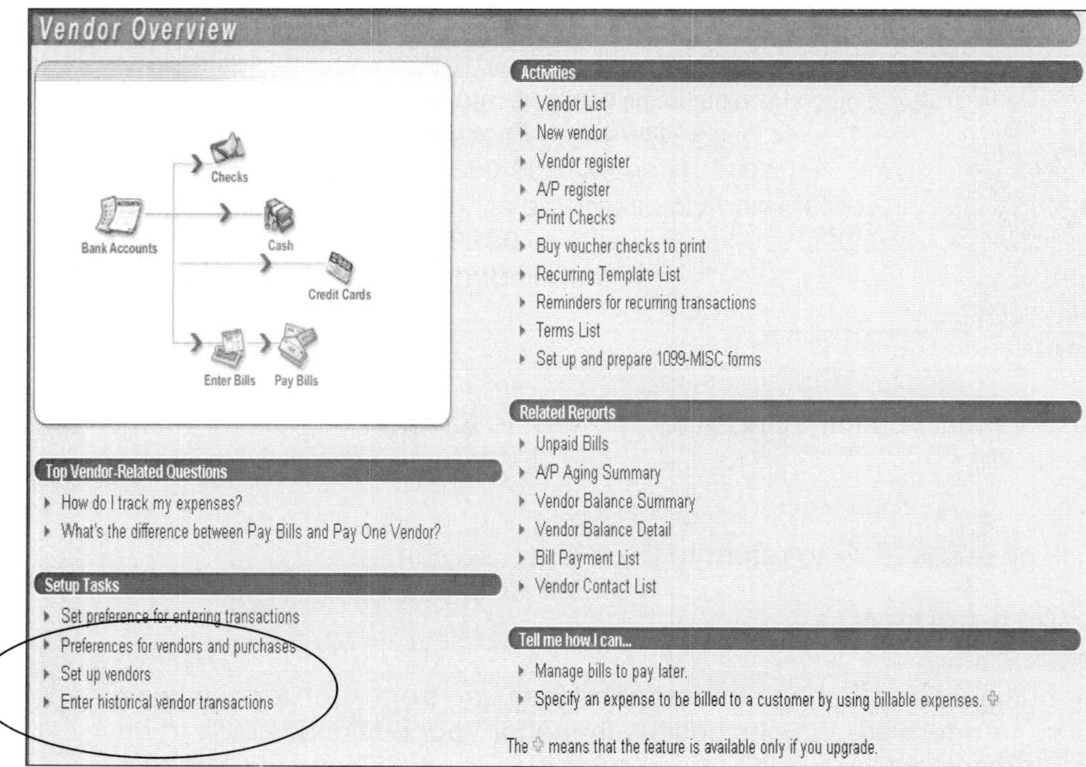

Set Preferences for Entering Transactions

1. From the "Vendor Overview" screen, click on the link Set preferences for entering transactions. After a few moments a "Mini Interview—Web Page Dialog" box appears asking "Do you want to automatically recall transactions." If necessary, click on the "Yes" radio button and then click on Finish at the bottom of the box to save vendor transaction preferences.

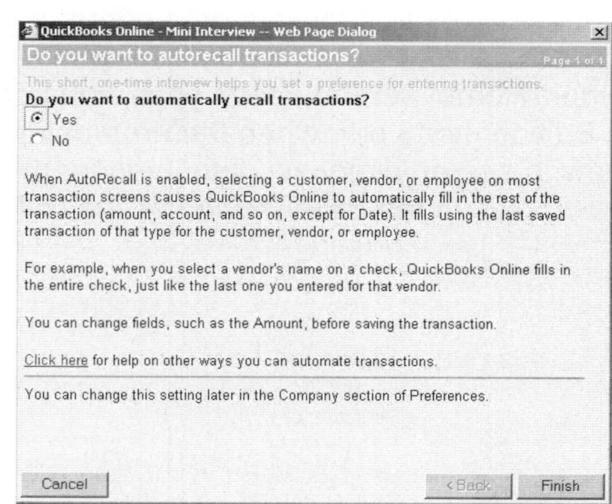

Set up Vendors

Follow these steps to add vendors used by your business to purchase supplies.

1. From the "Vendor Overview" screen, click on the link Set up vendors. After a few moments, a blank "Vendor Information" screen appears. Continue with step 2 to add a vendor.
2. Complete the vendor information for "Big Bytes Supplies," a supplier that sells your business computer supplies using the screen below as a guide. Remember, to select the company name (Big Bytes Supplies) in the "Display Name As" field. Check that you have entered the information correctly, then click on **Save** to save the vendor information for Big Bytes Supplies.

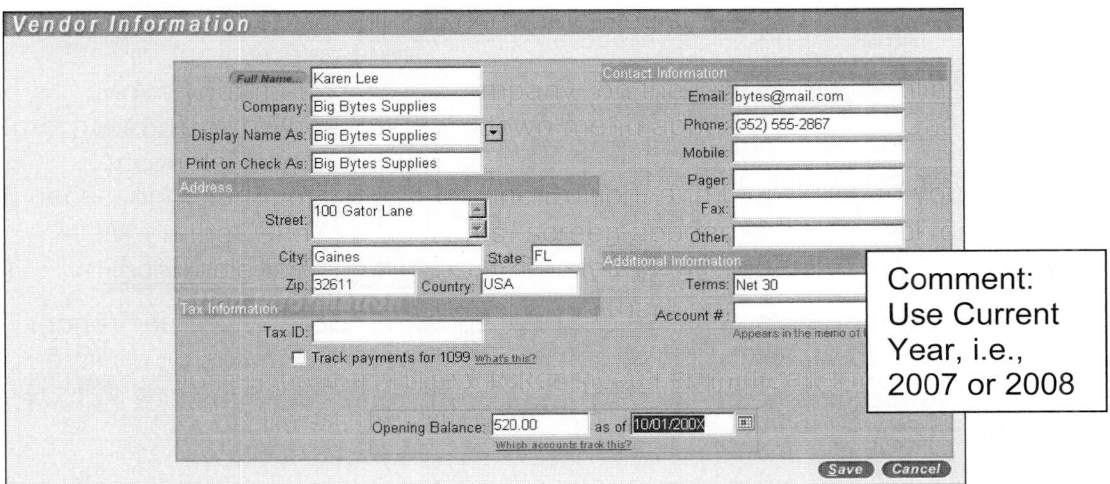

3. Complete the vendor information for "Sales Products Supply," a supplier that sells your business office supplies using the next screen as a guide. Use your tab key to move between data fields. Check that you have entered the information correctly, then click on **Save** to save the vendor information for Sales Products Supply.

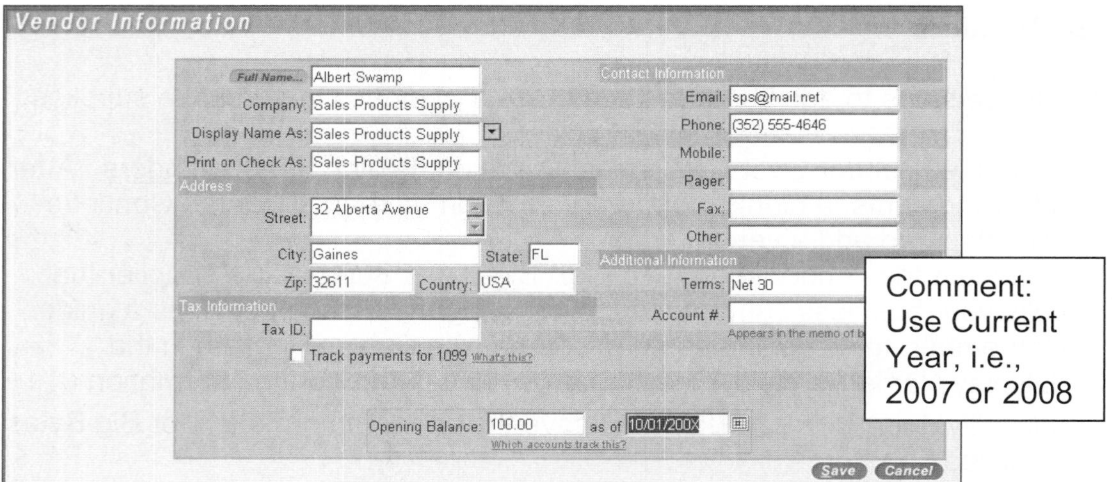

4. Another blank "Vendor Information" screen appears. Move your mouse over "Vendors" on the QuickBooks Online Edition menu bar. When the drop-down menu appears, click on "Vendor List."

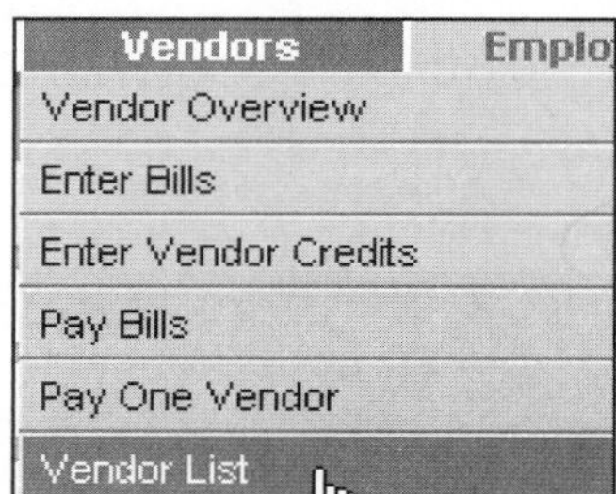

5. After a few moments, the "Vendor List" appears. Compare your "Vendor List" screen to the following screen. Correct any differences by clicking on the vendor line needing correction to highlight it and then click Edit at the bottom of the screen.

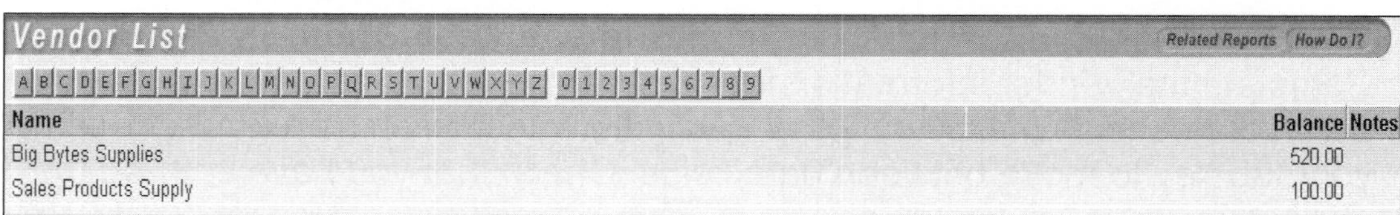

Observe that the balance for each vendor is shown on this screen. When you check the balance sheet below, you will see that the accounts payable account has a balance of $620.

6. Move your mouse over "Vendors" on the QuickBooks Online Edition menu bar. When the drop-down menu appears, click on "Vendor Overview."

7. The "Vendor Overview" screen appears. From the "Setup Tasks" list, you have completed set preference for entering transactions and set up vendors. Next you will display your balance sheet report.

DISPLAYING THE BALANCE SHEET

To display your balance sheet as of October 1, 20XX (your current year), follow the following steps.

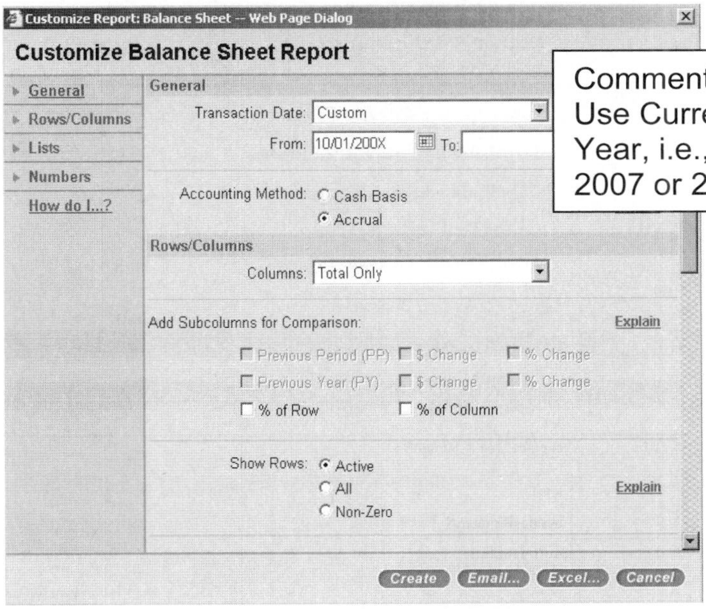

Comment: Use Current Year, i.e., 2007 or 2008

1. Click on "Reports" on the QuickBooks Online Edition menu bar, when the drop-down menu appears click on Balance Sheet.

2. When the "Report" screen appears, click Customize... . In the "Dates" filed, select "Custom."

3. When the "Customize Report: Balance Sheet—Web Page Dialog" box appears, change the date "From" and "To" dates to 10/01/20XX.

4. Click on Create . Your October 1, 20XX (your current year) balance sheet appears. Compare it to the one shown on the next page.

Note:
The Net income $255 which appears on the balance sheet is due to previous sales activity and resulted in the accounts receivable and accounts payable opening balances.

Your Name Service Corporation
Balance Sheet
As of October 1, 2007

Comment:
Will display your name and year, i.e., 2007 or 2008

	Total
ASSETS	
Current Assets	
Bank Accounts	
Your Name Service Corporation	3,000.00
Total Bank Accounts	**$3,000.00**
Accounts Receivable	
Accounts Receivable	875.00
Total Accounts Receivable	**$875.00**
Other Current Assets	
Prepaid Insurance	200.00
Total Other Current Assets	**$200.00**
Total Current Assets	**$4,075.00**
Fixed Assets	
Computer Equipment	
Accumulated Depreciation	-1,200.00
Original Cost	6,000.00
Total Computer Equipment	**4,800.00**
Total Fixed Assets	**$4,800.00**
TOTAL ASSETS	**$8,875.00**
LIABILITIES AND EQUITY	
Liabilities	
Current Liabilities	
Accounts Payable	
Accounts Payable	620.00
Total Accounts Payable	**$620.00**
Total Current Liabilities	**$620.00**
Total Liabilities	**$620.00**
Equity	
Common Stock	1,000.00
Paid in Capital	7,000.00
Retained Earnings	
Net Income	255.00
Total Equity	**$8,255.00**
TOTAL LIABILITIES AND EQUITY	**$8,875.00**

4. Verify that Accounts Receivable shows a balance of $875 and that Accounts Payable shows a balance of $620. Your company name should show "Your First and Last name Service Corporation" and the date should show your current year.

5. Logoff or continue.

CHECK YOUR PROGRESS

Flashcard Review

Prepare flashcards for the following tasks:

1. Set up customers.
2. Set up products and services.
3. Set up vendors.

Internet Homework

To learn more about the types of questions most frequently asked about managing customers and vendors in QuickBooks Online Edition, follow these steps:

1. Click "Customers" on the QuickBooks Online Edition menu bar. When the drop-down menu appears, click on "Customer Overview."

2. From the "Customer Overview" screen click on at least two of the links under "Top Customer-Related Questions." For each of the selected links, write a short essay on what you learned. The minimum length of each essay should be 25 words; the maximum length 50 words. Use a word-processing program to type your reports. Start each essay with the question.

3. From your "Home" screen, click "Vendors" on the QuickBooks Online Edition menu bar. When the drop-down menu appears, click on Vendor Overview.

4. From the "Vendor Overview" screen click on at least two of the links under "Top Vendor-Related Questions." For each of the selected links, write a short essay on what you learned. The minimum length of each essay should be 25 words; the maximum length 50 words. Use a word-processing program to type your reports. Start each essay with the question.

5. For steps 2. and 4., print one of the questions and answers and attach it to your report. *(Hint: To print, select "Print" from the tool bar menu at the top of the "Help Topics—Web Page Dialog" box.)*

Multiple-Choice. Write the letter that best answers each question.

_____1. To enter customer records, you select:

a. Click on "New" on the "Customers List" screen.
b. Link to Set up customers on the "Customer Overview" screen.
c. Link to New customer on the "Customer Overview" screen.
d. All of the above.
e. None of the above.

_____2. QuickBooks Online Edition information is saved via your Internet browser, when you click on:
a. Finish.
b. Help.
c. Setup.
d. Submit.
e. None of the above.

_____3. The Products & Services List contains all of the following except:

a. Maintenance service.
b. Repair service.
c. Emergency service.
d. All of the above are included.
e. None of the above.

_____4. All of the following are customers except:

a. NFP Access.
b. Big Bytes Supplies.
c. Cyberconnect Cafe.
d. Twin Sisters B & B.
e. All of the above.

______5. All of the following are vendors except:

a. Big Bytes Supplies.
b. Sales Products Supply.
c. Cyberconnect Cafe.
d. All of the above.
e. None of the above.

______6. Service businesses purchase supplies from suppliers known as:

a. Customers.
b. Vendors.
c. Salespeople.
d. Clients.
e. None of the above.

______7. The amount of money a business owes to its vendors is called:

a. Accounts payable.
b. Accounts receivable.
c. Inventory accounts.
d. Service accounts.
e. None of the above.

______8. An "Accounts Payable" is classified as a/an:

a. Expense account.
b. Liability account.
c. Equity account.
d. Cost of goods sold account.
e. None of the above.

______9. The amount of money credit customers owe to a business is called:

a. Accounts payable.
b. Accounts receivable.
c. Inventory account.
d. Service account.
e. None of the above.

_____10. The October 1, 20XX balance sheet shows an accounts receivable balance of:

a. $200.00.
b. $875.00
c. $975.00.
d. $2,000.00
e. None of the above.

True/False. Write T for True and F for false in the space provided.

_____11. Before you can enter credit sales transactions, you need to set up information about customers.

_____12. Accounts receivable is what vendors owe to the business.

_____13. Each time you click on the "Print" button, you are also saving.

_____14. QuickBooks Online Edition refers to default settings as preferences.

_____15. The opening balance for Cyberconnect Cafe is $280.00.

_____16. When a service business makes purchases on account from vendors, the transactions are called accounts payable transactions.

_____17. The types of service that service businesses sell to their customers are referred to as products and services.

_____18. The opening balance for Twin Sisters B & B is $300.00

_____19. The opening balance for Big Bytes Supplies is $520.00.

_____20. The opening balance for the Sales Products Supply is $400.00.

Exercise 3-1: Follow these steps to print the customer list.

1. If necessary, log in to your QuickBooks Online Edition account.
2. From the "Home" screen, move your mouse over "Reports" on the QuickBooks Online Edition menu bar. When the drop-down menu appears, click on "Customer Balance Detail."
3. Click on Print... to print the "Customer Balance Detail" report.
4. *Optional: Email your report to your instructor.*
5. Continue with Exercise 3-2.

Exercise 3-2: Follow these steps to print the "Product/Service Price List."

1. Click on "Reports, then select All Reports (Report Overview). In the "Sales" section, link to Product/Service Price List.
2. Click on Print... to print the Product/Service Price List report.
3. *Optional: Email your report to your instructor.*
4. Continue with Exercise 3-3.

Exercise 3-3: Follow these steps to print the vendor list.

1. Click on "Reports," then select "Vendor Balance Detail" from the QuickBooks Online Edition menu bar.
2. Click on Print... to print the Vendor Balance Detail report.
3. *Optional: Email your report to your instructor.*
4. Continue with Exercise 3-4.

Exercise 3-4: Follow these steps to print the balance sheet as of October 1, 20XX.

1. From the "Home" screen, move your mouse over "Reports" on the QuickBooks Online Edition menu bar, when the drop-down menu appears click on "Balance Sheet."

2. When the "Report" screen appears, click on Customize... . Select "Custom" for the "Dates" field.

3. Type **10/01/20XX (Your current year)** in the "From" field, and **10/01/20XX (Your current year)** in the "To" field. Then click on Create .

4. Make the selections to print your report.

5. *Optional: Email your report to your instructor.*

6. Back up your balance sheet using Excel. (*Hint: See the steps on pages 42, Copying Report Data to Excel.*) Use **Your Name** and **Exercise 3-4** as the file name.

7. Print your spreadsheet balance sheet using Excel.

CHAPTER 3 INDEX

Accounts payable 64, 67
Accounts payable transactions 64, 67
Accounts receivable 53, 67
Accounts receivable transactions 53
Check your progress 67
Computer accounting essentials website 51
Customer information 56, 57,58,59
Customer list 58
Customer overview 53, 55, 56, 59, 67
Defaults 51, 52
Displaying the balance sheet 65
Getting started 52
Flashcard review 67
Home page 52
Internet homework 67
Preferences 51
Set preferences for customer statements 55
Set preferences for entering transactions 55, 62
Set up customers 56
Set up products and services 59
Set up tasks 53, 56, 59, 63
Set up vendors 63
Software objectives 51
Vendor information 66, 68
Vendor list 68
Vendor overview 61, 62, 63, 64, 65, 67
Vendors 61, 67
Web objectives 51

4 Fourth Quarter Transactions

In Chapter 4 of *Computer Accounting Essentials Using QuickBooks Online Edition*, you will record transactions for the fourth quarter of the year: October, November and December. You will record accounts payable, accounts receivable, and cash transactions. At the end of each month's transactions, you will also reconcile the bank statement.

SOFTWARE OBJECTIVES: In Chapter 4, you use the software to:

1. Record accounts payable transactions.
2. Record accounts receivable transactions.
3. Record cash transactions.
4. Reconcile October, November, and December bank statements.
5. Print reports.
6. Copy report data to Excel.
7. Complete activities for Chapter 4, Fourth Quarter Transactions.

WEB OBJECTIVES: In Chapter 4, you use the Internet to:

1. Access the Computer Accounting Essentials web site at www.mhhe.com/yachtessentials3e to check for updates.
2. Log in to your QuickBooks Online Edition account.
3. Record fourth quarter transactions.
4. Complete Flashcard review.
5. Complete Internet activities.

COMPUTER ACCOUNTING ESSENTIALS WEBSITE

Before you begin your work in Chapter 4, Fourth Quarter Transactions, access the Computer Accounting Essentials website at www.mhhe.com/yachtessentials3e. Select the QuickBooks link, and then link to Text Updates. Check this website regularly for reference and study.

GETTING STARTED

Follow these steps to start QuickBooks Online Edition. You *must* complete Chapters 1, 2, and 3, pages 3 - 73, before starting Chapter 4, Fourth Quarter Transactions. *The exercises at the end of each Chapter must be completed, too.*

1. Start your Internet browser and log in to QuickBooks Online Edition in the usual way.

2. Move your mouse over "Vendors" on the QuickBooks Online Edition menu bar. When the drop-down menu appears, click on Enter Bills. The "Enter Bills" screen appears.

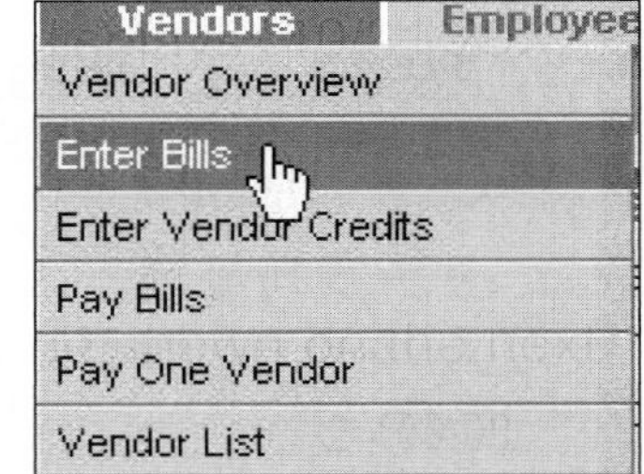

3. Scroll down the "Enter Bills" page to the section on "How Do I…" Click on the various links to learn more about vendor-related transactions.

3. For example, link to Edit a bill. A "Help Topics--Web Page Dialog" box appears. Compare your screen to the one shown on the right.

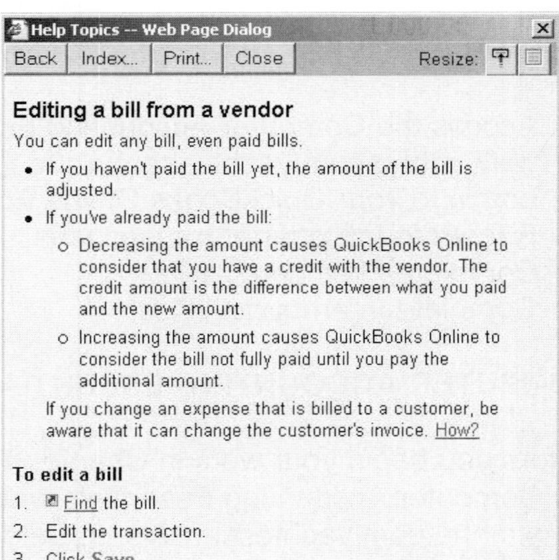

4. After reading the information in the box, click [X] in the upper right of the box to close the box and return to the "Enter Bills" screen.

5. Repeat Steps 4 and 5 until all the links to the various "How Do I…" questions have been read.
6. Return to the "Enter Bills" screen.

VENDOR TRANSACTIONS: ENTER BILLS

Service businesses purchase the supplies they use from suppliers known as vendors. Some of these vendors offer your business credit to buy supplies and/or assets, or credit for expenses incurred. When your business makes purchases on account from these vendors, the transactions are known as accounts payable transactions. Accounts payable, also known as the business' bills, is the amount of money the business owes to vendors or suppliers.

The "Enter Bills" screen is where you will enter information about the bills you receive from vendors. (Hint: Your screen illustration will differ somewhat—the "Bill Date" and "Due Date" fields will show the current date, *not* the dates shown below. Make no changes to the "Enter Bills" screen at this time.)

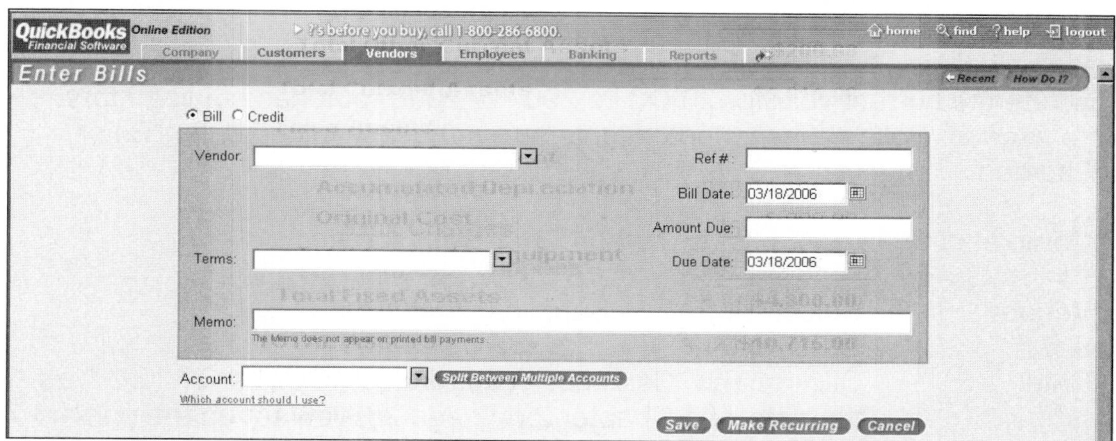

Your business purchases supplies on account from two vendors: Big Bytes Supplies and Sales Products Supply. You use the "Enter Bills" screen to record credit purchases.

Using QuickBooks Online Edition to track accounts payable is a two-step process:

1. You use the "Enter Bills" window to record bills. Entering bills as soon as you receive them keeps your cash flow reports up to date.

2. You use the "Pay Bills" window to pay your bills to vendors. The "Pay Bills" window writes the checks for you.

PURCHASES OF SUPPLIES: ENTER BILLS

Follow these steps to enter bills from vendors.

1. The "Enter Bills" screen should be shown on your screen.

2. The transaction you are going to work with is

Date	*Transaction*
10/02/20XX[1]	Received Invoice 66JE and shipment from Big Bytes Supplies for the purchase of computer supplies that included the purchase of usb drives on credit, Net 30, $300.

Here is how QuickBooks Online Edition journalizes this October 2, 20XX (substitute the current year for 20XX, i.e.2007 or 2008) purchase of inventory from a vendor. Follow these steps to enter a purchase invoice on the "Enter Bills" screen.

1. Complete the following fields on the "Enter Bills" screen:

Vendor	Select "Big Bytes Supplies"
Ref #	**66JE**
Date	Click on the "Calendar" icon. Select "October 2, 20XX" as the date. (In Chapter 2 on page 28, you set up the primary checking account as of 10/01/200X. If you used a different year, for example, 2007, be consistent.)
Amount	**300.00**
Terms	Observe that "Net 30" is shown in this field.
Due Date	Since this vendor is set up with terms of Net 30, 11/01/20XX" will appear in the "Due Date" field.
Memo:	usb drives
Account:	Select "Computer Supplies" (Note that this is an Expense account)

[1]In Chapter 2 on page 28, you set up the primary checking account to start as of 10/01/20XX (your current year). Make sure you use the same year consistently.

2. Compare your screen to the one shown below.

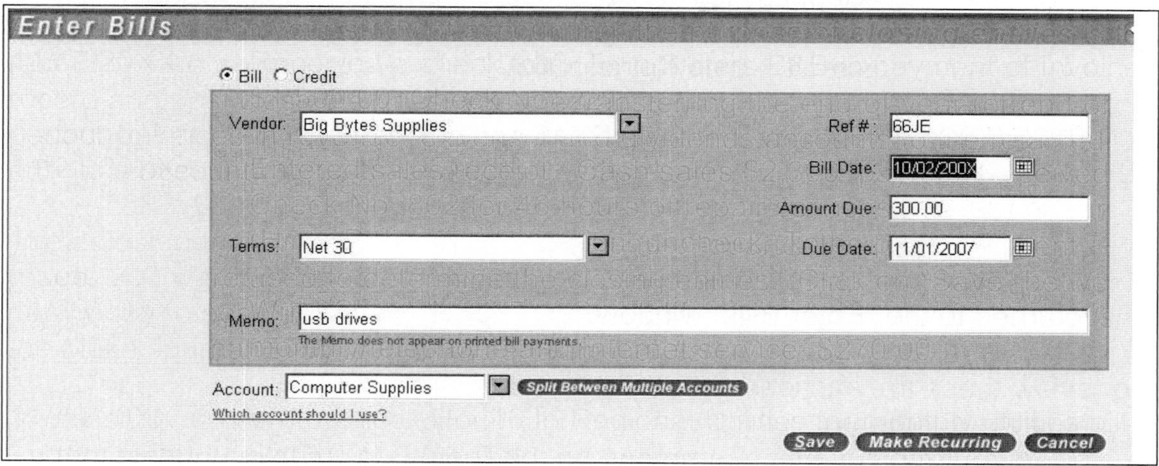

3. When you are satisfied with your entry, click Save to post the information to your QuickBooks Online Edition account.

4. After a few moments, a new "Enter Bills" window appears and you are ready to record the next transaction. Record the following transactions using Steps 1-3 as your guide.

Date	*Transaction*
10/03/20XX	Received Invoice EX32 and shipment from Sales Products Supply for the purchase of office expenses that included the purchase of paper, printer cartridges, and message pads on credit, terms Net 30, $245.

10/04/20XX Received Invoice 89JE and shipment from Big Bytes Supplies for the purchase of computer supplies that included the purchase of memory cartridges and memory sticks on credit, terms Net 30, $520.

10/05/20XX Received Invoice EX45 and shipment from Sales Products Supply for the credit purchase of office expenses that included the purchase of office supplies, Net 30, $385.

6. When you have completed the each transaction, click on "Save." You are returned to the "Enter Bills" window.

To review these transactions, follow these steps.

1. Move your mouse over "Company" on the QuickBooks Online Edition menu bar. When the drop-down menu appears, click on Chart of Accounts. When the "Chart of Accounts" screen appears, double click on Accounts Payable.

2. After a few moments, the "A/P Register" screen appears. This screen shows the total bills for your business, the four purchases made from vendors for $1,450 plus the opening balances in the two vendor accounts for a total Accounts payable of $2,070.00. This is the amount owed to vendors as of October 5, 20XX.

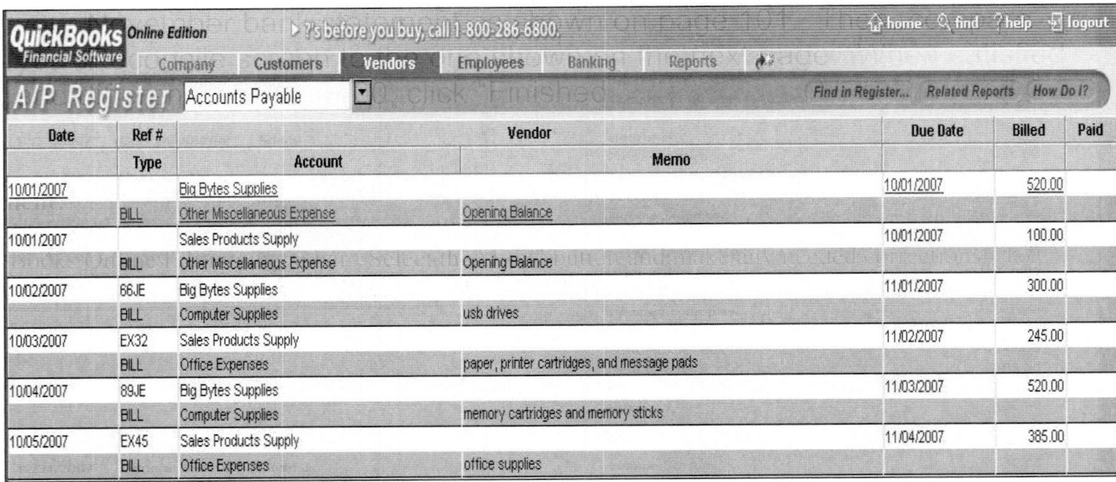

Date	Ref # / Type	Vendor / Account	Memo	Due Date	Billed	Paid
10/01/2007		Big Bytes Supplies		10/01/2007	520.00	
	BILL	Other Miscellaneous Expense	Opening Balance			
10/01/2007		Sales Products Supply		10/01/2007	100.00	
	BILL	Other Miscellaneous Expense	Opening Balance			
10/02/2007	66JE	Big Bytes Supplies		11/01/2007	300.00	
	BILL	Computer Supplies	usb drives			
10/03/2007	EX32	Sales Products Supply		11/02/2007	245.00	
	BILL	Office Expenses	paper, printer cartridges, and message pads			
10/04/2007	89JE	Big Bytes Supplies		11/03/2007	520.00	
	BILL	Computer Supplies	memory cartridges and memory sticks			
10/05/2007	EX45	Sales Products Supply		11/04/2007	385.00	
	BILL	Office Expenses	office supplies			

Purchase Returns: **Enter Vendor Credits**

When supplies or an asset is returned to a vendor, the vendor issues a vendor credit to document the return. In the next transaction, you are going to record a purchase return and revise your accounts to reflect the vendor credit.

Follow these steps to enter purchase returns.

1. Move your mouse over "Vendors" on the QuickBooks Online Edition menu bar. When the drop-down menu appears, click on Enter Vendor Credits. The "Enter Vendor Credits" screen appears.

2. The transaction you are going to work with is:

Date	*Transaction*
10/05/20XX	Returned 1 usb drive to Big Bytes Supplies, Invoice 66JE, $50.

Follow these steps to record the October 5, 20XX return of supplies.

1. The "Enter Vendor Credits" screen should be shown on your screen.

2. Complete the following fields:

Vendor	Select "Big Bytes Supplies"
Reference No.	**66JE**
Date	Select October 5, 20XX
Credit Amount	**50.00**
Memo	**Returned 1 usb drive**
Account	Computer Supplies

Compare your screen to the one shown on the next page.

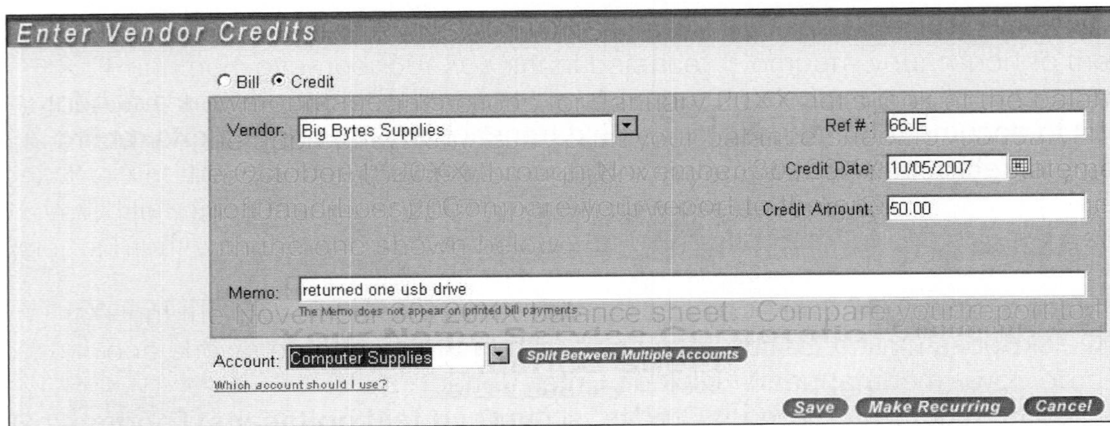

3. When you are satisfied with your entry, click Save.

4. To check that this vendor credit was entered in to your accounts, move your mouse over "Reports" on the QuickBooks Online Edition menu bar. When the drop-down menu appears, click on Transaction Detail by Account. Customize the report so that "Display Options" are grouped by "Account;" General shows "All Dates." When you locate the accounts payable information, observe that "Vendor Credit" reflects the $50 return of computer supplies on October 5, 20XX.

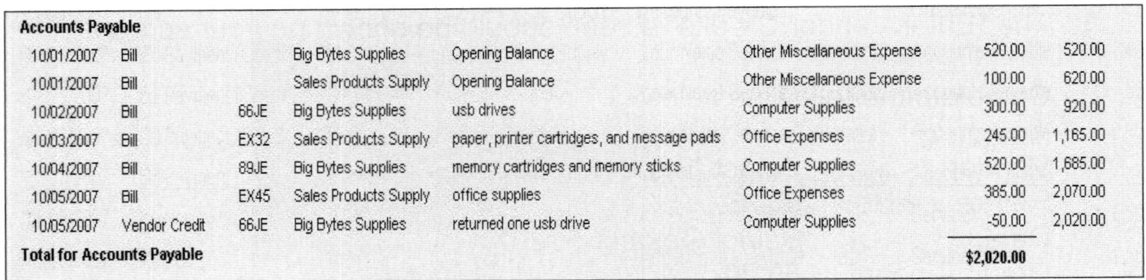

Accounts Payable							
10/01/2007	Bill		Big Bytes Supplies	Opening Balance	Other Miscellaneous Expense	520.00	520.00
10/01/2007	Bill		Sales Products Supply	Opening Balance	Other Miscellaneous Expense	100.00	620.00
10/02/2007	Bill	66JE	Big Bytes Supplies	usb drives	Computer Supplies	300.00	920.00
10/03/2007	Bill	EX32	Sales Products Supply	paper, printer cartridges, and message pads	Office Expenses	245.00	1,165.00
10/04/2007	Bill	89JE	Big Bytes Supplies	memory cartridges and memory sticks	Computer Supplies	520.00	1,685.00
10/05/2007	Bill	EX45	Sales Products Supply	office supplies	Office Expenses	385.00	2,070.00
10/05/2007	Vendor Credit	66JE	Big Bytes Supplies	returned one usb drive	Computer Supplies	-50.00	2,020.00
Total for Accounts Payable						**$2,020.00**	

5. Move your mouse over "Vendors" on the QuickBooks Online Edition menu bar. When the drop-down menu appears, click on Vendor Overview. The "Vendor Overview" screen appears.

Vendor Payments: Pay Bills

You have recorded four bills to vendors and one return. The credit terms offered to your business by each vendor is Net 30.

You are going to record the following vendor payment:

Date	*Transaction*
10/06/20XX	Paid Big Bytes Supplies' $520 opening balance by hand- writing a check (# 1) for $470 and applying the October 5 vendor credit for $50. (*Hint: Your business' opening balance was $520. On October 5, you returned one usb drive for a $50 credit. The balance owed to Big Bytes Supplies after the return is $470, excluding any purchases made during October.*)

Follow these steps to record vendor payments.

1. Move your mouse over "Vendors" on the QuickBooks Online Edition menu bar. When the drop-down menu appears, click on Pay Bills. The "Pay Bills" window appears.

2. Click on the radio button to show all bills.

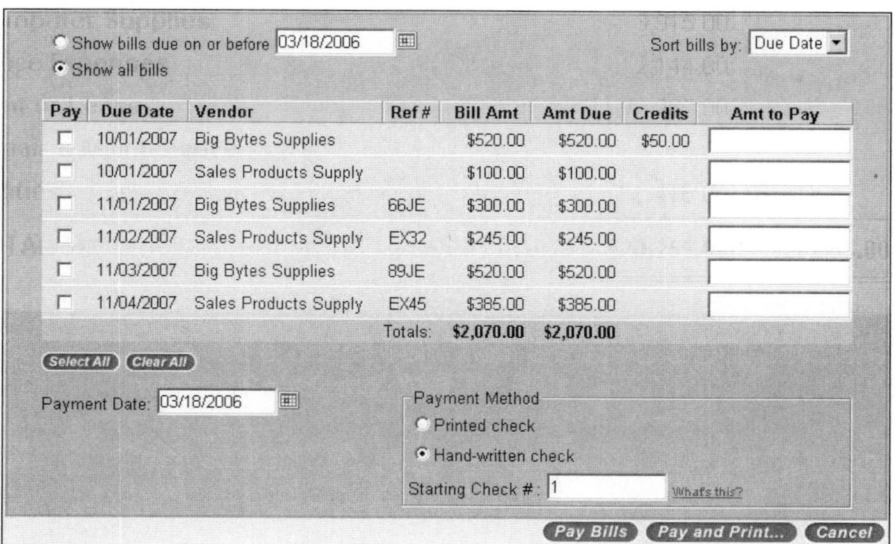

3. Complete the following:

Pay	Place a check mark in the box next to the first vendor "Big Bytes Supplies" on the list.
Amount to Pay	$470 (Observe that this amount is completed automatically.)
Payment Date	**10/06/20XX**
Payment Method	Select Hand-written check
Starting Check #	1

4. Compare your screen to the one shown below.

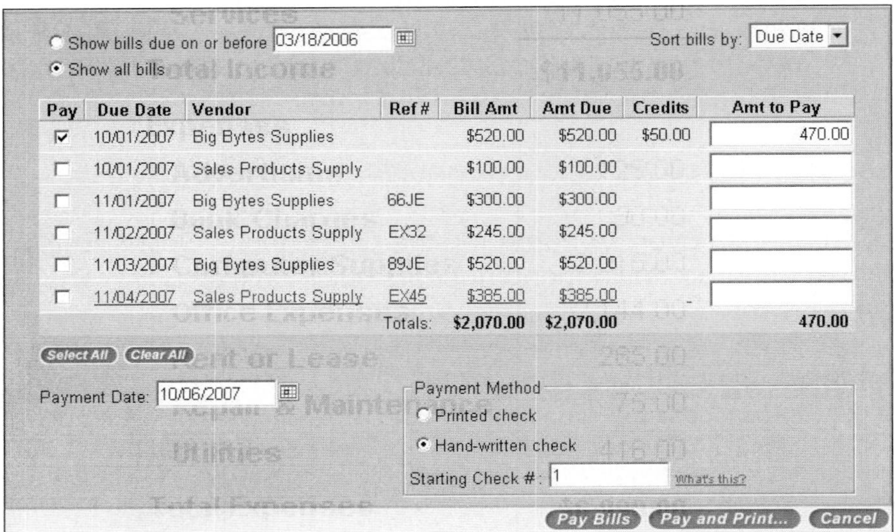

5. When you are satisfied with your work, click Pay Bills. The following screen shows that 1 bill is paid. Go to the "Bill Payment List" screen by clicking on it. (*Hint:* The "Created" line will show the current date.)

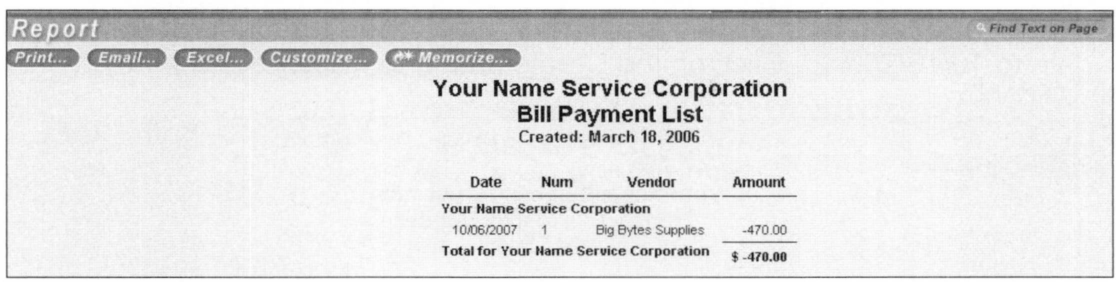

Your Name Service Corporation
Bill Payment List
Created: March 18, 2006

Date	Num	Vendor	Amount
Your Name Service Corporation			
10/06/2007	1	Big Bytes Supplies	-470.00
Total for Your Name Service Corporation			**$ -470.00**

6. Using Steps 1-4 as a guide, pay the following bills with hand-written checks. (*Hint*: Remember to select "Show all bills.")

Date	*Transactions*
10/07/20XX	Paid Sales Products Supply, Invoice EX32, $245 for the October 3 purchase with check number 2.
10/07/20XX	Paid Big Bytes Supplies, Invoice 66JE, $300 for the October 4 purchase with check number 3.

7. Compare your "Bill Payment List" report to the one shown below.

Your Name Service Corporation
Bill Payment List
Created: March 18, 2006

Date	Num	Vendor	Amount
Your Name Service Corporation			
10/06/2007	1	Big Bytes Supplies	-470.00
10/07/2007	2	Sales Products Supply	-245.00
10/07/2007	3	Big Bytes Supplies	-300.00
Total for Your Name Service Corporation			**$ -1,015.00**

8. To check that the vendor payments were made, display the "Transaction List by Vendor." (*Hint:* Move your mouse over "Reports" on the QuickBooks Online Edition menu bar. When the drop-down menu appears, click on All Reports (Report Overview). When the "Reports Overview" screen appears, click on the link to Transaction List by Vendor. Remember to customize the

report in General by changing the "From:" date to 10/01/20XX and the “To” date to 10/10/20XX. Click on the Create button to display the report.)

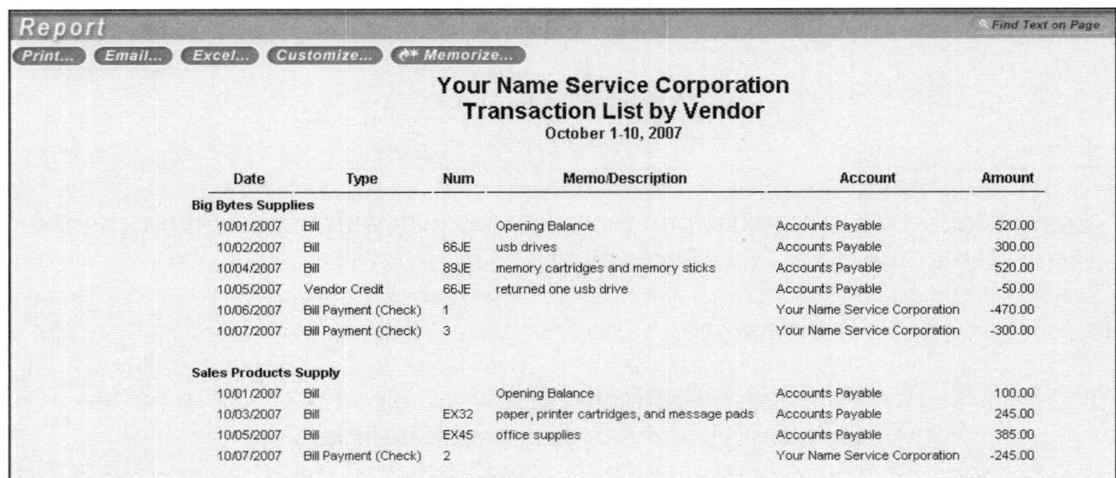

Your Name Service Corporation
Transaction List by Vendor
October 1-10, 2007

Date	Type	Num	Memo/Description	Account	Amount
Big Bytes Supplies					
10/01/2007	Bill		Opening Balance	Accounts Payable	520.00
10/02/2007	Bill	66JE	usb drives	Accounts Payable	300.00
10/04/2007	Bill	89JE	memory cartridges and memory sticks	Accounts Payable	520.00
10/05/2007	Vendor Credit	66JE	returned one usb drive	Accounts Payable	-50.00
10/06/2007	Bill Payment (Check)	1		Your Name Service Corporation	-470.00
10/07/2007	Bill Payment (Check)	3		Your Name Service Corporation	-300.00
Sales Products Supply					
10/01/2007	Bill		Opening Balance	Accounts Payable	100.00
10/03/2007	Bill	EX32	paper, printer cartridges, and message pads	Accounts Payable	245.00
10/05/2007	Bill	EX45	office supplies	Accounts Payable	385.00
10/07/2007	Bill Payment (Check)	2		Your Name Service Corporation	-245.00

9. Compare your “Transaction List by Vendor” to the one shown above. (In the “Account” column your company name will show.)

10. You may want to log off or continue with the next section.

CUSTOMER TRANSACTIONS: CREATE INVOICE

When you sell services to credit customers, the amount of those sales is recorded in an account called accounts receivable. In the following section, you will record credit customer transactions.

In QuickBooks Online Edition, the second selection in the “Customers” drop-down menu is “Create Invoice.” You use the Create Invoice link to record credit customer transactions.

Before you start, let’s review your business’ credit customers.

- Twin Sisters B&B: Your business has offered credit terms of “Net 30” meaning the full amount is due within 30 days of the invoice date.
- Cyberconnect Cafe: This customer also has credit terms of “Net 30” extended to them.
- NFP Access: This facility also has credit terms of “Net 30.”

The transaction you are going to work with is:

Date	*Transaction*
10/08/20XX	Sold services on account to Twin Sisters B&B, Invoice No. 1004 for $1,200 which included 12 hours new service at $100 per hour due to the installation of a wireless network.

> **Comment**
> QuickBooks automatically numbers invoices, unless you change the default to custom. On the next page, you accept the default for "Automatic." The invoice number for the 10/8/20XX transaction is 1004. Invoice numbers 1001, 1002 and 1003 were applied to the opening balances.

Follow these steps to record credit sales.

1. From the menu bar, click on Customers, then Create Invoice. The "Create Invoice" screen appears.

2. A "Mini-Interview—Web Page Dialog" screen pops up. Make sure that "No" is selected in answer to the question "Would you like to provide estimates to your customers?" Click Next >.

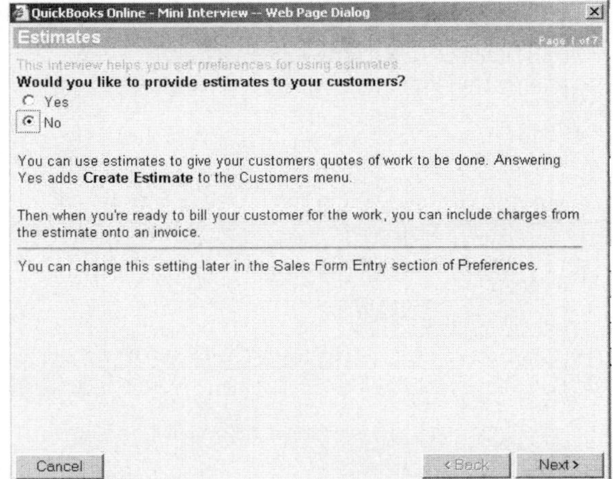

3. A "Mini-Interview—Web Page Dialog" screen pops up. Make sure that "No" is selected in answer to the question "Do you track service dates?" Click Next >.

4. A "Mini-Interview—Web Page Dialog" screen pops up. Make sure that boxes remain unchecked in answer to the question "Do you offer discounts, ship products, or take deposits?" Click Next >.

5. A "Mini-Interview—Web Page Dialog" screen pops up. Make sure that "No" is selected in answer to the question "Do you charge sales tax?" Click Next >.

6. A "Mini-Interview—Web Page Dialog" screen pops up. Make sure that boxes remain unchecked in answer to the question "Do you need more fields?" Click Next >.

7. The "Custom transaction numbers" screen appears.

8. Read the information on this screen. Take no action. Then click Finish. The "Create Invoice" screen appears. Compare it to the one shown.

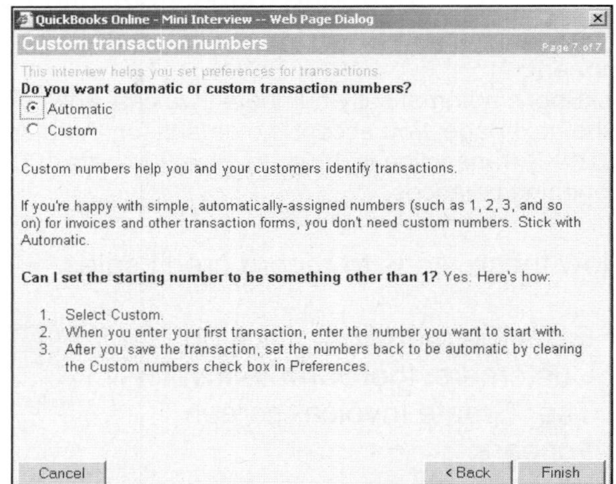

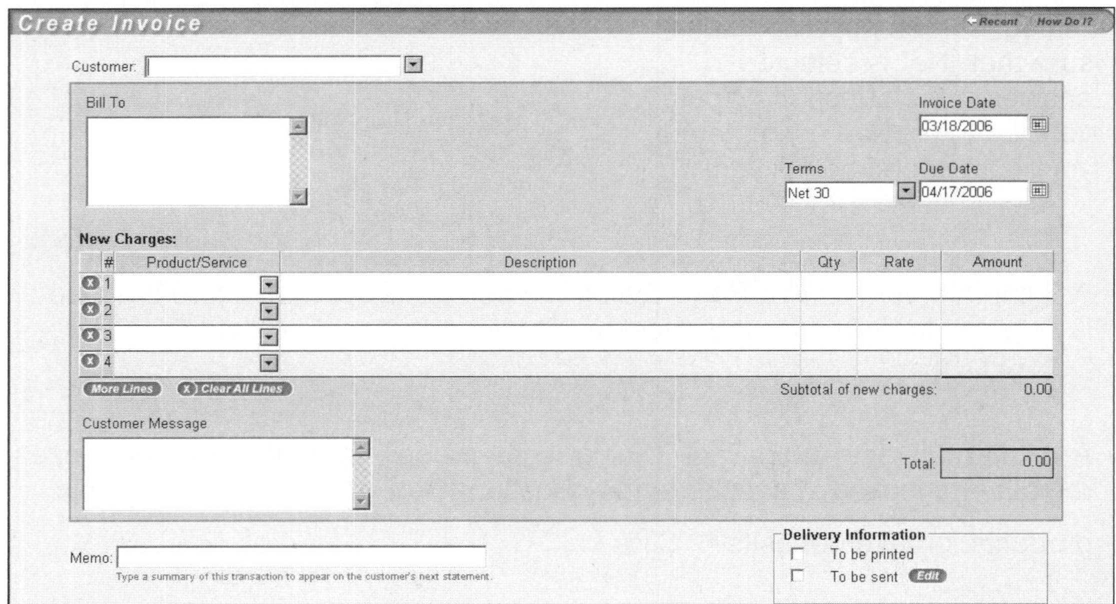

9. Complete the following fields:

Customer	Select "Twin Sisters B&B"
Date:	**10/8/20XX** (Use the current year)
Product/Service 1	Select "New service"
Quantity	**12**
Rate	100 is completed automatically
Amount	1,200.00 is completed automatically.
Memo	Install wireless network.

10. Compare your "Create Invoice" screen to the one shown.

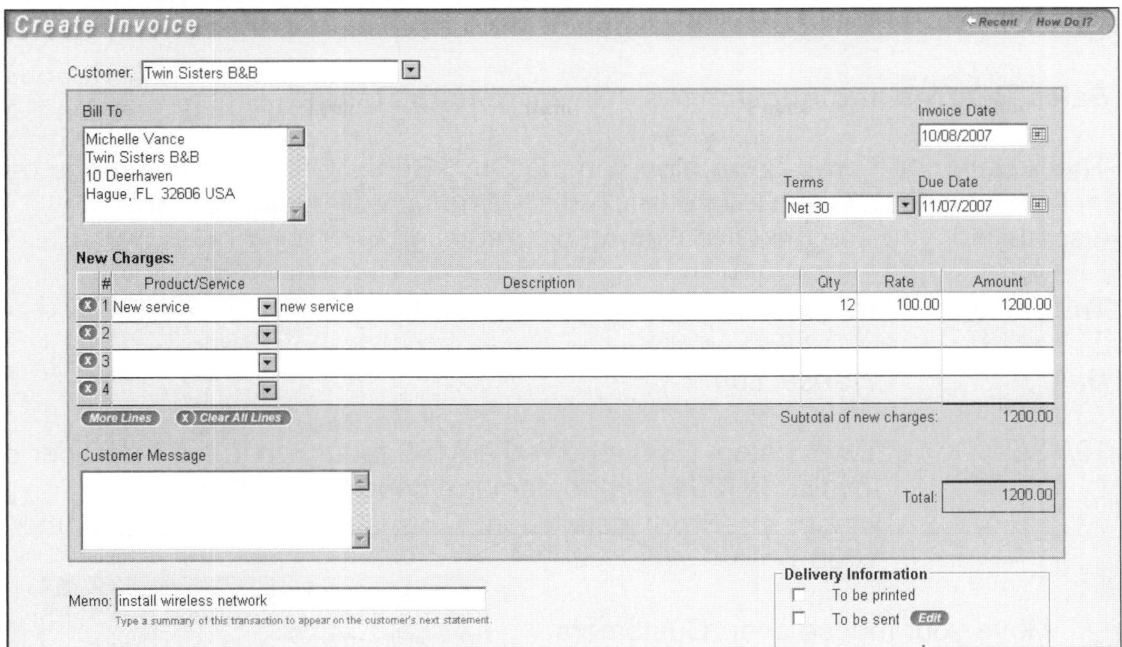

16. Make sure "To be printed" is unchecked. When you are satisfied with your work, click **Save** to post the information to your QuickBooks Online Edition account.

17. After a few moments, a new "Create Invoice" window appears and you are ready to record the next transaction. Record the following accounts receivable transactions using Steps 1-3 as your guide.

Date	*Transactions*
10/09/20XX	Sold maintenance services on account to NFP Access, Invoice No. 1005, for a total of $300 for 10 hours of maintenance work at $30 per hour. (Hint: Remember, "To be printed" should be unchecked.)
10/10/20XX	Sold services on account to Cyberconnect Cafe, Invoice No. 1006, $780 for 6 hours of maintenance services at $30 per hour and 12 hours of repair services at $50 per hour.
10/11/20XX	Sold services on account to Twin Sisters B&B, Invoice 1007, $540 for 8 hours of maintenance services at $30 per hour and 1.5 hours of emergency services at $200 per hour.

Sales Returns and Allowances: Give Credit or Refund

The "Customers" drop-down menu on the QuickBooks Online Edition menu bar includes a link to "Give Refund or Credit." When credit customers are dissatisfied, you use the Give Refund or Credit link.

The sales credit transaction you are going to work with is:

Date	*Transaction*
10/13/20XX	Twin Sisters B&B received a $150 reduction in their October 8 Invoice (#1004) due to damage done to a wall during the wireless network installation. (This is numbered Credit Memo 1008.)

1. Move your mouse over "Customers" on the QuickBooks Online Edition menu bar. When the drop-down menu appears, click on "Give Refund or Credit."

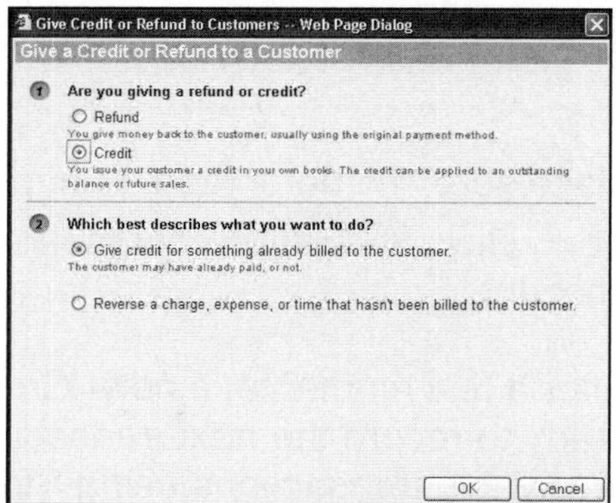

2. The "Give a Credit or Refund to a Customer" screen appears. Select "Credit."

3. Make sure that “Give credit for something already billed to the customer is selected.” Then click OK. If the “Web Page Dialog screen on “Automatically Apply Credits” appears, confirm that this preference is not selected and click Finish. The “Enter Credit Memo” screen appears.

4. Complete the following fields:

Customer	Select "Twin Sisters B&B"
Date	10/13/20XX
Product/Service 1	New service
Quantity	**1.5**
Rate	100
Amount	150.00
Memo	Credit due to wall damage. Uncheck “To be printed.”

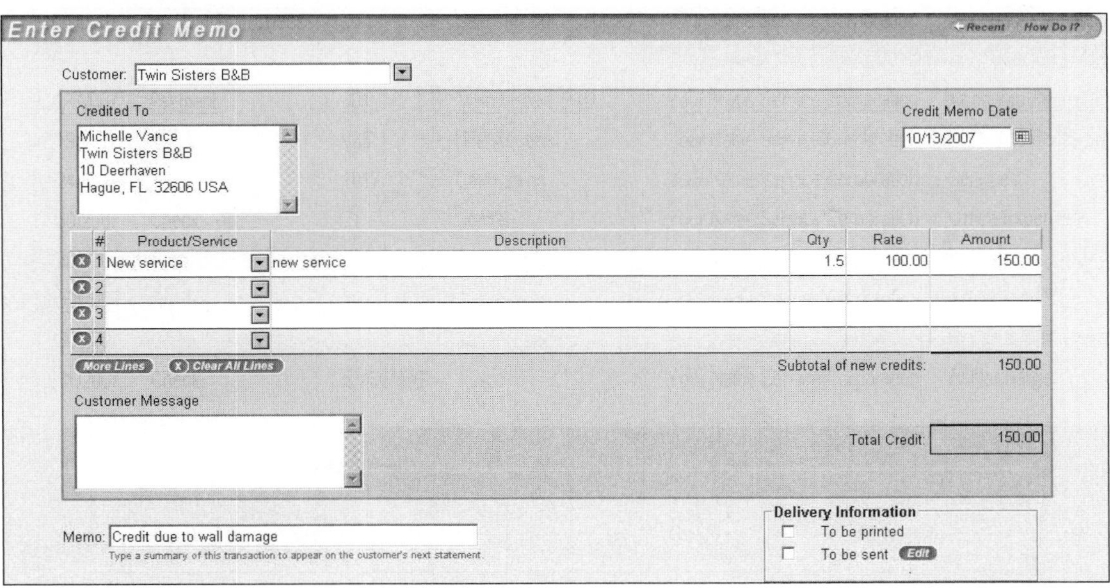

5. Click Save.

Displaying the Accounts Receivable Register

To see that your customer transactions and credit memo have been recorded, display the "Transaction List by Customer."

1. Move your mouse over "Reports" on the QuickBooks Online Edition menu bar. When the drop-down menu appears, click on All Reports (Report Overview).

2. When the "Reports Overview" screen appears, click on the link to Transaction List by Customer.

3. Click Customize... button on the "Transaction List by Customer" screen. When the "Customize Report—Web Page Dialog" box pops up, for General select "Custom" for the Transaction Date Options. For the "From:" date enter 10/01/20XX and for the "To:" date enter 10/15/20XX. Click <Create> at the bottom of the screen to display the report.

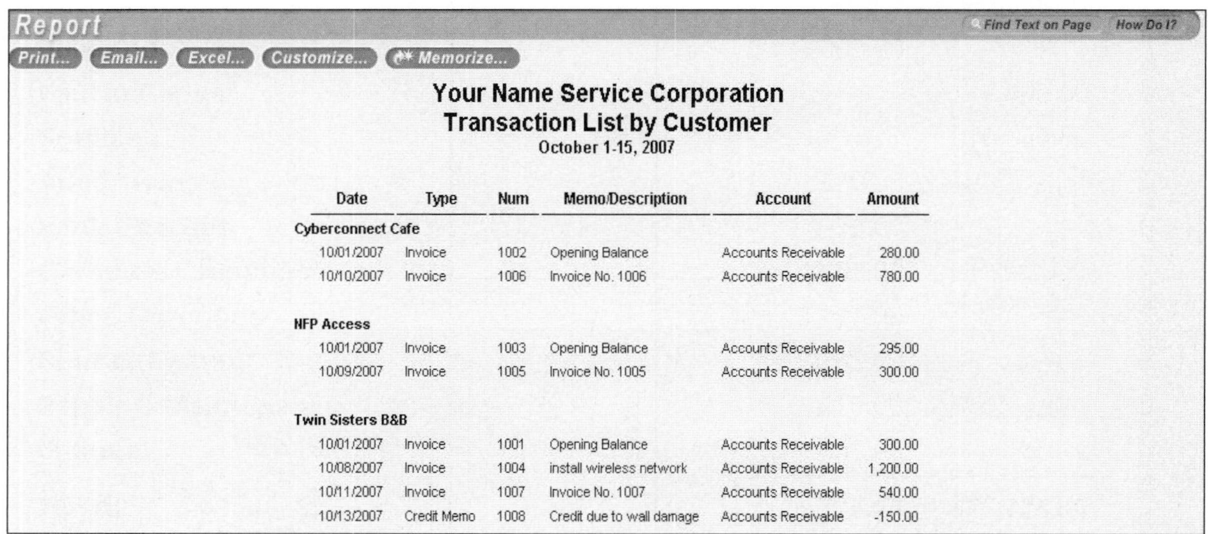

Your Name Service Corporation
Transaction List by Customer
October 1-15, 2007

Date	Type	Num	Memo/Description	Account	Amount
Cyberconnect Cafe					
10/01/2007	Invoice	1002	Opening Balance	Accounts Receivable	280.00
10/10/2007	Invoice	1006	Invoice No. 1006	Accounts Receivable	780.00
NFP Access					
10/01/2007	Invoice	1003	Opening Balance	Accounts Receivable	295.00
10/09/2007	Invoice	1005	Invoice No. 1005	Accounts Receivable	300.00
Twin Sisters B&B					
10/01/2007	Invoice	1001	Opening Balance	Accounts Receivable	300.00
10/08/2007	Invoice	1004	install wireless network	Accounts Receivable	1,200.00
10/11/2007	Invoice	1007	Invoice No. 1007	Accounts Receivable	540.00
10/13/2007	Credit Memo	1008	Credit due to wall damage	Accounts Receivable	-150.00

Comment

Your "Num" column may differ. You can ignore these differences; they are usually insignificant. Remember QB Online Edition assigns numbers automatically.

If you move your mouse over the date of any of the transactions, you can link to that record and edit the entry, if necessary.

Receipts From Customers: Receive Customer Payments

Once you issue an invoice to a customer that customer owes your business money. It is easy to apply customer payments in QuickBooks Online Edition. From the "Customers" drop-down menu you select the link to "Receive Payments."

In Chapter 3, you entered an opening balance for Twin Sisters B&B of $300. The transaction that follows shows you how to record payment from Twin Sisters B&B of that opening balance and apply the $150 credit memo to their account.

1. Move your mouse over "Customers" on the QuickBooks Online Edition menu bar. When the drop-down menu appears, click on the link to Receive Payments. The "Receive Payments" screen appears.

2. Select the date "10/13/20XX" from the calendar icon and select "Twin Sisters B&B" as the customer. A "Please wait. Retrieving customer information" box appears. In a few moments, the "Receive Payments" screen reappears with Twin Sisters B&B credits and outstanding statement charges.

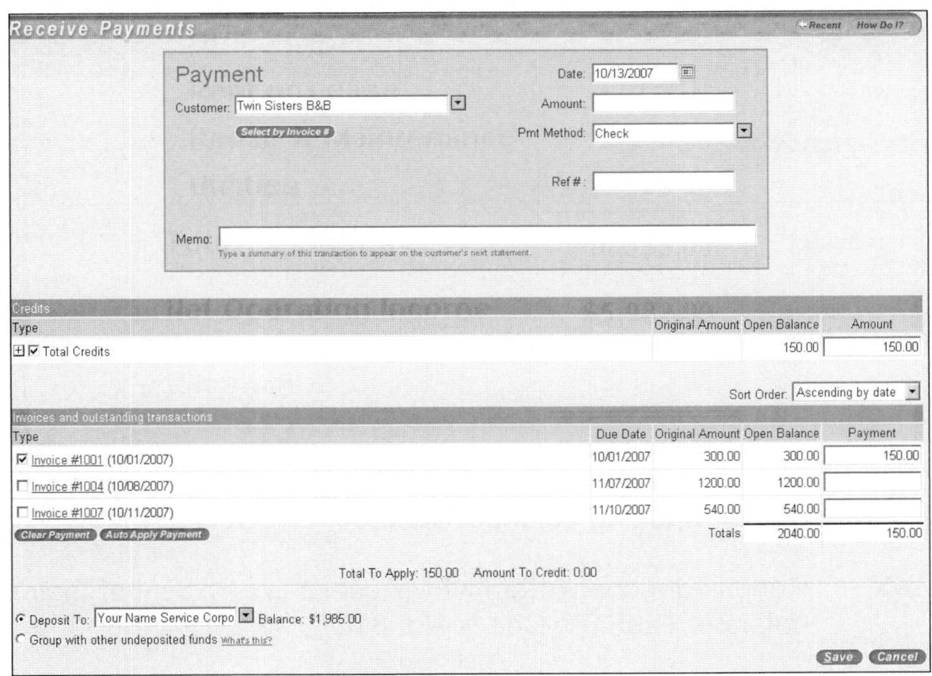

3. Complete the following fields:

Deposit To	"Your Name Service Corporation" is automatically completed.
Amount	Type **300.00**
Pmt Method:	"Check" is automatically completed.
Ref #	Type **9290**
Memo	Opening balance

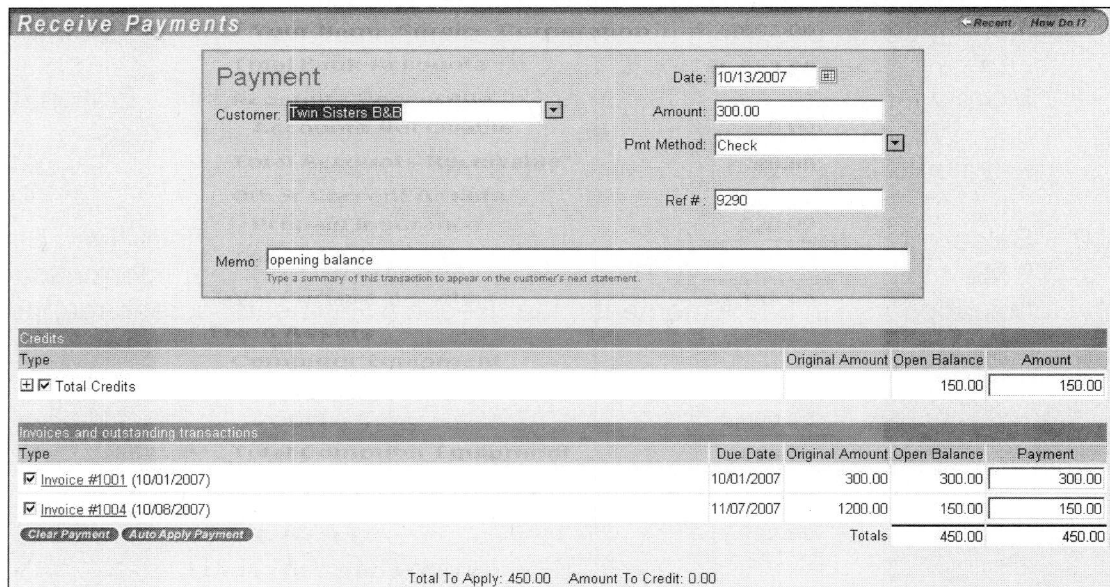

4. Click Save. A new "Receive Payments" screen appears.

5. Complete the following transactions:

Date	*Transactions*
10/16/20XX	Received a check from Cyberconnect Cafe in payment of their opening balance, $280.00, Check No. 4522.
10/16/20XX	Received a check from NFP Access in payment of their opening balance, $295.00, Check No. 816.

10/16/20XX	Received a $1,050 check from Twin Sisters B&B in payment of October 7 invoice, less the October 13 credit memo, Check No. 9346.
10/18/20XX	Received a $300 check from NFP Access in payment of October 9 Invoice, Check No. 901.
10/19/20XX	Received a $780 check from Cyberconnect Cafe in payment of October 10 Invoice, Check No. 5001.
10/19/20XX	Received a $540 check from Twin Sisters B&B in payment of October 11 Invoice, Check No. 9401.

To verify that these payments were recorded in accounts receivable, follow these steps to display the "Accounts Receivable Register":

1. Move your mouse over "Company" on the QuickBooks Online Edition menu bar. When the drop-down menu appears, click on Chart of Accounts.

2. When the "Chart of Accounts" screen appears, double click on Accounts Receivable to view the "A/R Register."

> **Hint:**
> To have a one-line view of the A/R Register, click in the "1-Line" box in the lower right of the A/R Register screen.

3. Scroll down the "A/R Register" screen. The "Balance" shows "$0.00." Compare your screen to the one shown on the next page.

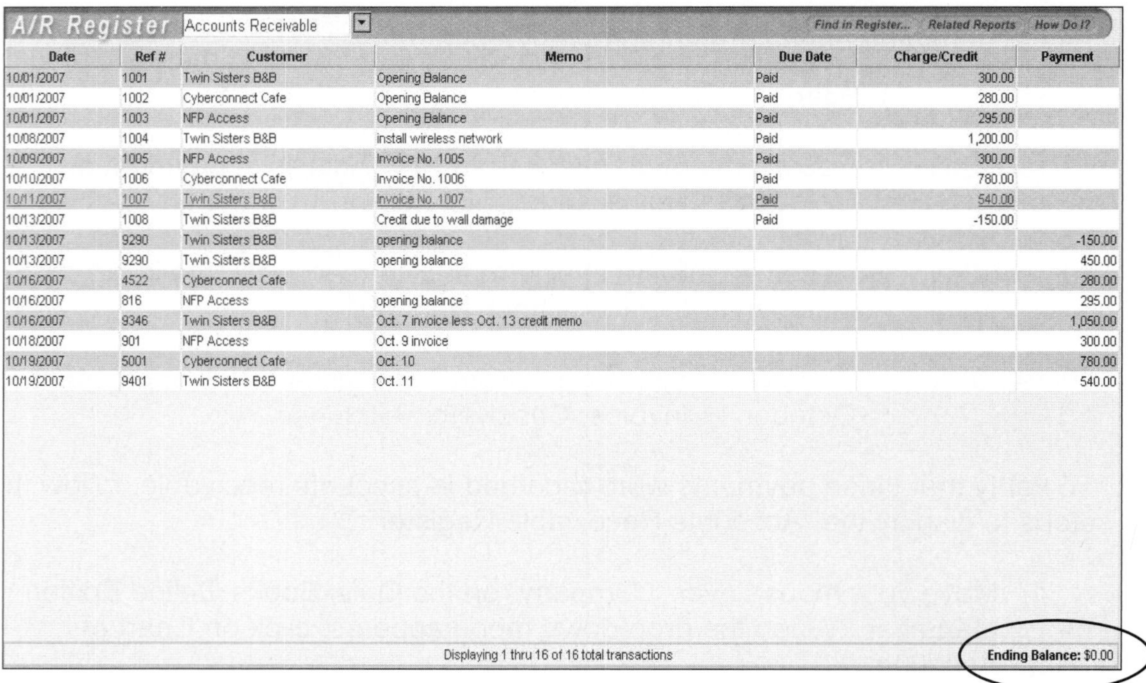

A/R Register | Accounts Receivable | Find in Register... | Related Reports | How Do I?

Date	Ref #	Customer	Memo	Due Date	Charge/Credit	Payment
10/01/2007	1001	Twin Sisters B&B	Opening Balance	Paid	300.00	
10/01/2007	1002	Cyberconnect Cafe	Opening Balance	Paid	280.00	
10/01/2007	1003	NFP Access	Opening Balance	Paid	295.00	
10/08/2007	1004	Twin Sisters B&B	install wireless network	Paid	1,200.00	
10/09/2007	1005	NFP Access	Invoice No. 1005	Paid	300.00	
10/10/2007	1006	Cyberconnect Cafe	Invoice No. 1006	Paid	780.00	
10/11/2007	1007	Twin Sisters B&B	Invoice No. 1007	Paid	540.00	
10/13/2007	1008	Twin Sisters B&B	Credit due to wall damage	Paid	-150.00	
10/13/2007	9290	Twin Sisters B&B	opening balance			-150.00
10/13/2007	9290	Twin Sisters B&B	opening balance			450.00
10/16/2007	4522	Cyberconnect Cafe				280.00
10/16/2007	816	NFP Access	opening balance			295.00
10/16/2007	9346	Twin Sisters B&B	Oct. 7 invoice less Oct. 13 credit memo			1,050.00
10/18/2007	901	NFP Access	Oct. 9 invoice			300.00
10/19/2007	5001	Cyberconnect Cafe	Oct. 10			780.00
10/19/2007	9401	Twin Sisters B&B	Oct. 11			540.00

Displaying 1 thru 16 of 16 total transactions | **Ending Balance:** $0.00

CASH TRANSACTIONS

Your business makes cash sales and cash payments. The transactions that follow will show you how to use the Enter "Sales Receipts" link under "Customers" and use the "Write Checks" link under "Banking" on the QuickBooks Online Edition menu bar.

Cash Sales: Enter Sales Receipt

The transaction for a cash sale follows.

Date	*Transaction*
10/20/20XX	Cash sales of various repairs, $2,150, received check No. 801.

1. Move your mouse over "Customers" on the QuickBooks Online Edition menu bar. When the drop-down menu appears, click on Enter Sales Receipt. The "Enter Sales Receipt" window appears.

2. In the "Customer" field, type **Cash Sales**. A "Web Page Dialog" box pops up asking if you want to do a quick add of "Cash Sales." Click Quick Add.

3. In the "Sale Date" field, type **10/20/20XX** or use the calendar icon to enter the date.

4. For the "Product/Service," "Quantity," "Rate," "Amount" and Memo" fields, use the following screen as a guide.

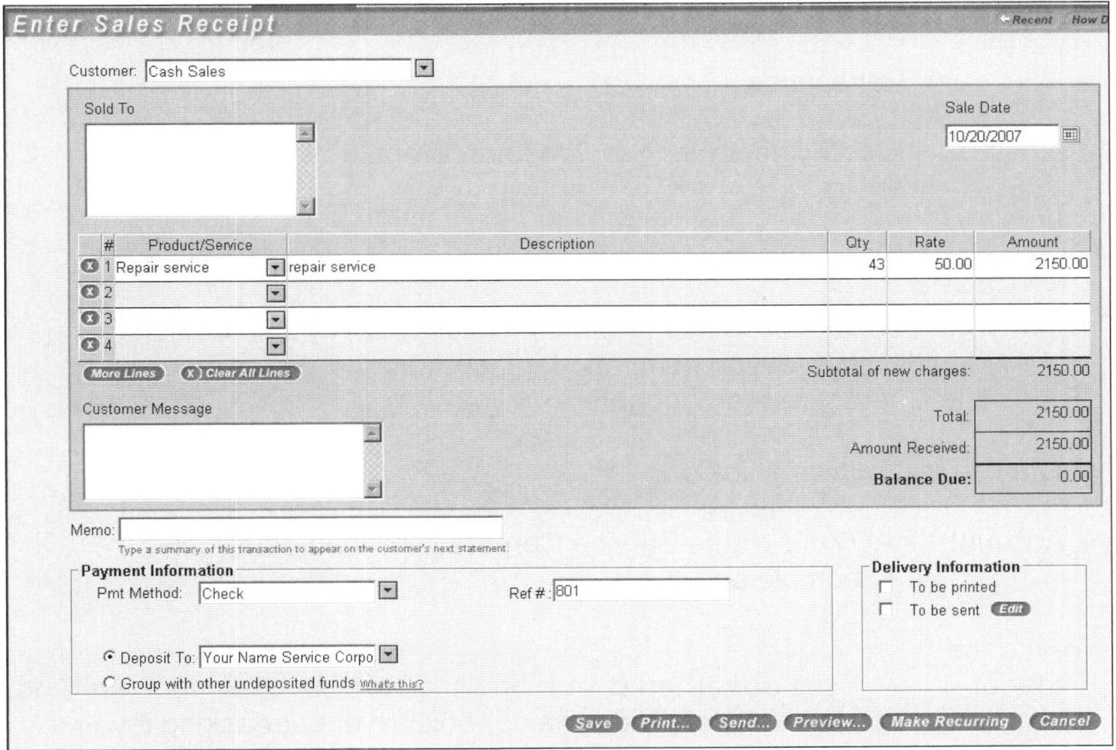

5. Scroll down the "Enter Sales Receipt" screen to complete the following fields.
   a. In the "Pmt Method" field, select "Check."
   b. Type **801** in the "Ref #" field.
   c. In the "Deposit to" field, make sure that "Your Name Service Corporation" appears.

6. Make sure your screen matches the one shown on previous page, then click Save.

Now that you have received cash from a cash sale, it is time to learn about making cash payments by writing checks.

Cash Payments: Write Checks

Your business also makes cash payments. Usually these cash payments are for expenses. All payments of cash are recorded in the "Write Checks" window. The transaction you are going to work with is

Date	*Transaction*
10/21/20XX	Issued Check No. 4 to Jonathan Brent, a new vendor, for repairs, $75.

Follow these steps to write checks:

1. Move your mouse over "Banking" on the QuickBooks Online Edition menu bar. When the drop-down menu appears, click on the Write Checks link. The "Write Checks" screen appears.

2. Complete the following fields:

Bank Account	"Your Name Service Corporation" is automatically completed.
Pay to the Order of	Type **Jonathan Brent**, press <Tab>. In a moment, an "Add Name—Web Page Dialog" box will appear asking if you want to add "Jonathan Brent" and if he is a "Vendor." Click Quick Add.
Check #	"4" is automatically displayed.
Date	Select "10/21/20XX"
Amount	**75.00** (Observe that the check is automatically written.)
Memo	Type "Repairs"

Account Select "Repairs & Maintenance."

3. Compare your "Write Checks" screen to the one below.

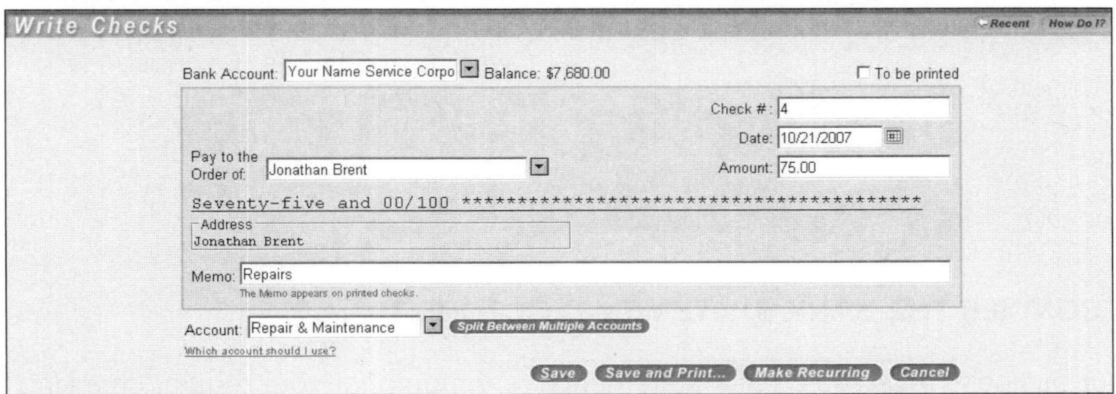

4. If necessary, make any needed changed. Then click Save. A blank "Write Checks" screen appears. Complete the following transactions.

Date	*Transaction*
10/21/20XX	Issued Check No. 5 to the Sun News, a new vendor, for advertising, $125.
10/21/20XX	Issued Check No. 6 to Santa Fe Rentals, a new vendor, for equipment rental, $265. Use the "Rent or Lease" expense account.
10/22/20XX	Issued Check No. 7 to Comtel, a new vendor, for the monthly telephone and Internet service, $269. Use the "Office expense" account.
10/30/20XX	Issued Check No. 8 to Regional Utilities, a new vendor, for monthly utilities bill, $206. Use the "Utilities Expense" account.
10/30/20XX	Issued Check No. 9 to the sole stockholder in payment of a $1,000 cash dividend. Since you are the sole stockholder in your corporation, type **your first and last name** after "Pay to the order of"**,** then **Dividends** in the account field. Complete

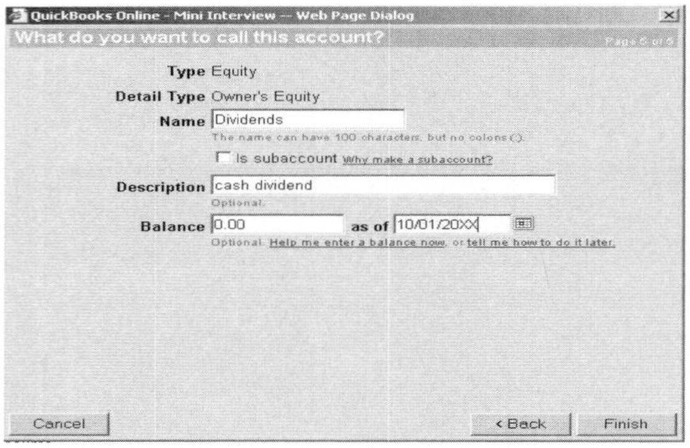

the "Mini Interview—Web Page Dialog" boxes to add the Dividends account to your chart of accounts. Remember Dividends is an "Equity" type of account, its detail type is "Owner's Equity," its description is "cash dividend," and it had a "0" balance as of "10/01/20XX."

RECONCILE THE BANK STATEMENT: OCTOBER

Your business receives a bank statement every month for your regular checking account. Bank statements show which checks and deposits have cleared the bank. Use the bank statement below to complete account reconciliation with QuickBooks Online Edition.

REGULAR CHECKING ACCOUNT October 1 - 31, 20XX			
Previous Balance		3,000.00	
7 Deposits (+)		5,155.00	
6 checks (-)		1,480.00	
Service Charges (-)	10/31/XX	25.00	
Ending Balance	10/31/XX	**$6,650.00**	
DEPOSITS			
	10/14	300.00	
	10/17	280.00	
	10/17	295.00	
	10/17	1,050.00	
	10/19	300.00	
	10/20	780.00	
	10/22	2,150.00	
CHECKS (Asterisk * indicates break in check number sequence)			
10/15	1	470.00	
10/15	2	245.00	
10/17	3	300.00	
10/29	4	75.00	
10/29	5	125.00	
10/29	6	265.00	

Follow these steps to reconcile the bank statement.

1. Move your mouse over "Banking" on the QuickBooks Online Edition menu bar. When the drop-down menu appears, click on Banking Overview. When the "Banking Overview" screen appears, move your mouse over the word "Reconcile" then double click.

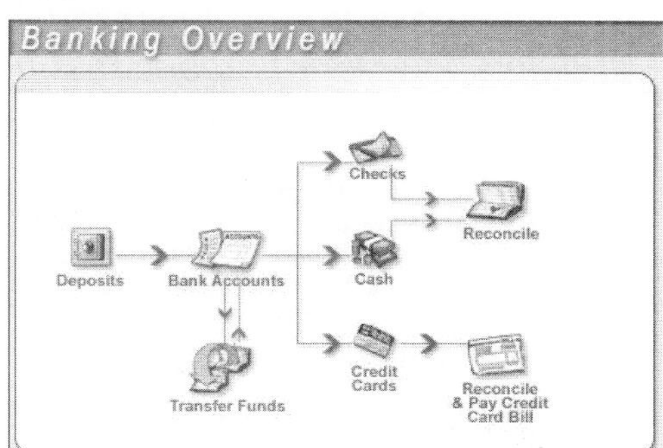

2. A "Choose an account to reconcile -- Web Page Dialog" box appears. Select the account "Your Name Service Corporation" and click OK.

3. A "--Web Page Dialog" box appears. For Question 1 refer to your October bank statement on the previous page. Type **10/31/20XX** (your current year) for the "Statement Ending Date," verify the "Opening Balance" is "3000.00" and type **6650.00** as the "Ending Balance."

4. For Question 2 refer to your October bank statement. Type **25.00** for the "Service Charge;" type **10/31/20XX** for the "Date," and select **Bank Charges** for the "Expense Account."

5. IMPORTANT! Verify that you have entered all information correctly. Errors made when reconciling the bank statement are difficult to correct. Click OK when you are satisfied.

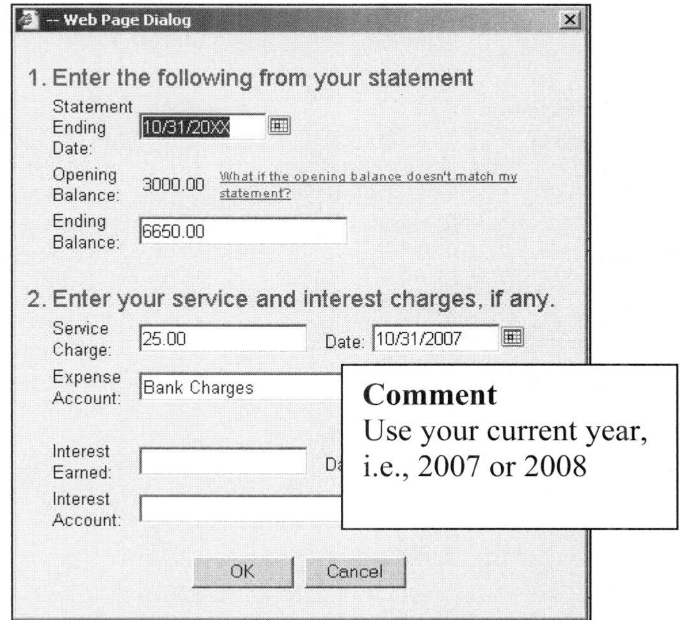

6. The "Reconcile" screen appears. Click in the "√" column to place a check mark next to each deposit that is shown on your bank statement.

7. Using the bank statement, click in the "√" column to place a check mark next to each check that has cleared your bank. (*Hint: Your company name should show your first and last name Service Corporation*. Your "Num" column may differ. This is okay; the differences are insignificant.)

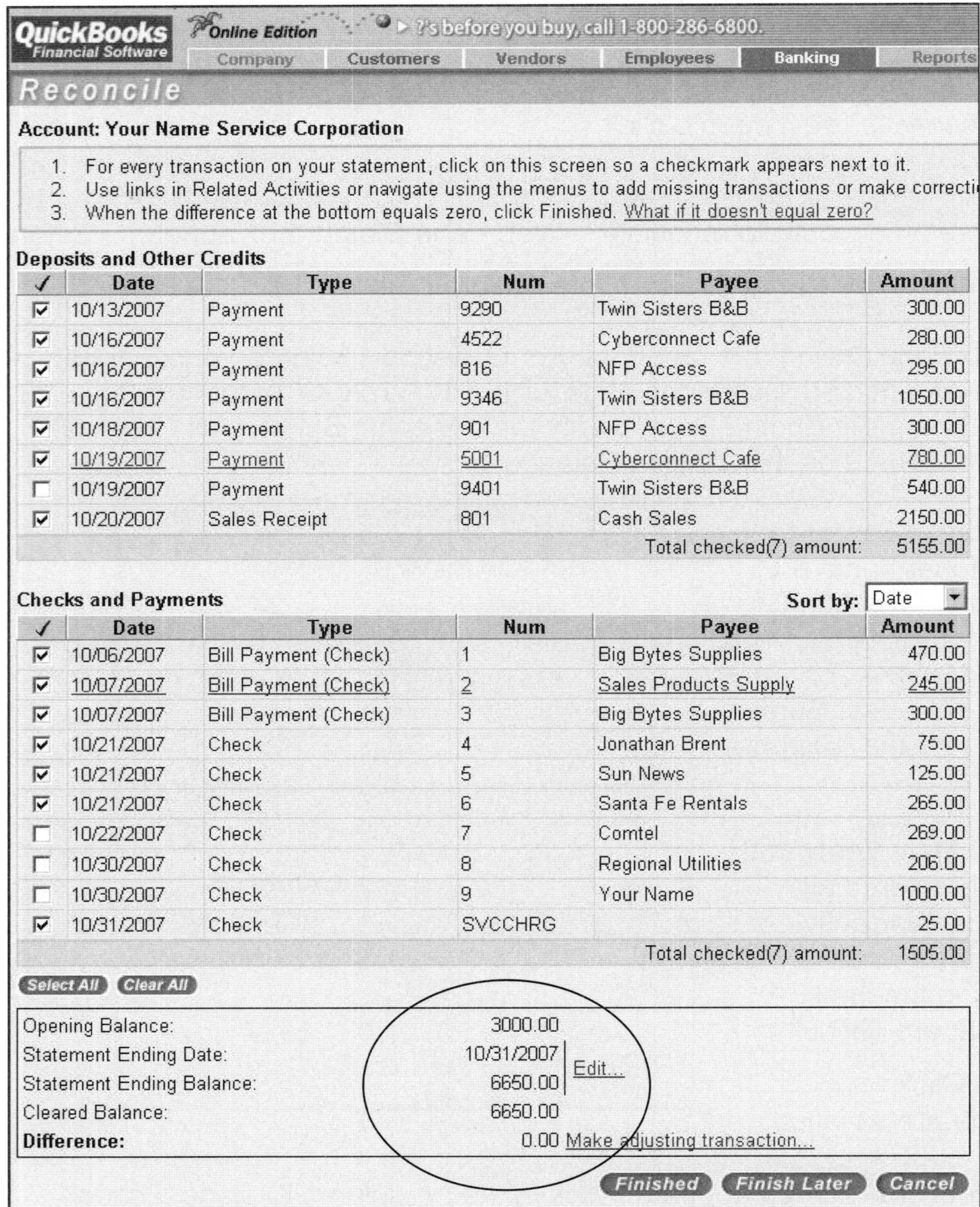

QuickBooks Financial Software | Online Edition | ?'s before you buy, call 1-800-286-6800.

Company | Customers | Vendors | Employees | Banking | Reports

Reconcile

Account: Your Name Service Corporation

1. For every transaction on your statement, click on this screen so a checkmark appears next to it.
2. Use links in Related Activities or navigate using the menus to add missing transactions or make correcti
3. When the difference at the bottom equals zero, click Finished. What if it doesn't equal zero?

Deposits and Other Credits

✓	Date	Type	Num	Payee	Amount
☑	10/13/2007	Payment	9290	Twin Sisters B&B	300.00
☑	10/16/2007	Payment	4522	Cyberconnect Cafe	280.00
☑	10/16/2007	Payment	816	NFP Access	295.00
☑	10/16/2007	Payment	9346	Twin Sisters B&B	1050.00
☑	10/18/2007	Payment	901	NFP Access	300.00
☑	10/19/2007	Payment	5001	Cyberconnect Cafe	780.00
☐	10/19/2007	Payment	9401	Twin Sisters B&B	540.00
☑	10/20/2007	Sales Receipt	801	Cash Sales	2150.00
				Total checked(7) amount:	5155.00

Checks and Payments Sort by: Date

✓	Date	Type	Num	Payee	Amount
☑	10/06/2007	Bill Payment (Check)	1	Big Bytes Supplies	470.00
☑	10/07/2007	Bill Payment (Check)	2	Sales Products Supply	245.00
☑	10/07/2007	Bill Payment (Check)	3	Big Bytes Supplies	300.00
☑	10/21/2007	Check	4	Jonathan Brent	75.00
☑	10/21/2007	Check	5	Sun News	125.00
☑	10/21/2007	Check	6	Santa Fe Rentals	265.00
☐	10/22/2007	Check	7	Comtel	269.00
☐	10/30/2007	Check	8	Regional Utilities	206.00
☐	10/30/2007	Check	9	Your Name	1000.00
☑	10/31/2007	Check	SVCCHRG		25.00
				Total checked(7) amount:	1505.00

Select All | Clear All

Opening Balance:	3000.00
Statement Ending Date:	10/31/2007 Edit...
Statement Ending Balance:	6650.00
Cleared Balance:	6650.00
Difference:	0.00 Make adjusting transaction...

Finished | Finish Later | Cancel

8. Make sure the "Difference" field shows "0.00." Click [Finished]. The "Reconcile Report for Your Name Service Corporation" screen appears. Let's learn how to print it.

PRINTING OCTOBER'S RECONCILATION REPORT

1. The "Reconcile Report for YOUR NAME Service Corporation" screen should be displayed. Make sure that the statement date is 10/31/20XX.

2. Click [Print...]. Your report starts to print.

3. Your "Register Balance as of Reconcile Date" shows 5715.00.

PRINTING TRANSACTION LIST BY DAY: OCTOBER

Follow these steps to print the "Transaction List by Day" report.

1. Move your mouse over "Reports" on the QuickBooks Online Edition menu bar. When the drop-down menu appears, click on All Reports (Report Overview). From the "Accountant & Taxes" list, click on Transaction List by Date.

2. Click [Customize...]. A "Customize Report: Transaction List by Date—Web Page Dialog" box appears asking about General, Rows/Columns, and Dates options.

3. For "General," select "Custom" for the "Transaction Date." In the "From" box, select "10/01/20XX" as the date. In the "To," box, select "10/31/20XX" as the date.

4. Click [Change Columns...]. Then, remove the Memo/Description column. Click "OK."

5. Click on [Create]

7. Click [Print...]. Make the selections to print in Landscape orientation. Compare your report with the one shown on the next page.

Comment
Your first and last name and current year will be displayed.

Your Name Service Corporation
Transaction List by Date
October 2007

Date	Type	Num	Name	Account	Split	Amount
10/01/2007	Deposit			Your Name Service Corporation	Paid in Capital	3,000.00
10/01/2007	General Journal				-SPLIT-	
10/01/2007	Deposit			Prepaid Insurance	Paid in Capital	200.00
10/01/2007	General Journal				-SPLIT-	
10/01/2007	Invoice	1001	Twin Sisters B&B	Accounts Receivable	Services	300.00
10/01/2007	Invoice	1002	Cyberconnect Cafe	Accounts Receivable	Services	280.00
10/01/2007	Invoice	1003	NFP Access	Accounts Receivable	Services	295.00
10/01/2007	Bill		Big Bytes Supplies	Accounts Payable	Other Miscellaneous Expense	520.00
10/01/2007	Bill		Sales Products Supply	Accounts Payable	Other Miscellaneous Expense	100.00
10/02/2007	Bill	66JE	Big Bytes Supplies	Accounts Payable	Computer Supplies	300.00
10/03/2007	Bill	EX32	Sales Products Supply	Accounts Payable	Office Expenses	245.00
10/04/2007	Bill	89JE	Big Bytes Supplies	Accounts Payable	Computer Supplies	520.00
10/05/2007	Bill	EX45	Sales Products Supply	Accounts Payable	Office Expenses	385.00
10/05/2007	Vendor Credit	66JE	Big Bytes Supplies	Accounts Payable	Computer Supplies	-50.00
10/06/2007	Bill Payment (Check)	1	Big Bytes Supplies	Your Name Service Corporation	-SPLIT-	-470.00
10/07/2007	Bill Payment (Check)	2	Sales Products Supply	Your Name Service Corporation	Accounts Payable	-245.00
10/07/2007	Bill Payment (Check)	3	Big Bytes Supplies	Your Name Service Corporation	Accounts Payable	-300.00
10/08/2007	Invoice	1004	Twin Sisters B&B	Accounts Receivable	Services	1,200.00
10/09/2007	Invoice	1005	NFP Access	Accounts Receivable	Services	300.00
10/10/2007	Invoice	1006	Cyberconnect Cafe	Accounts Receivable	-SPLIT-	780.00
10/11/2007	Invoice	1007	Twin Sisters B&B	Accounts Receivable	-SPLIT-	540.00
10/13/2007	Credit Memo	1008	Twin Sisters B&B	Accounts Receivable	Services	-150.00
10/13/2007	Payment	9290	Twin Sisters B&B	Your Name Service Corporation	-SPLIT-	300.00
10/16/2007	Payment	4522	Cyberconnect Cafe	Your Name Service Corporation	Accounts Receivable	280.00
10/16/2007	Payment	816	NFP Access	Your Name Service Corporation	Accounts Receivable	295.00
10/16/2007	Payment	9346	Twin Sisters B&B	Your Name Service Corporation	Accounts Receivable	1,050.00
10/18/2007	Payment	901	NFP Access	Your Name Service Corporation	Accounts Receivable	300.00
10/19/2007	Payment	5001	Cyberconnect Cafe	Your Name Service Corporation	Accounts Receivable	780.00
10/19/2007	Payment	9401	Twin Sisters B&B	Your Name Service Corporation	Accounts Receivable	540.00
10/20/2007	Sales Receipt	1009	Cash Sales	Your Name Service Corporation	Services	2,150.00
10/21/2007	Check	4	Jonathan Brent	Your Name Service Corporation	Repair & Maintenance	-75.00
10/21/2007	Check	5	Sun News	Your Name Service Corporation	Advertising	-125.00
10/21/2007	Check	6	Santa Fe Rentals	Your Name Service Corporation	Rent or Lease	-265.00
10/22/2007	Check	7	Comtel	Your Name Service Corporation	Office Expenses	-269.00
10/30/2007	Check	8	Regional Utilities	Your Name Service Corporation	Utilities	-206.00
10/30/2007	Check	9	Your Name	Your Name Service Corporation	Dividends	-1,000.00
10/31/2007	Check	SVCCHRG		Your Name Service Corporation	Bank Charges	-25.00

PRINTING OCTOBER'S TRIAL BALANCE

1. Move your mouse over "Reports" on the QuickBooks Online Edition menu bar. When the drop-down menu appears, click on All Reports (Report Overview). Scroll down to the "Accountant & Taxes" list and link to Trial Balance.

2. Click Customize... . In a few moments, a "Customize Report: Trial Balance—Web Page Dialog" box appears asking about general and date options.

3. For "General," select "Custom" for "Transaction Date." Make sure the "From" date is "10/01/20XX" and the "To" date displays "10/31/20XX."

4. Click Create.

Comment
Your first and last name and current year will be displayed.

Your Name Service Corporation
Trial Balance
As of October 31, 2007

	Debit	Credit
Your Name Service Corporation	5,715.00	
Accounts Receivable	0.00	
Prepaid Insurance	200.00	
Computer Equipment:Accumulated Depreciation		1,200.00
Computer Equipment:Original Cost	6,000.00	
Accounts Payable		1,005.00
Common Stock		1,000.00
Dividends	1,000.00	
Paid in Capital		7,000.00
Services		5,695.00
Advertising	125.00	
Bank Charges	25.00	
Computer Supplies	770.00	
Office Expenses	899.00	
Rent or Lease	265.00	
Repair & Maintenance	75.00	
Utilities	206.00	
Other Miscellaneous Expense	620.00	
TOTAL	$15,900.00	$15,900.00

EDITING THE OCTOBER 31 TRIAL BALANCE

Observe that your trial balance shows a 620.00 balance in the "Other miscellaneous expense account." This is because QuickBooks Online recorded the opening balance for Big Bytes Supplies and Sales Products Supply in this account: $520 (Big Bytes Supplies) + $100 (Sales Products Supply) = $620.00.

Follow these steps to change this default to the appropriate accounts.

1. Place your mouse over 620.00. Double-click on 620.00.

2. Notice that the two vendors are listed: Big Bytes Supplies and Sales Products Supply. Link to each vendor. Then edit the information in the Account field as follows:

   Big Bytes Supplies: Computer Supplies – Expense
   Sales Products Supply: Office Expense

3. Save each change. Then follow steps 1-4 on the previous page to reprint your 10/01/20XX to 10/31/20XX trial balance. Compare it to the one shown below.

Your Name Service Corporation
Trial Balance
As of October 31, 2007

	Debit	Credit
Your Name Service Corporation	5,715.00	
Accounts Receivable	0.00	
Prepaid Insurance	200.00	
Computer Equipment:Accumulated Depreciation		1,200.00
Computer Equipment:Original Cost	6,000.00	
Accounts Payable		1,005.00
Common Stock		1,000.00
Dividends	1,000.00	
Paid in Capital		7,000.00
Services		5,695.00
Advertising	125.00	
Bank Charges	25.00	
Computer Supplies	1,290.00	
Office Expenses	999.00	
Rent or Lease	265.00	
Repair & Maintenance	75.00	
Utilities	206.00	
TOTAL	$15,900.00	$15,900.00

PRINTING OCTOBER'S INCOME STATEMENT

1. Move your mouse over "Reports" on the QuickBooks Online Edition menu bar. When the drop-down menu appears, click on Profit & Loss (what QuickBooks calls the Income Statement).

2. Click Customize... . In a few moments, a "Customize Report: Profit & Loss—Web Page Dialog" box appears asking about display options and date options.

3. For "General," select "Custom" for "Transaction Date." Make sure the "From" date is "10/01/20XX" and the "To" date displays "10/31/20XX."

4. Click Create .

5. Click Print... .

Your Name Service Corporation
Profit & Loss
October 2007

	Total
Income	
Services	5,695.00
Total Income	**$5,695.00**
Expenses	
Advertising	125.00
Bank Charges	25.00
Computer Supplies	1,290.00
Office Expenses	999.00
Rent or Lease	265.00
Repair & Maintenance	75.00
Utilities	206.00
Total Expenses	**$2,985.00**
Net Operating Income	**$2,710.00**
Net Income	**$2,710.00**

PRINTING OCTOBER'S BALANCE SHEET

1. Move your mouse over "Reports" on the QuickBooks Online Edition menu bar. When the drop-down menu appears, click on Balance Sheet.

2. Click Customize... . In a few moments, a "Customize Report: Balance Sheet—Web Page Dialog" box appears asking about display options and date options.

3. For "General," select "Custom" for "Transaction Date." Make sure the "From" date is "10/01/20XX" and the "To" date displays "10/31/20XX."

4. Click Create.

5. Click Print... . Compare your printout to the one shown on the next page.

Your Name Service Corporation
Balance Sheet
As of October 31, 2007

	Total
ASSETS	
Current Assets	
Bank Accounts	
Your Name Service Corporation	5,715.00
Total Bank Accounts	**$5,715.00**
Accounts Receivable	
Accounts Receivable	0.00
Total Accounts Receivable	**$0.00**
Other Current Assets	
Prepaid Insurance	200.00
Total Other Current Assets	**$200.00**
Total Current Assets	**$5,915.00**
Fixed Assets	
Computer Equipment	
Accumulated Depreciation	-1,200.00
Original Cost	6,000.00
Total Computer Equipment	**4,800.00**
Total Fixed Assets	**$4,800.00**
TOTAL ASSETS	**$10,715.00**
LIABILITIES AND EQUITY	
Liabilities	
Current Liabilities	
Accounts Payable	
Accounts Payable	1,005.00
Total Accounts Payable	**$1,005.00**
Total Current Liabilities	**$1,005.00**
Total Liabilities	**$1,005.00**
Equity	
Common Stock	1,000.00
Dividends	-1,000.00
Paid in Capital	7,000.00
Retained Earnings	
Net Income	2,710.00
Total Equity	**$9,710.00**
TOTAL LIABILITIES AND EQUITY	**$10,715.00**

Comment
Your first and last name and current year will be displayed.

6. Log off or continue.

NOVEMBER TRANSACTIONS

Complete the following transactions for November.

Date	*Transaction*
11/02/20XX	Paid vendor bill. Issued Check No. 10 to the Sales Products Supply in payment of Invoice EX45, $385.
11/04/20XX	Entered vendor bill. Received Invoice 98JE and shipment from Big Bytes Supplies for the purchase of computer supplies, Net 30, $2,625.
11/04/20XX	Entered vendor bill. Received Invoice EX55 and shipment from Sales Products Supply for the purchase of office supplies, Net 30, $875.
11/05/20XX	Paid vendor bill. Paid Sales Products Supply the 10/01/20XX $100 opening balance with hand-written Check No. 11.
11/05/20XX	Paid Big Bytes Supplies, Invoice 89JE, for the October 4 purchase, $520.00, hand-written Check No. 12.
11/06/20XX	Paid Big Bytes Supplies, Invoice 98JE, for the November 4 purchase, $2,625.00, hand-written Check No. 13.
11/07/20XX	Paid Sales Products Supply, Invoice EX55, for the November 4 purchase, $875.00, Check No. 14.
11/8/20XX	Created invoice. Sold maintenance services on account to Twin Sisters B&B, Invoice, Net 30, $1,500 for 50 hours of maintenance services at $30 an hour. (Hint: Delivery Information, uncheck "To be printed.")
11/8/20XX	Sold maintenance services on account to Cyberconnect Cafe, Invoice, Net 30, $1,560 for 52 hours of maintenance at $30 an hour. (Hint: Delivery Information, uncheck "To be printed.")

11/17/20XX	Received payments. Received a check from Cyberconnect Cafe in payment of Invoice, $1560.00, Check No. 5110.
11/17/20XX	Received a check from Twin Sisters B&B in payment of Invoice, $1,500.00, Check No. 221.
11/21/20XX	Entered sales receipt. Cash sales $2,300, payment received by Check No. 802 for 46 hours of repair services at $50 an hour. (Hint: Delivery Information, uncheck "To be printed.")
11/29/20XX	Write Check No. 15 to Comtel from bank account for the monthly telephone and Internet service, $270.00.
11/29/20XX	Write Check No. 16 to Regional Utilities for monthly utilities bill, $210.00.
11/29/20XX	Write Check No. 17 for a cash dividend to the sole stockholder (you), $1,000 from checking account.

RECONCILE THE BANK STATEMENT: NOVEMBER

Your business receives a bank statement every month from the bank for your regular checking account. The bank statement shows that checks and deposits have cleared the bank. Use the bank statement on the next page to complete account reconciliation for November.

Comment:
The check dates shown on the bank statement will differ from the dates the checks were written since the bank statement shows when the checks were processed by the bank not when they was written. Only checks that have been processed by the bank, the cleared checks, will be listed on the bank statement. Uncleared checks will not appear since they have not been processed by the bank.

REGULAR CHECKING ACCOUNT November 1 - 30, 20XX			
Previous Balance		$6,650.00	
4 Deposits (+)		5,900.00	
9 checks (-)		6,250.00	
Service Charges (-)	11/30/XX	25.00	
Ending Balance	11/30/XX	**$6,275.00**	
DEPOSITS			
	11/02	540.00	
	11/18	1,560.00	
	11/20	1,500.00	
	11/22	2,300.00	
CHECKS (Asterisk * indicates break in check number sequence)			
11/02	7	269.00	
11/02	8	206.00	
11/03	9	1,000.00	
11/04	10	385.00	
110/6	11	100.00	
11/06	12	520.00	
11/08	13	2,625.00	
11/08	14	875.00	
11/23	15	270.00	

From the "Banking" drop-down menu on the QuickBooks Online Edition menu bar, go to the link for Reconcile. Complete the steps for reconciling your November bank statement as shown on page 101. Then, compare your Reconcile screen to the one shown on the next page. When satisfied and difference shows 0.00, click "Finished."

Comment:
If a check or deposit does *not* appear on your "Reconcile" screen, click on the appropriate link on the QuickBooks Online Edition menu bar. Select the "Edit" button and make any needed corrections. To update the record, click on "Save."

November Reconcile Screen

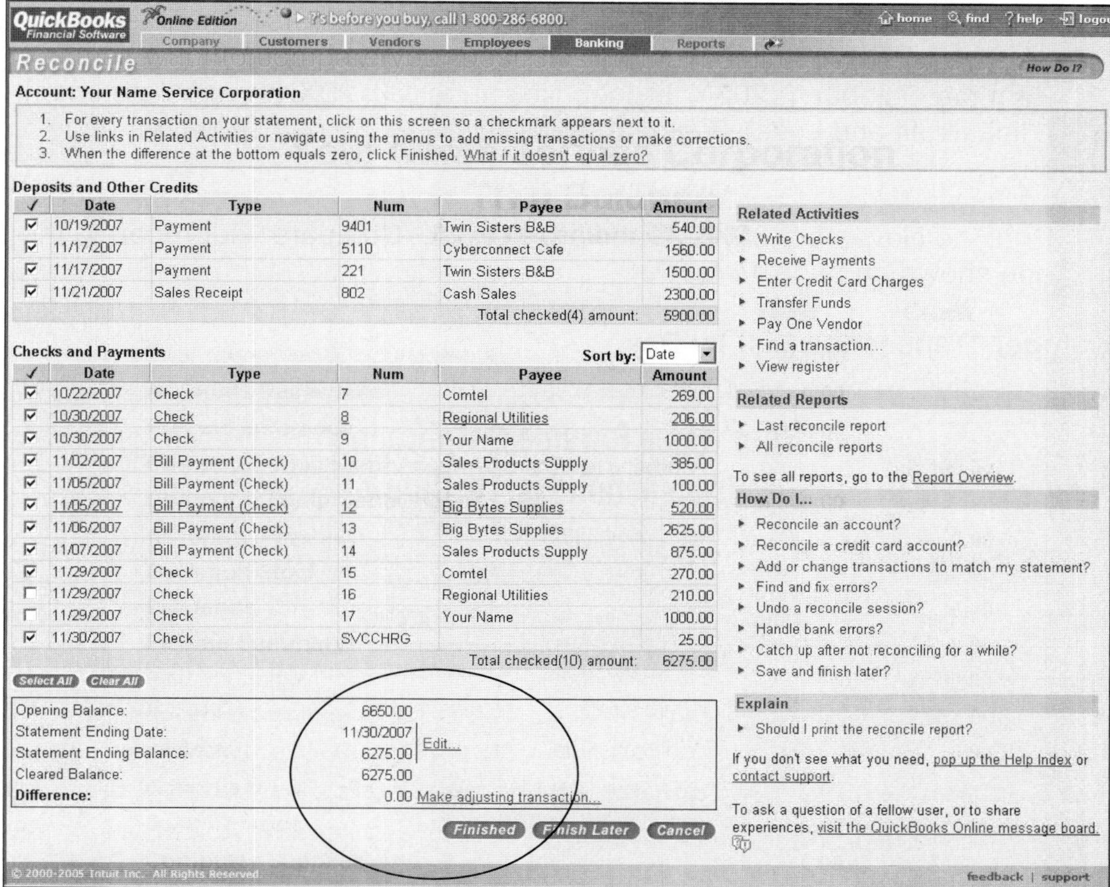

✓	Date	Type	Num	Payee	Amount
✓	10/19/2007	Payment	9401	Twin Sisters B&B	540.00
✓	11/17/2007	Payment	5110	Cyberconnect Cafe	1560.00
✓	11/17/2007	Payment	221	Twin Sisters B&B	1500.00
✓	11/21/2007	Sales Receipt	802	Cash Sales	2300.00
				Total checked(4) amount:	5900.00

✓	Date	Type	Num	Payee	Amount
✓	10/22/2007	Check	7	Comtel	269.00
✓	10/30/2007	Check	8	Regional Utilities	206.00
✓	10/30/2007	Check	9	Your Name	1000.00
✓	11/02/2007	Bill Payment (Check)	10	Sales Products Supply	385.00
✓	11/05/2007	Bill Payment (Check)	11	Sales Products Supply	100.00
✓	11/05/2007	Bill Payment (Check)	12	Big Bytes Supplies	520.00
✓	11/06/2007	Bill Payment (Check)	13	Big Bytes Supplies	2625.00
✓	11/07/2007	Bill Payment (Check)	14	Sales Products Supply	875.00
✓	11/29/2007	Check	15	Comtel	270.00
	11/29/2007	Check	16	Regional Utilities	210.00
	11/29/2007	Check	17	Your Name	1000.00
✓	11/30/2007	Check	SVCCHRG		25.00
				Total checked(10) amount:	6275.00

November Reconciliation Summary

Click on "Print" to print your November Reconcile Report.

PRINTING NOVEMBER REPORTS

1. Print "Transaction List by Day" report for November 1, 20XX through November 30, 20XX. Compare your report to the one shown on page 114. (Hints: For General--select "Custom" from the pull-down menu for Transaction Date. Click on Change columns—remove "Memo/Description.")

2. Print the November 30, 20XX trial balance. Compare your report to the one shown on page 115.

3. Print the October 1, 20XX through November 30, 20XX income statement (Hint: Profit and Loss). Compare your report to the one shown on page 116.

4. Print the November 30, 20XX balance sheet. Compare your report to the one shown on page 117.

November Transaction List by Day

Your Name Service Corporation
Transaction List by Date
November 2007

Date	Type	Num	Name	Account	Split	Amount
11/02/2007	Bill Payment (Check)	10	Sales Products Supply	Your Name Service Corporation	Accounts Payable	-385.00
11/04/2007	Bill	98JE	Big Bytes Supplies	Accounts Payable	Computer Supplies	2,625.00
11/04/2007	Bill	EX55	Sales Products Supply	Accounts Payable	Office Expenses	875.00
11/05/2007	Bill Payment (Check)	11	Sales Products Supply	Your Name Service Corporation	Accounts Payable	-100.00
11/05/2007	Bill Payment (Check)	12	Big Bytes Supplies	Your Name Service Corporation	Accounts Payable	-520.00
11/06/2007	Bill Payment (Check)	13	Big Bytes Supplies	Your Name Service Corporation	Accounts Payable	-2,625.00
11/07/2007	Bill Payment (Check)	14	Sales Products Supply	Your Name Service Corporation	Accounts Payable	-875.00
11/08/2007	Invoice	1010	Twin Sisters B&B	Accounts Receivable	Services	1,500.00
11/08/2007	Invoice	1011	Cyberconnect Cafe	Accounts Receivable	Services	1,560.00
11/17/2007	Payment	5110	Cyberconnect Cafe	Your Name Service Corporation	Accounts Receivable	1,560.00
11/17/2007	Payment	221	Twin Sisters B&B	Your Name Service Corporation	Accounts Receivable	1,500.00
11/21/2007	Sales Receipt	1012	Cash Sales	Your Name Service Corporation	Services	2,300.00
11/29/2007	Check	15	Comtel	Your Name Service Corporation	Office Expenses	-270.00
11/29/2007	Check	16	Regional Utilities	Your Name Service Corporation	Utilities	-210.00
11/29/2007	Check	17	Your Name	Your Name Service Corporation	Dividends	-1,000.00
11/30/2007	Check	SVCCHRG		Your Name Service Corporation	Bank Charges	-25.00

November Trial Balance

Your Name Service Corporation
Trial Balance
As of November 30, 2007

	Debit	Credit
Your Name Service Corporation	5,065.00	
Accounts Receivable	0.00	
Prepaid Insurance	200.00	
Computer Equipment:Accumulated Depreciation		1,200.00
Computer Equipment:Original Cost	6,000.00	
Accounts Payable		0.00
Common Stock		1,000.00
Dividends	2,000.00	
Paid in Capital		7,000.00
Services		11,055.00
Advertising	125.00	
Bank Charges	50.00	
Computer Supplies	3,915.00	
Office Expenses	2,144.00	
Rent or Lease	265.00	
Repair & Maintenance	75.00	
Utilities	416.00	
TOTAL	**$20,255.00**	**$20,255.00**

November Income Statement

Your Name Service Corporation
Profit & Loss
October - November, 2007

	Total
Income	
Services	11,055.00
Total Income	**$11,055.00**
Expenses	
Advertising	125.00
Bank Charges	50.00
Computer Supplies	3,915.00
Office Expenses	2,144.00
Rent or Lease	265.00
Repair & Maintenance	75.00
Utilities	416.00
Total Expenses	**$6,990.00**
Net Operating Income	**$4,065.00**
Net Income	**$4,065.00**

Comment:

QuickBooks Online Edition uses the title "Profit & Loss" to refer to the income statement. The income statement is where business reports its revenues and expenses and determines its net income or loss for the period.

November Balance Sheet

Your Name Service Corporation
Balance Sheet
As of November 30, 2007

	Total
ASSETS	
Current Assets	
Bank Accounts	
Your Name Service Corporation	5,065.00
Total Bank Accounts	**$5,065.00**
Accounts Receivable	
Accounts Receivable	0.00
Total Accounts Receivable	**$0.00**
Other Current Assets	
Prepaid Insurance	200.00
Total Other Current Assets	**$200.00**
Total Current Assets	**$5,265.00**
Fixed Assets	
Computer Equipment	
Accumulated Depreciation	-1,200.00
Original Cost	6,000.00
Total Computer Equipment	**4,800.00**
Total Fixed Assets	**$4,800.00**
TOTAL ASSETS	**$10,065.00**
LIABILITIES AND EQUITY	
Liabilities	
Current Liabilities	
Accounts Payable	
Accounts Payable	0.00
Total Accounts Payable	**$0.00**
Total Current Liabilities	**$0.00**
Total Liabilities	**$0.00**
Equity	
Common Stock	1,000.00
Dividends	-2,000.00
Paid in Capital	7,000.00
Retained Earnings	
Net Income	4,065.00
Total Equity	**$10,065.00**
TOTAL LIABILITIES AND EQUITY	**$10,065.00**

DECEMBER TRANSACTIONS

Complete the following transactions for December.

Date	*Transaction*
12/02/20XX	Write Check No. 18 to Pro Insurance, a new vendor, in payment of next year's insurance premiums, $320. *(Hint: Use the "Prepaid insurance" account.)*
12/02/20XX	Received vendor bill. Invoice 113JE and shipment from Big Bytes Supplies for the purchase of computer supplies on credit, Net 30, $2,050.
12/03/20XX	Received Invoice EX82 and shipment from Sales Products Supply for the purchase of office supplies on credit, Net 30, $700.
12/08/20XX	Create invoice. Sold repair and maintenance services on account to Twin Sisters B & B, Invoice Net 30, $1,800 for 30 hours of repairs and 10 hours of maintenance. (Hint: Delivery Information, uncheck "To be printed.")
12/08/20XX	Sold repair and maintenance services on account to Cyberconnect Cafe, Invoice Net 30, $970 for 14 hours of repairs and 9 hours of maintenance. (Hint: Delivery Information, uncheck "To be printed.")
12/09/20XX	Sold 10 hours of maintenance services on account to the NFP Access, Invoice Net 30, for a total of $300.
12/10/20XX	Sold 4 hours of repair services on account to NFP Access, Invoice Net 30, for a total of $200.
12/11/20XX	Paid vendor bill to Big Bytes Supplies, Invoice 113JE for the December 2 purchase, $2,050.00, hand-written Check No. 19.
12/11/20XX	Paid Sales Products Supply, Invoice EX82, for the December 3 purchase, $700.00, hand-written Check No. 20.

12/17/20XX	Received customer payment. Received a check from Cyberconnect Cafe in payment of Invoice, $970, Check No. 5225.
12/17/20XX	Received a check from Twin Sisters B & B in payment of Invoice, $1,800, Check No. 301.
12/19/20XX	Received a check from NFP Access in payment of Invoices, $500, Check No. 935.
12/24/20XX	Enter sales receipt. Cash sales $2,200, received check No. 803 for 44 hours of repair services. (Hint: Delivery Information, uncheck "To be printed.")
12/30/20XX	Write Check No. 21 to Comtel for monthly telephone and Internet service, $303.
12/30/20XX	Write Check No. 22 to Regional Utilities for monthly utilities bill, $190.
12/30/20XX	Write Check No. 23 to Sun News for advertising $145.
12/30/20XX	Write Check No. 24 to Jonathan Brent for repairs $140.

Remember:
Uncheck "To be printed" in the Delivery Information box each time you create an invoice (credit sales) or enter a sales receipt (cash sales).

RECONCILE THE BANK STATEMENT: DECEMBER

You business receives a bank statement every month from the bank for your regular checking account. The bank statement shows that checks and deposits have cleared the bank. Use the bank statement below to complete account reconciliation for December.

REGULAR CHECKING ACCOUNT December 1 - 31, 20XX			
Previous Balance		$6,275.00	
4Deposits (+)		5,470.00	
5checks (-)		4,280.00	
Service Charges (-)	12/31/XX	25.00	
Ending Balance	12/31/XX	$7,440.00	
DEPOSITS			
	12/18	970.00	
	12/19	1,800.00	
	12/20	500.00	
	12/26	2,200.00	
CHECKS (Asterisk * indicates break in check number sequence)			
12/5	16	210.00	
12/5	17	1,000.00	
12/7	18	320.00	
12/15	19	2,050.00	
12/18	20	700.00	

From the "Banking" drop-down menu, go to the link for Reconcile. Complete the steps for reconciling your December bank statement as shown on page 101. Then, compare your Reconcile screen to the one shown on the next page. When satisfied and difference shows 0.00, click "Finished."

Comment:
If a check or deposit does *not* appear on your "Reconcile" screen, click on the "Transactions" tab. Then, select the appropriate link. Select the "Edit" button and make any needed corrections. To update the record, click on "Submit."

December's Reconcile Screen

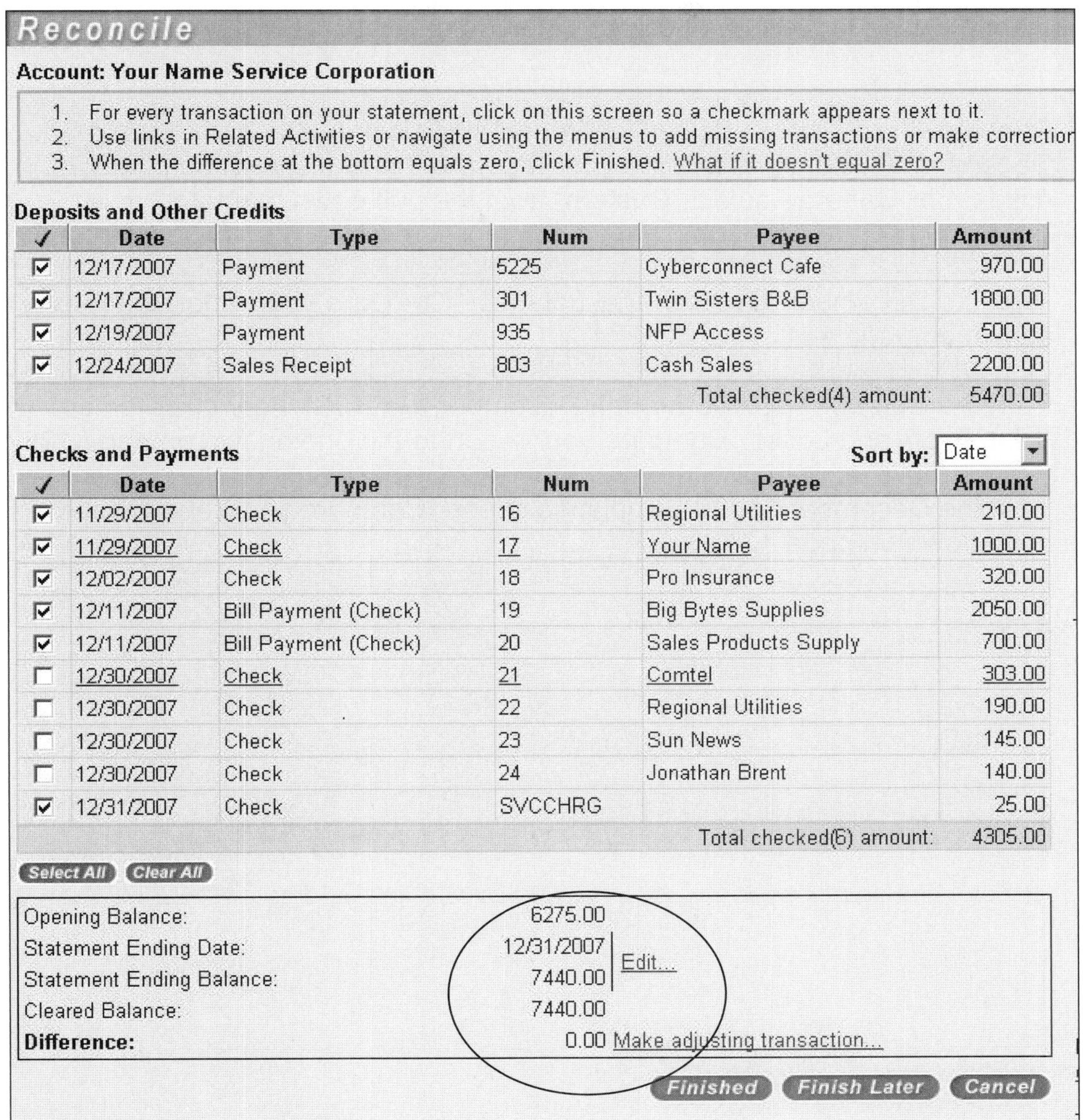

Reconcile

Account: Your Name Service Corporation

1. For every transaction on your statement, click on this screen so a checkmark appears next to it.
2. Use links in Related Activities or navigate using the menus to add missing transactions or make correctio
3. When the difference at the bottom equals zero, click Finished. What if it doesn't equal zero?

Deposits and Other Credits

✓	Date	Type	Num	Payee	Amount
☑	12/17/2007	Payment	5225	Cyberconnect Cafe	970.00
☑	12/17/2007	Payment	301	Twin Sisters B&B	1800.00
☑	12/19/2007	Payment	935	NFP Access	500.00
☑	12/24/2007	Sales Receipt	803	Cash Sales	2200.00
				Total checked(4) amount:	5470.00

Checks and Payments — Sort by: Date

✓	Date	Type	Num	Payee	Amount
☑	11/29/2007	Check	16	Regional Utilities	210.00
☑	11/29/2007	Check	17	Your Name	1000.00
☑	12/02/2007	Check	18	Pro Insurance	320.00
☑	12/11/2007	Bill Payment (Check)	19	Big Bytes Supplies	2050.00
☑	12/11/2007	Bill Payment (Check)	20	Sales Products Supply	700.00
☐	12/30/2007	Check	21	Comtel	303.00
☐	12/30/2007	Check	22	Regional Utilities	190.00
☐	12/30/2007	Check	23	Sun News	145.00
☐	12/30/2007	Check	24	Jonathan Brent	140.00
☑	12/31/2007	Check	SVCCHRG		25.00
				Total checked(6) amount:	4305.00

Select All | Clear All

Opening Balance:	6275.00
Statement Ending Date:	12/31/2007 Edit...
Statement Ending Balance:	7440.00
Cleared Balance:	7440.00
Difference:	0.00 Make adjusting transaction...

Finished | Finish Later | Cancel

December Reconciliation Summary

Click on "Print" to print your December Reconcile Report.

PRINTING DECEMBER REPORTS

Print the following reports and compare them to the ones shown on pages 123 - 126.

1. Print the "Transaction List by Day" report for December 1, 20XX through December 31, 20XX. Compare your report to the one shown on page123. (Hints: For General--select “Custom” from the pull-down menu for Transaction Date. Click on Change columns—remove “Memo/Description.”)

2. Print the December 31, 20XX trial balance. Compare your report to the one shown on page 124.

3. Print the October 1, 20XX through December 31, 20XX income statement (Hint: Profit and Loss). Compare your report to the one shown on page 125.

4. Print the December 31, 20XX balance sheet. Compare your report to the one shown on page 126.

December's Transaction List by Day

Your Name Service Corporation
Transaction List by Date
December 2007

Date	Type	Num	Name	Account	Split	Amount
12/02/2007	Check	18	Pro Insurance	Your Name Service Corporation	Prepaid Insurance	-320.00
12/02/2007	Bill	113JE	Big Bytes Supplies	Accounts Payable	Computer Supplies	2,050.00
12/03/2007	Bill	EX82	Sales Products Supply	Accounts Payable	Office Expenses	700.00
12/08/2007	Invoice	1013	Twin Sisters B&B	Accounts Receivable	-SPLIT-	1,800.00
12/08/2007	Invoice	1014	Cyberconnect Cafe	Accounts Receivable	-SPLIT-	970.00
12/09/2007	Invoice	1015	NFP Access	Accounts Receivable	Services	300.00
12/10/2007	Invoice	1016	NFP Access	Accounts Receivable	Services	200.00
12/11/2007	Bill Payment (Check)	19	Big Bytes Supplies	Your Name Service Corporation	Accounts Payable	-2,050.00
12/11/2007	Bill Payment (Check)	20	Sales Products Supply	Your Name Service Corporation	Accounts Payable	-700.00
12/17/2007	Payment	5225	Cyberconnect Cafe	Your Name Service Corporation	Accounts Receivable	970.00
12/17/2007	Payment	301	Twin Sisters B&B	Your Name Service Corporation	Accounts Receivable	1,800.00
12/19/2007	Payment	935	NFP Access	Your Name Service Corporation	Accounts Receivable	500.00
12/24/2007	Sales Receipt	1017	Cash Sales	Your Name Service Corporation	Services	2,200.00
12/30/2007	Check	21	Comtel	Your Name Service Corporation	Office Expenses	-303.00
12/30/2007	Check	22	Regional Utilities	Your Name Service Corporation	Utilities	-190.00
12/30/2007	Check	23	Sun News	Your Name Service Corporation	Advertising	-145.00
12/30/2007	Check	24	Jonathan Brent	Your Name Service Corporation	Repair & Maintenance	-140.00
12/31/2007	Check	SVCCHRG		Your Name Service Corporation	Bank Charges	-25.00

December's Trial Balance

Your Name Service Corporation
Trial Balance
As of December 31, 2007

	Debit	Credit
Your Name Service Corporation	6,662.00	
Accounts Receivable	0.00	
Prepaid Insurance	520.00	
Computer Equipment:Accumulated Depreciation		1,200.00
Computer Equipment:Original Cost	6,000.00	
Accounts Payable		0.00
Common Stock		1,000.00
Dividends	2,000.00	
Paid in Capital		7,000.00
Services		16,525.00
Advertising	270.00	
Bank Charges	75.00	
Computer Supplies	5,965.00	
Office Expenses	3,147.00	
Rent or Lease	265.00	
Repair & Maintenance	215.00	
Utilities	606.00	
TOTAL	**$25,725.00**	**$25,725.00**

October 1 through December 31, 20XX Income Statement

Your Name Service Corporation
Profit & Loss
October - December, 2007

	Total
Income	
Services	16,525.00
Total Income	**$16,525.00**
Expenses	
Advertising	270.00
Bank Charges	75.00
Computer Supplies	5,965.00
Office Expenses	3,147.00
Rent or Lease	265.00
Repair & Maintenance	215.00
Utilities	606.00
Total Expenses	**$10,543.00**
Net Operating Income	**$5,982.00**
Net Income	**$5,982.00**

December's Balance Sheet

Your Name Service Corporation
Balance Sheet
As of December 31, 2007

	Total
ASSETS	
Current Assets	
Bank Accounts	
Your Name Service Corporation	6,662.00
Total Bank Accounts	**$6,662.00**
Accounts Receivable	
Accounts Receivable	0.00
Total Accounts Receivable	**$0.00**
Other Current Assets	
Prepaid Insurance	520.00
Total Other Current Assets	**$520.00**
Total Current Assets	**$7,182.00**
Fixed Assets	
Computer Equipment	
Accumulated Depreciation	-1,200.00
Original Cost	6,000.00
Total Computer Equipment	**4,800.00**
Total Fixed Assets	**$4,800.00**
TOTAL ASSETS	**$11,982.00**
LIABILITIES AND EQUITY	
Liabilities	
Current Liabilities	
Accounts Payable	
Accounts Payable	0.00
Total Accounts Payable	**$0.00**
Total Current Liabilities	**$0.00**
Total Liabilities	**$0.00**
Equity	
Common Stock	1,000.00
Dividends	-2,000.00
Paid in Capital	7,000.00
Retained Earnings	
Net Income	5,982.00
Total Equity	**$11,982.00**
TOTAL LIABILITIES AND EQUITY	**$11,982.00**

CHECK YOUR PROGRESS

Flashcard Review

1. Enter bills
2. Receive vendor credit
3. Pay bills
4. Create invoice
5. Give customer credit
6. Receive customer payments
7. Enter sales receipts
8. Write checks
9. Reconcile bank statement
10. Print transaction list by day
11. Print trial balance
12. Print income statement

Internet Homework

If necessary, start QuickBooks Online Edition, and then log in to your account.

1. On the QuickBooks Online Edition home page under Subscription Information click on What happens after my trial?

2. Read to learn about the three actions you can take after your trial period expires.

3. When you are finished reading the information in the box, return to the home page screen by closing the box.

4. Link to Privacy and Security and read to learn more about these important issues.

5. Write a summary of what you learned about what QuickBooks Online Edition is doing about privacy and security. The minimum length of each essay should be 25 words; the maximum length 75 words. Use a word-processing program to type your reports.

Multiple-Choice. In the space provided, write the letter that best answers each question.

______1. Fourth quarter transactions are for the months of:

a. January, February, and March.
b. April, May, and June.
c. July, August, and September.
d. October, November, and December.
e. None of the above.

______2. The Accounting Essentials website is located at:

a. www.mhhe.com/yachtessentials3e
b. www.QuickBooks Online Edition.com
c. www.google.com
d. www.QuickBooks Online Editionsupport.com
e. None of the above.

______3. Which QuickBooks Online Edition menu bar areas do you access to complete fourth-quarter recordkeeping?

a. Banking.
b. Customers.
c. Vendors.
d. Report.
e. All of the above.

______4. Another word used for supplier is:

a. Vendor.
b. Customer.
c. Sales discount.
d. Inventory.
e. All of the above.

______5. Which of the following is the name of one of your vendors?

a. Twin Sisters B & B
b. Cyberconnect Cafe
c. Big Bytes Supplies
d. NFP Access
e. None of the above.

______6. Which of the following is the name of one of your customers?

a. Twin Sisters B & B
b. Sales Products Supply
c. Big Bytes Supplies
d. Student name.
e. None of the above.

______7. To record purchases of supplies from vendors, you use which of the following links?

a. Enter invoices.
b. Pay sales tax.
c. Enter bills.
d. Make vendor payment.
e. None of the above.

______8. To return supplies purchased from a vendor, you use which of the following links?

a. Return supplies.
b. Enter credits.
c. Enter vendor credits.
d. Pay bills.
e. None of the above.

_____9. What report would you display or print to see the balance in your accounts payable account?

a. A/R Register.
b. A/P Register.
c. Income Statement.
d. Reconciliation Summary.
e. None of the above.

_____10. What report would you display or print to see the balance in your accounts receivable account?

a. A/R Register.
b. A/P Register.
c. Income Statement.
d. Reconciliation Summary.
e. None of the above.

True/False. Write T for True and F for false in the space provided.

_____11. When your business makes purchases on account from vendors, the transactions are known as accounts receivable transactions.

_____12. When your business makes sales on account to customers, these transactions are knows as accounts payable transactions.

_____13. Entering bills as soon as you receive them, keeps your cash flow reports up to date.

_____14. You can use the "Pay Bills" link and the "Pay One Vendor" link to pay amounts owed to vendors.

_____15. The "Products and Services List" link under “Customers” on the QuickBooks Online Edition menu bar allows you to access the prices of your services.

_____16. To record customer transactions, you use the "Create Invoices" link.

_____17. To edit customer information, you use the “Customer List.”

_____18. To write checks, you link to “Write Checks” under “Company” on the QuickBooks Online Edition menu bar.

_____19. If a customer returns supplies to you, you use the "Give Refund or Credit" link to record this return.

_____20. Once you issue an invoice to a customer, that customer owes your business money.

Exercise 4-1. Using the reports that you printed for December, answer the following questions.

1. Your business' Net Income at the end of the fourth quarter is: __________

1. On December 31, 20XX, your prepaid insurance account shows the following balance: __________

3. On December 31, 20XX, your accounts receivable account shows the following balance: __________

4. On December 31, 20XX, your checking account shows the following balance: __________

5. On December 31, 20XX, your accounts payable account shows the following balance: __________

Exercise 4-2. Copy your December 31, 20XX balance sheet to Excel. Use **Your Name** and **Exercise 4-2** as the file name. Print your Excel balance sheet.

CHAPTER 4 INDEX

Cash payments: write checks....98
Cash sales: enter sales receipts....96
Cash transactions....96
Check your progress....127
Computer accounting essentials website....75
Customer transactions: create invoice....86
December transactions....118
Displaying the accounts receivable register....92
Editing trial balance....106
Enter bills....78
Exercise 4-1....132
Exercise 4-2....132
Flashcard review....127
Getting started....76
Internet homework....127
Multiple-choice....128
November transactions....110
Printing December reports....122
Printing November reports....113
Printing October's balance sheet....108
Printing October's income statement....107
Printing October's reconciliation report....103
Printing October's trial balance....105
Printing transaction listing by day: October....103
Purchase returns: enter vendor credits....81
Receive customer payments....93
Reconcile the bank statement: December....120
Reconcile the bank statement: November....111
Reconcile the bank statement: October....100
Sales returns and allowances: give credit or refund....90
Software objectives....75
True/False....131
Vendor payments: pay bills....83
Vendor transactions: Enter bills....77
Web objectives....75

5 End-of-Year & Beginning-of-Year Transactions

In Chapter 5 of *Computer Accounting Essentials Using QuickBooks Online Edition*, you will complete end-of-year adjusting entries and print financial statements. Chapter 5 also includes transactions for the start of the new year – January 1 - 31, 20XX.

SOFTWARE OBJECTIVES: In Chapter 5, you use the software to:

1. Record end-of-year adjusting entries.
2. Print the adjusted trial balance and end-of-quarter reports.
3. Record end-of-year closing entries.
4. Print the post-closing trial balance.
5. Close the accounting period.
6. Complete January 1 - 31, 20XX transactions.
7. Copy data to Excel.
8. Complete activities for Chapter 5, End-of-Year & Beginning-of-Year transactions.

WEB OBJECTIVES: In Chapter 5, you use the Internet to:

1. Access the Computer Accounting Essentials website at www.mhhe.com/yachtessentials3e to check for updates.
2. Log in to your QuickBooks Online Edition account.
3. Record end-of-year and beginning-of-year transactions.
4. Complete Flashcard review.
5. Complete Internet activities.

COMPUTER ACCOUNTING ESSENTIALS WEBSITE

Before you begin your work in Chapter 5, End-of-Year and Beginning-of-Year Transactions, access the Computer Accounting Essentials website at **www.mhhe.com/yachtessentials3e**. Software and book updates will be shown. Check this website regularly for reference and study.

GETTING STARTED

Follow these steps to start QuickBooks Online Edition. You *must* complete Chapters 1, 2, 3, and 4, pages 3 – 132, before starting Chapter 5, End-of-Year & Beginning-of-Year Transactions. *The exercises at the end of each Chapter must be completed, too.*

1. Start your Internet browser and log in to QuickBooks Online Edition in the usual way.

2. Move your mouse over "Banking" on the QuickBooks Online Edition menu bar. When the drop-down menu appears, click on Make Journal Entry.

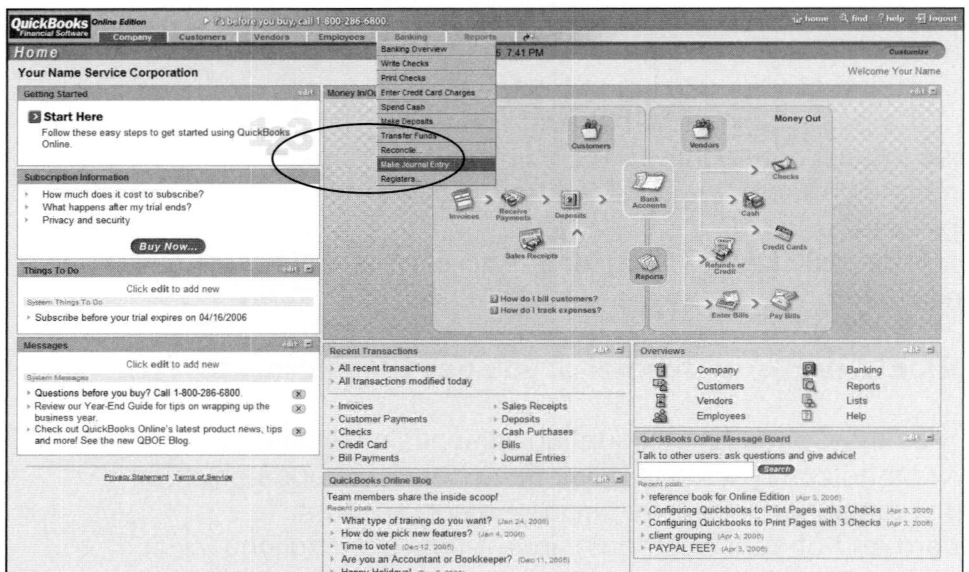

The "Make Journal Entry" screen appears.

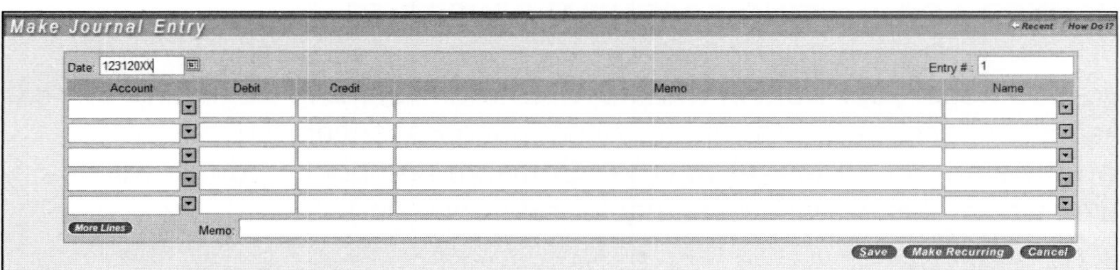

END-OF-YEAR ADJUSTING ENTRIES

The ***general journal*** shows the debits and credits of transactions, and can be used to record any type of transaction. For purposes of this exercise, you will use the general journal to record adjusting entries.

In Chapters 4 of *Computer Accounting Essentials Using QuickBooks Online Edition,* you used selections from the "Customers," "Vendors," and "Banking" drop-down menus to record business transactions. For adjusting entries, you will use the Make Journal Entry link from the "Banking" list, which takes you to QuickBooks Online Edition's "Make Journal Entry" screen. Compare your screen to the one shown on page 136.

> **Comment:**
> Journal entries are in debit/credit format and must always be in balance. QuickBooks Online Edition will show you any out-of-balance amount at the top of the "Make Journal Entry" screen and will *not* let you submit the entry until it is balanced.

Follow these steps to record adjusting entries in the general journal for December 31, 20XX:

1. The "Make Journal Entry" window should be displayed on your screen. Change the date to December 31, 20XX.

2. Type **Adjust 1** in the "Entry No." field. (For the subsequent adjusting entry, type **Adjust 2**.)

3. In the "Account" field, select or type the appropriate account to debit.

4. In the "Debit" amount field, type the appropriate amount.

5. In the next "Account" field, select or type the appropriate account to credit.

6. When you click on the "Credit" field, the amount is automatically completed or you can type in the appropriate amount.

7. Type any memo information, optional.

8. Click on "Save."

9. In a few moments, a new "Make Journal Entry" screen will appear to record the next entry.

Record the following adjusting entries for December 31, 20XX:

1. Adjust 1: Use straight-line depreciation for the business' equipment. The equipment has a five-year service life and no salvage value. To depreciate the equipment for the year, use this calculation: $6,000/5 years = $1,200.00. (*Hint: For Account: First line-- scroll to bottom of the pull-down menu and select "Depreciation Expense—Other Expense." For second line—from the pull-down menu select "Computer Equipment—Accumulated Depreciation—Fixed Assets."*)

Account Name	Debit	Credit
Depreciation Expense – Other Expense	1,200.00	
Computer Equipment - Accumulated Depreciation—Fixed Assets		1,200.00

Compare your screen to the following then click on <u>Save</u>.

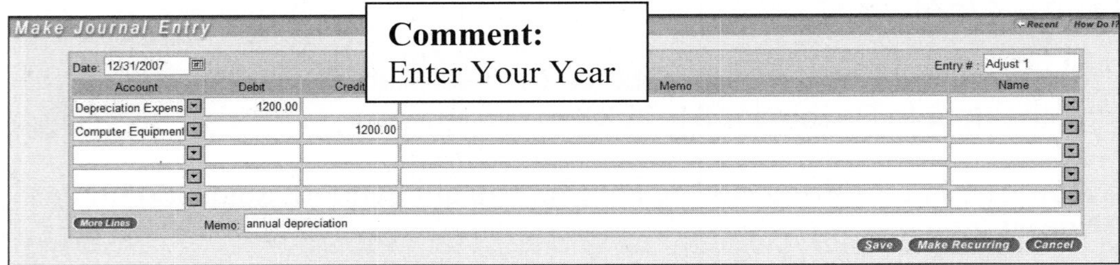

2. Adjust 2: During the year, $250 of Prepaid insurance expired.

Account Name	Debit	Credit
Insurance - Expense	250.00	
Prepaid Insurance – Other Current Asset		250.00

Compare your screen to the following then click on <u>Save</u>.

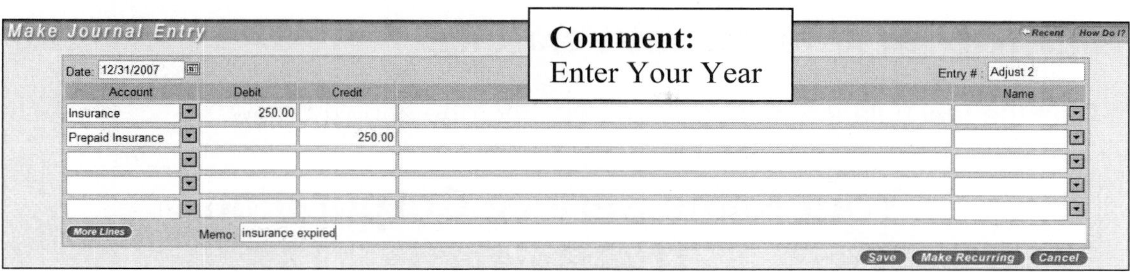
Make Journal Entry

Comment:
Enter Your Year

Date: 12/31/2007 Entry #: Adjust 2

Account	Debit	Credit		Name
Insurance	250.00			
Prepaid Insurance		250.00		

Memo: insurance expired

Save · Make Recurring · Cancel

3. Display or print the "Transaction List with Splits" report for December 31, 20XX. Compare with the one shown below.

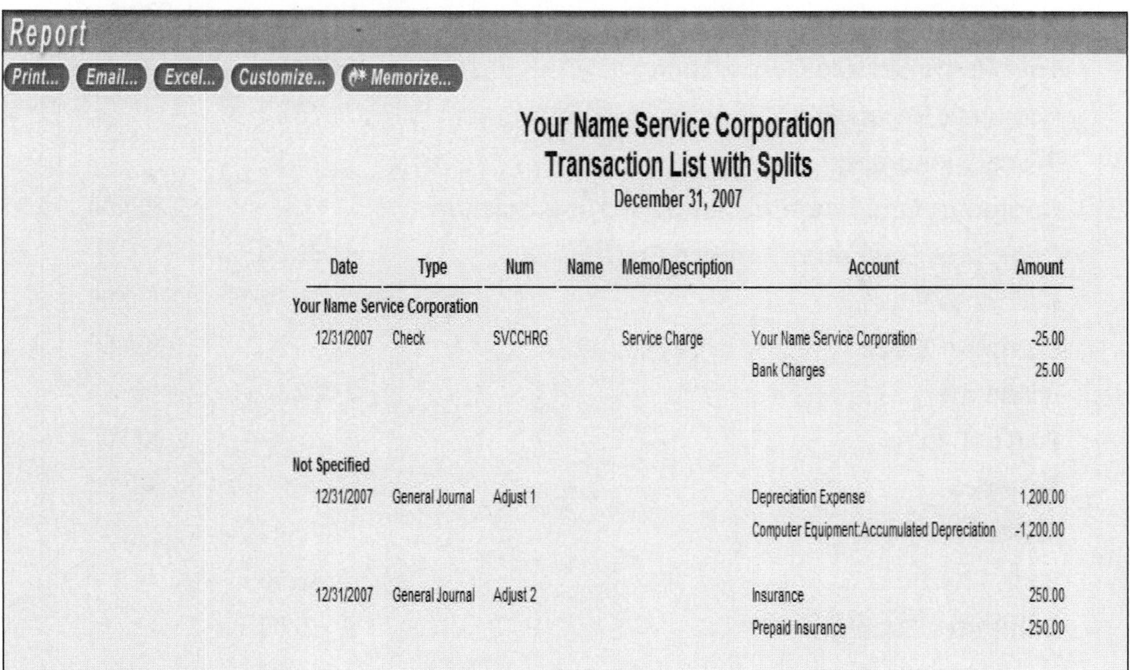
Report

Print... Email... Excel... Customize... Memorize...

Your Name Service Corporation
Transaction List with Splits
December 31, 2007

Date	Type	Num	Name	Memo/Description	Account	Amount
Your Name Service Corporation						
12/31/2007	Check	SVCCHRG		Service Charge	Your Name Service Corporation	-25.00
					Bank Charges	25.00
Not Specified						
12/31/2007	General Journal	Adjust 1			Depreciation Expense	1,200.00
					Computer Equipment:Accumulated Depreciation	-1,200.00
12/31/2007	General Journal	Adjust 2			Insurance	250.00
					Prepaid Insurance	-250.00

Observe that the first entry for December 31 is the bank service charge. Adjustments 1 and 2 are shown after the service charge.

PRINTING THE ADJUSTED TRIAL BALANCE

Print the trial balance and compare with the one shown below.

Your Name Service Corporation
Trial Balance
As of December 31, 2007

	Debit	Credit
Your Name Service Corporation	6,662.00	
Accounts Receivable	0.00	
Prepaid Insurance	270.00	
Computer Equipment:Accumulated Depreciation		2,400.00
Computer Equipment:Original Cost	6,000.00	
Accounts Payable		0.00
Common Stock		1,000.00
Dividends	2,000.00	
Paid in Capital		7,000.00
Services		16,525.00
Advertising	270.00	
Bank Charges	75.00	
Computer Supplies	5,965.00	
Insurance	250.00	
Office Expenses	3,147.00	
Rent or Lease	265.00	
Repair & Maintenance	215.00	
Utilities	606.00	
Depreciation Expense	1,200.00	
TOTAL	**$26,925.00**	**$26,925.00**

PRINTING END-OF-YEAR FINANCIAL STATEMENTS

1. Print the Income Statement from 10/1/20XX to 12/31/0X. Compare your printout with the one shown below.

Income Statement

Your Name Service Corporation
Profit & Loss
October - December, 2007

	Total
Income	
Services	16,525.00
Total Income	**$16,525.00**
Expenses	
Advertising	270.00
Bank Charges	75.00
Computer Supplies	5,965.00
Insurance	250.00
Office Expenses	3,147.00
Rent or Lease	265.00
Repair & Maintenance	215.00
Utilities	606.00
Total Expenses	**$10,793.00**
Net Operating Income	**$5,732.00**
Other Expenses	
Depreciation Expense	1,200.00
Total Other Expenses	**$1,200.00**
Net Other Income	**$ -1,200.00**
Net Income	**$4,532.00**

2. Print the balance sheet and compare with the one shown on next page.

Balance Sheet

Your Name Service Corporation
Balance Sheet
As of December 31, 2007

	Total
ASSETS	
Current Assets	
Bank Accounts	
Your Name Service Corporation	6,662.00
Total Bank Accounts	**$6,662.00**
Accounts Receivable	
Accounts Receivable	0.00
Total Accounts Receivable	**$0.00**
Other Current Assets	
Prepaid Insurance	270.00
Total Other Current Assets	**$270.00**
Total Current Assets	**$6,932.00**
Fixed Assets	
Computer Equipment	
Accumulated Depreciation	-2,400.00
Original Cost	6,000.00
Total Computer Equipment	**3,600.00**
Total Fixed Assets	**$3,600.00**
TOTAL ASSETS	**$10,532.00**
LIABILITIES AND EQUITY	
Liabilities	
Current Liabilities	
Accounts Payable	
Accounts Payable	0.00
Total Accounts Payable	**$0.00**
Total Current Liabilities	**$0.00**
Total Liabilities	**$0.00**
Equity	
Common Stock	1,000.00
Dividends	-2,000.00
Paid in Capital	7,000.00
Retained Earnings	
Net Income	4,532.00
Total Equity	**$10,532.00**
TOTAL LIABILITIES AND EQUITY	**$10,532.00**

END-OF-YEAR CLOSING ENTRIES

As you know from your study of accounting, the purpose of ***closing entries*** is to reset revenue, expense, and dividends account balances to zero. When you record and post closing entries, you are transferring the end-of-year (or end-of-period) balances in revenue, expense, and dividends accounts to the retained earnings account.

The adjusted trial balance (page 140) and end-of-quarter Income Statement (page 141) were used to determine the closing entries. Click on "Save" between each entry to post. Record the closing entries in the **general journal** *(Hint: Use the* Make Journal Entry *link from the* "Banking" *list).*

1. Close 1: Close revenue accounts. (*Hint: After typing "Income Summary" in the account field, a "Mini Interview will appear to guide you through the process of adding this new account. The answers to the mini interview include: "Choose from all account types" for the account type, "equity" for detail type of expense, "accumulated adjustment" for the type of equity, and "Income Summary" for the name of the account. Leave the description and balance information blank.*)

Date	Account Name	Debit	Credit
12/31/20XX	Services-Income	16,525.00	
	Income Summary		16,525.00

2. Close 2: Close expense accounts.

Date	Account Name	Debit	Credit
12/31/20XX	Income Summary	11,993.00	
	Advertising		270.00
	Bank Charges		75.00
	Computer Supplies		5,965.00
	Utilities		606. 00
	Insurance Expense		250.00
	Office Expenses		3,147.00
	Rent or Lease		265.00
	Repairs & Maintenance		215.00
	Depreciation		1,200.00

3. Close 3: Close Income Summary account.

Date	Account Name	Debit	Credit
12/31/20XX	Income Summary	4,532.00	
	Retained Earnings		4,532.00

4. Close 4: Close Dividends account.

Date	Account Name	Debit	Credit
12/31/20XX	Retained Earnings	2,000.00	
	Dividends		2,000.00

TRANSACTION LIST BY DAY REPORT

To make sure that you have entered all the closing entries, you should display your "Transaction List with Splits" report and compare it with the one shown below. This report will show all your December 31 entries: bank service charges, adjusting entries, and closing entries.

December 31, 20XX Transaction List

Your Name Service Corporation
Transaction List with Splits
December 31, 2007

Date	Type	Num	Name	Memo/Description	Account	Amount
Your Name Service Corporation						
12/31/2007	Check	SVCCHRG		Service Charge	Your Name Service Corporation	-25.00
					Bank Charges	25.00
Not Specified						
12/31/2007	General Journal	Adjust 1			Depreciation Expense	1,200.00
					Computer Equipment:Accumulated Depreciation	-1,200.00
12/31/2007	General Journal	Adjust 2			Insurance	250.00
					Prepaid Insurance	-250.00
12/31/2007	General Journal	Close 1			Services	-16,525.00
					Income Summary	16,525.00
12/31/2007	General Journal	Close 2			Income Summary	-11,993.00
					Advertising	-270.00
					Bank Charges	-75.00
					Computer Supplies	-5,965.00
					Insurance	-250.00
					Office Expenses	-3,147.00
					Rent or Lease	-265.00
					Repair & Maintenance	-215.00
					Utilities	-606.00
					Depreciation Expense	-1,200.00
12/31/2007	General Journal	Close 3			Income Summary	-4,532.00
					Retained Earnings	4,532.00
12/31/2007	General Journal	Close 4			Retained Earnings	-2,000.00
					Dividends	2,000.00

POST-CLOSING TRIAL BALANCE

Make the appropriate selections to print a trial balance for December 31, 20XX. You may want to compare your post-closing trial balance to the one below:

Your Name Service Corporation
Trial Balance
As of December 31, 2007

	Debit	Credit
Your Name Service Corporation	6,662.00	
Accounts Receivable	0.00	
Prepaid Insurance	270.00	
Computer Equipment:Accumulated Depreciation		2,400.00
Computer Equipment:Original Cost	6,000.00	
Accounts Payable		0.00
Common Stock		1,000.00
Dividends		0.00
Income Summary		0.00
Paid in Capital		7,000.00
Retained Earnings		2,532.00
Services		0.00
Advertising	0.00	
Bank Charges	0.00	
Computer Supplies	0.00	
Insurance	0.00	
Office Expenses	0.00	
Rent or Lease	0.00	
Repair & Maintenance	0.00	
Utilities	0.00	
Depreciation Expense	0.00	
TOTAL	**$12,932.00**	**$12,932.00**

Observe that your dividends, income, and expense accounts all have zero balances. Also, your Retained Earnings account now has a balance $2,532.00.

BEGINNING-OF-YEAR TRANSACTIONS

Before you start entering transactions for January 20XX, let's look at the balance sheet. Make the appropriate entries to print your balance sheet for January 1, 20XX. (*Hint: Remember to use the next year in your date.* For example, if you have been using December 2007, you will now use January 2008.) Compare your printout with the one shown below.

Your Name Service Corporatio
Balance Sheet
As of January 1, 2008

> **Comment**
> Your new year, i.e., 2007 or 2008

	Total
ASSETS	
Current Assets	
Bank Accounts	
Your Name Service Corporation	6,662.00
Total Bank Accounts	$6,662.00
Accounts Receivable	
Accounts Receivable	0.00
Total Accounts Receivable	$0.00
Other Current Assets	
Prepaid Insurance	270.00
Total Other Current Assets	$270.00
Total Current Assets	$6,932.00
Fixed Assets	
Computer Equipment	
Accumulated Depreciation	-2,400.00
Original Cost	6,000.00
Total Computer Equipment	3,600.00
Total Fixed Assets	$3,600.00
TOTAL ASSETS	$10,532.00
LIABILITIES AND EQUITY	
Liabilities	
Current Liabilities	
Accounts Payable	
Accounts Payable	0.00
Total Accounts Payable	$0.00
Total Current Liabilities	$0.00
Total Liabilities	$0.00
Equity	
Common Stock	1,000.00
Dividends	0.00
Income Summary	0.00
Paid in Capital	7,000.00
Retained Earnings	2,532.00
Net Income	0.00
Total Equity	$10,532.00
TOTAL LIABILITIES AND EQUITY	$10,532.00

Date	*Transaction*
1/02/20XX	Issued hand-written Check No. 25 to Santa Fe Rentals for equipment rental, $192.
1/02/20XX	Received Invoice 135JE and shipment from Big Bytes Supplies for the purchase of computer supplies on account, Net 30, $1,775.
1/03/20XX	Received Invoice EX99 and shipment from Sales Products Supply for the purchase of office supplies on account, Net 30, $175.
1/08/20XX	Sold 50 hours of maintenance services on account to Twin Sisters B & B, Invoice Net 30, $1,500.
1/08/20XX	Sold 2 hours of maintenance services, 10 hours of repair services, and 10 hours of new service on account to Cyberconnect Cafe, Invoice Net 30, $1,560.
1/08/20XX	Returned to Big Bytes Supplies computer supplies, Invoice 135JE, for vendor credit, $100.
1/11/20XX	Paid Big Bytes Supplies, Invoice 135JE, for the January 2 purchase less January 8 return, hand-written Check No. 26, $1,675.
1/11/20XX	Paid Sales Products Supply, Invoice EX99, for the January 3 purchase, hand-written Check No. 27, $175.
1/17/20XX	Received a check from Cyberconnect Cafe in payment of Invoice, Check No. 5510, $1,560.
1/17/20XX	Received a check from Twin Sisters B & B in payment of Invoice, Check No. 335, $1,500.
1/24/20XX	Cash sales $680, received check No. 804 for 10 hours of repair services and 6 hours of maintenance services.
1/30/20XX	Issued Check No. 28 to Comtel for monthly telephone and Internet service, $279.

1/30/20XX Issued Check No. 29 to Regional Utilities for monthly utilities bill, $201.

1/30/20XX Issued Check No. 30 for payment of dividends $2,000 from checking account.

RECONCILE THE BANK STATEMENT: JANUARY

The business receives a bank statement every month for your regular checking account. The bank statement shows that checks and deposits have cleared the bank. Use the bank statement below to complete account reconciliation for January.

REGULAR CHECKING ACCOUNT January 1 - 31, 20XX			
Previous Balance		$7,440.00	
3 Deposits (+)		3,740.00	
7 Checks (-)		2,820.00	
Service Charges (-)	1/31/XX	25.00	
Ending Balance	1/31/XX	**$8,335.00**	
DEPOSITS			
	1/19	1,560.00	
	1/19	1,500.00	
	1/25	680.00	
CHECKS (Asterisk * indicates break in check number sequence)			
1/5	21	303.00	
1/5	22	190.00	
1/5	23	145.00	
1/5	24	140.00	
1/5	25	192.00	
1/13	26	1,675.00	
1/13	27	175.00	

From the "Banking" drop-down menu, go to the link for Reconcile. Complete the steps for reconciling your January bank statement. Then, compare your Reconcile Screen to the one shown on the next page.

Comment:
If a check or deposit does *not* appear on your "Reconcile" screen, move your mouse over the QuickBooks Online Edition menu bar to access the appropriate drop-down menu. Then, select the appropriate link. Select the "Edit" button and make any needed corrections. To update the record, click on "Save."

January's Reconcile Screen

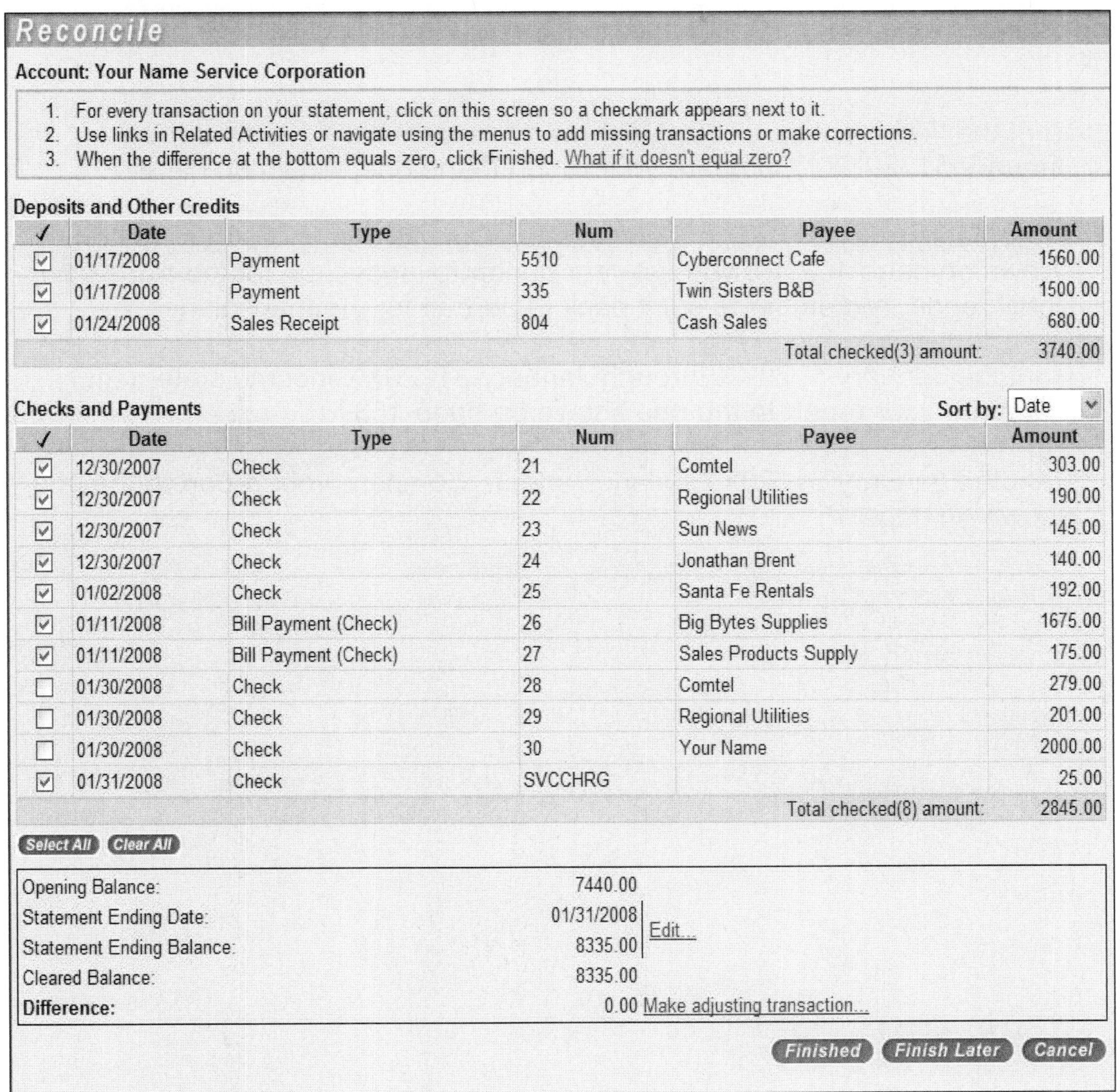

Reconcile

Account: Your Name Service Corporation

1. For every transaction on your statement, click on this screen so a checkmark appears next to it.
2. Use links in Related Activities or navigate using the menus to add missing transactions or make corrections.
3. When the difference at the bottom equals zero, click Finished. What if it doesn't equal zero?

Deposits and Other Credits

✓	Date	Type	Num	Payee	Amount
☑	01/17/2008	Payment	5510	Cyberconnect Cafe	1560.00
☑	01/17/2008	Payment	335	Twin Sisters B&B	1500.00
☑	01/24/2008	Sales Receipt	804	Cash Sales	680.00
				Total checked(3) amount:	3740.00

Checks and Payments — Sort by: Date

✓	Date	Type	Num	Payee	Amount
☑	12/30/2007	Check	21	Comtel	303.00
☑	12/30/2007	Check	22	Regional Utilities	190.00
☑	12/30/2007	Check	23	Sun News	145.00
☑	12/30/2007	Check	24	Jonathan Brent	140.00
☑	01/02/2008	Check	25	Santa Fe Rentals	192.00
☑	01/11/2008	Bill Payment (Check)	26	Big Bytes Supplies	1675.00
☑	01/11/2008	Bill Payment (Check)	27	Sales Products Supply	175.00
☐	01/30/2008	Check	28	Comtel	279.00
☐	01/30/2008	Check	29	Regional Utilities	201.00
☐	01/30/2008	Check	30	Your Name	2000.00
☑	01/31/2008	Check	SVCCHRG		25.00
				Total checked(8) amount:	2845.00

Select All | Clear All

Opening Balance:	7440.00
Statement Ending Date:	01/31/2008 Edit...
Statement Ending Balance:	8335.00
Cleared Balance:	8335.00
Difference:	0.00 Make adjusting transaction...

Finished | Finish Later | Cancel

When satisfied and difference shows 0.00, click "Finished."

January Reconciliation Summary

Click on "Print" to print your January Reconcile Report.

PRINTING JANUARY REPORTS

Print the following reports and compare them to the ones shown on pages 151 - 154.

1. Print the "Transaction List by Day" report for January 1, 20XX through January 31, 20XX. Compare your report to the one shown on page 151.

2. Print the January 31, 20XX trial balance. Compare your report to the one shown on page 152. (If you set your printer to landscape for the transaction detail report, remember to set it back to portrait for the trial balance.)

3. Print the January 1, 20XX through January 31, 20XX income statement. Compare your report to the one shown on page 153.

4. Print the January 31, 20XX balance sheet. Compare your report to the one shown on page 154.

January's Transaction List

Comment
Your new year, i.e., 2007 or 2008

Your Name Service Corporation
Transaction List by Date
January 2008

Date	Type	Num	Name	Memo/Description	Account	Split	Amount
01/02/2008	Check	25	Santa Fe Rentals	Equipment rental	Your Name Service Corporation	Rent or Lease	-192.00
01/02/2008	Bill	135JE	Big Bytes Supplies	computer supplies	Accounts Payable	Computer Supplies	1,775.00
01/03/2008	Bill	EX99	Sales Products Supply	office supplies	Accounts Payable	Office Expenses	175.00
01/08/2008	Invoice	1018	Twin Sisters B&B		Accounts Receivable	Services	1,500.00
01/08/2008	Invoice	1019	Cyberconnect Cafe		Accounts Receivable	-SPLIT-	1,560.00
01/08/2008	Vendor Credit	135JE	Big Bytes Supplies	returned computer supplies	Accounts Payable	Computer Supplies	-100.00
01/11/2008	Bill Payment (Check)	26	Big Bytes Supplies		Your Name Service Corporation	-SPLIT-	-1,675.00
01/11/2008	Bill Payment (Check)	27	Sales Products Supply		Your Name Service Corporation	Accounts Payable	-175.00
01/17/2008	Payment	5510	Cyberconnect Cafe		Your Name Service Corporation	Accounts Receivable	1,560.00
01/17/2008	Payment	335	Twin Sisters B&B		Your Name Service Corporation	Accounts Receivable	1,500.00
01/24/2008	Sales Receipt	1020	Cash Sales		Your Name Service Corporation	-SPLIT-	680.00
01/30/2008	Check	28	Comtel	Telephone and Internet	Your Name Service Corporation	Office Expenses	-279.00
01/30/2008	Check	29	Regional Utilities	monthly utilities	Your Name Service Corporation	Utilities	-201.00
01/30/2008	Check	30	Your Name	Dividends	Your Name Service Corporation	Dividends	-2,000.00
01/31/2008	Check	SVCCHRG		Service Charge	Your Name Service Corporation	Bank Charges	-25.00

January's Trial Balance

Your Name Service Corporation
Trial Balance
As of January 31, 2008

Comment
Your new year, i.e., 2007 or 2008

	Debit	Credit
Your Name Service Corporation	5,855.00	
Accounts Receivable	0.00	
Prepaid Insurance	270.00	
Computer Equipment:Accumulated Depreciation		2,400.00
Computer Equipment:Original Cost	6,000.00	
Accounts Payable		0.00
Common Stock		1,000.00
Dividends	2,000.00	
Income Summary		0.00
Paid in Capital		7,000.00
Retained Earnings		2,532.00
Services		3,740.00
Advertising	0.00	
Bank Charges	25.00	
Computer Supplies	1,675.00	
Insurance	0.00	
Office Expenses	454.00	
Rent or Lease	192.00	
Repair & Maintenance	0.00	
Utilities	201.00	
Depreciation Expense	0.00	
TOTAL	**$16,672.00**	**$16,672.00**

January's Income Statement

Your Name Service Corporation
Profit & Loss
January 2008

	Total
Income	
Services	3,740.00
Total Income	**$3,740.00**
Expenses	
Bank Charges	25.00
Computer Supplies	1,675.00
Office Expenses	454.00
Rent or Lease	192.00
Utilities	201.00
Total Expenses	**$2,547.00**
Net Operating Income	**$1,193.00**
Net Income	**$1,193.00**

Comment
Your new year, i.e., 2007 or 2008

January's Balance Sheet

Comment
Your new year, i.e., 2007 or 2008

Your Name Service Corporation
Balance Sheet
As of January 31, 2008

	Total
ASSETS	
Current Assets	
Bank Accounts	
Your Name Service Corporation	5,855.00
Total Bank Accounts	**$5,855.00**
Accounts Receivable	
Accounts Receivable	0.00
Total Accounts Receivable	**$0.00**
Other Current Assets	
Prepaid Insurance	270.00
Total Other Current Assets	**$270.00**
Total Current Assets	**$6,125.00**
Fixed Assets	
Computer Equipment	
Accumulated Depreciation	-2,400.00
Original Cost	6,000.00
Total Computer Equipment	**3,600.00**
Total Fixed Assets	**$3,600.00**
TOTAL ASSETS	**$9,725.00**
LIABILITIES AND EQUITY	
Liabilities	
Current Liabilities	
Accounts Payable	
Accounts Payable	0.00
Total Accounts Payable	**$0.00**
Total Current Liabilities	**$0.00**
Total Liabilities	**$0.00**
Equity	
Common Stock	1,000.00
Dividends	-2,000.00
Income Summary	0.00
Paid in Capital	7,000.00
Retained Earnings	2,532.00
Net Income	1,193.00
Total Equity	**$9,725.00**
TOTAL LIABILITIES AND EQUITY	**$9,725.00**

CHECK YOUR PROGRESS

Flashcard Review

1. Make adjusting journal entries.
2. Make closing journal entries.

Internet Homework

If necessary, start QuickBooks Online Edition, and then log in to your account. Using selections from your QuickBooks Online Edition account, answer the following questions. Answer each question in the space provided.

1. List ways you can get QuickBooks Online Edition to run faster. (*Hint: Click on the Can I make QuickBooks Online Edition run faster? link under "Common Questions" on your company's home page.)*

   ____

   ____

2. If you want to accept credit card payments, what does that feature cost? *(Hint: Click on the appropriate link on the oe.QuickBooks.com website)*

   ____

   ____

3. Briefly describe two other products offered by QuickBooks. (*Hint: Click on the "Additional links.")*.

   ____

   ____

4. Click on ? help on the QuickBooks Online Edition menu bar. Explain various ways to use this feature.

____

____

Multiple-Choice. In the space provided, write the letter that best answers each question.

_____1. In Chapter 5, the general journal is used to record which of the following transactions?

a. Purchases.
b. Sales.
c. Adjusting entries.
d. Credit memos for customers.
e. None of the above.

_____2. Adjusting entries are dated:

a. The first day of the month.
b. The last day of the month.
c. Any day of the month.
d. All of the above.
e. None of the above.

_____3. To depreciate your business's fixed assets, you used which one of the following deprecation methods?

a. Sum-of-the-years digits.
b. Units of production.
c. MACRS.
d. Straight-line.
e. None of the above.

_____4. The amount of the adjusting entry for depreciation expense--equipment was:

a. $5,000.00.
b. $1,200.00.
c. $2,333.33.
d. $1,000.00.
e. None of the above.

______5. The amount of the adjusting entry for expired insurance was:

a. $200.00.
b. $410.00.
c. $250.00.
d. $1,200.00.
e. None of the above.

______6. The total debit and credit balance on your adjusted trial balance is:

a. $26,925.00.
b. $16,672.00.
c. $9,658.00.
d. $12,932.00.
e. None of the above.

______7. The net income for the month of January is:

a. $1,675.00.
b. $1,193.00.
c. $3,740.00.
d. $4,532.00.
e. None of the above.

______8. When you reset revenue, expense, and dividends account balances to zero, this is known as:

a. Adjusting entries.
b. General journal entries.
c. Debits equaling credits.
d. Closing entries.
e. None of the above.

______9. Which two reports do you refer to when completing the closing entries?

a. Balance Sheet and Income Statement.
b. Unadjusted Trial Balance and Income Statement.
c. Adjusted Trial Balance and Income Statement.
d. You use just the unadjusted trial balance.
e. None of the above.

_____10. The total debit and credit balance on your January 31, 20XX trial balance is:

a. $9,658.00.
b. $12,932.00 .
c. $8,851.00.
d. $16,672.00.
e. None of the above.

True/False. Write T for True or F for false in the space provided.

_____11. You must complete Chapters 1 - 4 before doing the work in Chapter 5.

_____12. You use the Make Journal Entry link to record transactions in the General Journal.

_____13. QuickBooks Online Edition will allow you to submit entries that are out of balance.

_____14. Computer equipment has a five-year service life.

_____15. When you record and post closing entries, you are transferring the end-of-year balances in revenue, expense, and dividends accounts to the retained earnings account.

_____16. You click on "Submit" between each entry to post to the general ledger.

_____17. A good way to see if you have entered transactions is to print a Trial Balance.

_____18. Once the accounting period is closed, you will not be able to access transactions recorded before December 31, 20XX.

_____19. Your adjusted trial balance and post-closing trial balance are always prepared on the same date.

_____20. After recording closing entries, you should print a post-closing trial balance.

Exercise 5-1. Using the reports that you printed in Chapter 5, End-of-Quarter and End-of-Year Transactions, answer the following questions.

1. At the end of the quarter, your business's accumulated depreciation for the equipment is: ____________

2. The amount of accounts payable owed on January 1, 20XX is: ____________

3. The updated retained earnings account balance on January 1, 20XX is: ____________

4. On January 1, 20XX, your total fixed assets are: ____________

5. On January 1, 20XX, your total liabilities and equity are: ____________

Exercise 5-2. Complete the following.

1. Copy your January 1, 20XX balance sheet to Excel. Use **Exercise 5-2-1** as the file name. Print your Excel balance sheet.

2. Copy your January 31, 20XX balance sheet to Excel. Use **Exercise 5-2-2** as the file name. Print your Excel balance sheet.

CHAPTER 5 INDEX

Balance sheet 142, 146, 154
Beginning-of-year transactions 146
Check your progress 155
Closing entries 143, 144
Computer accounting essentials website 135
End-of-year adjusting entries 137
End-of-year closing entries 143
Exercise 5-1 159
Exercise 5-2 159
Flashcard review 155
Getting started 136
Income statement 141, 153
Internet Homework 155
Multiple-choice 156
Post-closing trial balance 145
Printing end-of-year financial statements 141
Printing January reports 150
Printing the adjusted trial balance 140
Reconcile the bank statement: January 148
Software objectives 135
Transaction list by day report 139, 144, 151
True/False 158
Web objectives 135

6 Advanced Features

In Chapter 6 of *Computer Accounting Essentials Using QuickBooks Online Edition*, you use QuickBooks Online Edition's memorize report feature, customize report feature, copy report data to a spreadsheet program and produce graphs, and use the activity log.

SOFTWARE OBJECTIVES: In Chapter 6, you use the software to:

1. Memorize reports.
2. Customize reports.
3. Create graphs.
4. Access activity log.
5. Complete activities for Chapter 6, Advanced Features.

WEB OBJECTIVES: In Chapter 6, you use the Internet to:

1. Access the Computer Accounting Essentials web site at www.mhhe.com/yachtessentials3e to check for updates.
2. Log in to your QuickBooks Online Edition account.
3. Access QuickBooks Online Edition's help feature.
4. Complete Flashcard review.
5. Complete Internet activities.

COMPUTER ACCOUNTING ESSENTIALS WEBSITE

Before you begin your work in Chapter 6, Advanced Features, access the Computer Accounting Essentials website at **www.mhhe.com/yachtessentials3e**. Software and book updates will be shown. Check this web site regularly for reference and study.

GETTING STARTED

Follow these steps to start QuickBooks Online Edition. You *must* complete Chapters 1, 2, 3, 4, and 5, pages 3 – 159, before starting Chapter 6, Advanced Features. *The exercises at the end of each Chapter must be completed, too.*

1. Start your Internet browser and log in to QuickBooks Online Edition in the usual way.

2. Move your mouse over "Reports" on the QuickBooks Online Edition menu bar. When the drop-down screen appears, click on Balance Sheet.

3. When the "Balance Sheet" screen appears, click on Customize in the upper center of the screen.

4. The "Customize Balance Sheet Report" screen pops up asking for Transaction Date options and Rows/Columns options. In General section's "Transaction Date," select "Custom." For "Rows/Columns," select "Total Only" for the date. Type 01/01/20XX for both the "From" and "To" dates.

5. Click on Create. Scroll down the screen to see your balance sheet. The year shown on your balance sheet may differ. Compare your balance sheet with the one shown on page 146.

MEMORIZING REPORTS

On every Report screen there are five buttons in the upper left corner. These buttons allow you to print, email, excel, customize, or memorize a report. You have already used the "Print," "Email," and "Customize" buttons. Let's learn about the Memorize... button.
The "Memorize" button creates a link on your home page to the memorized report and retains its customization.

Follow these steps to memorize a report. The January 1, 20XX balance sheet should be displayed on your screen.

1. Display the report you want to memorize and click Memorize.

2. When the "Add Shortcut – Web Page Dialog" appears, give the report a descriptive name.

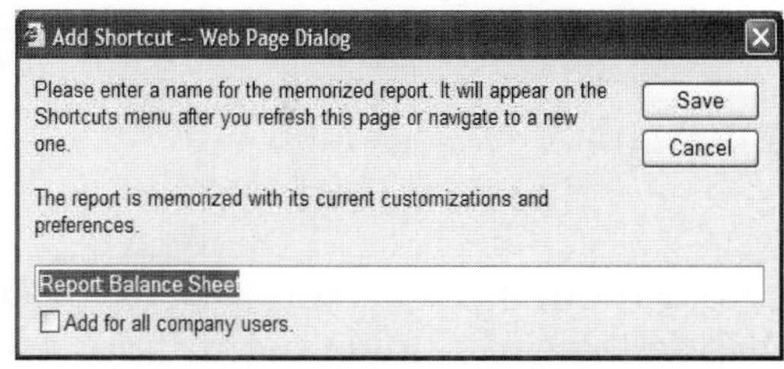

3. Click Save.

4. Return to your home page by clicking on home.

5. Click on Customize in the upper right of your screen to add the Shortcuts section to your home page. When the "Web Page Dialog" appears, highlight Shortcuts.

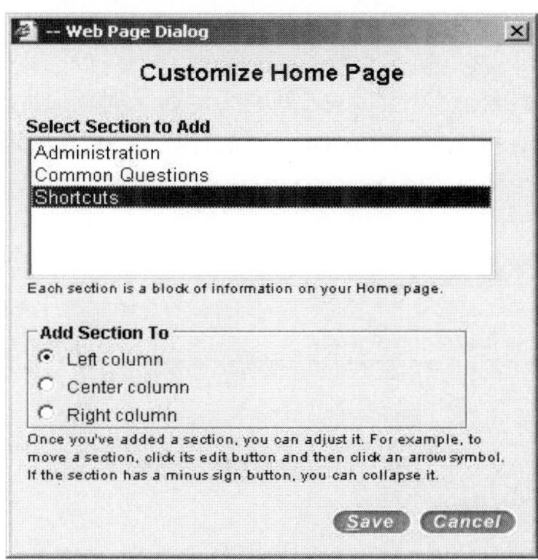

6. Click "Save."

7. A shortcut to the report is now available on your home page.

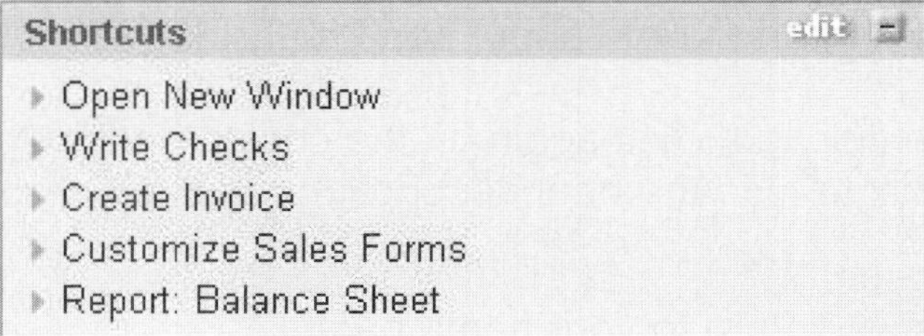

Later, if you want to change the customization on a memorized report, you must memorize it again to save the changes.

CUSTOMIZING REPORTS

QuickBooks Online Edition has many different reports available for customization. Customizing reports gives you the flexibility to create the reports you want. You have three ways you can customize a report: display options, date options, and filter options. Let's look at the various types of reports you can customize.

Reports

To learn more about the various reports you can customize, follow the following steps.

1. Move your mouse over "Reports" on the QuickBooks Online Edition menu bar. When the drop-down menu appears, click on All Reports (Report Overview).

2. When the "Report Overview" screen appears, place a check mark in the "Show Report Descriptions" box to display a brief description of each report if the descriptions are not displayed.

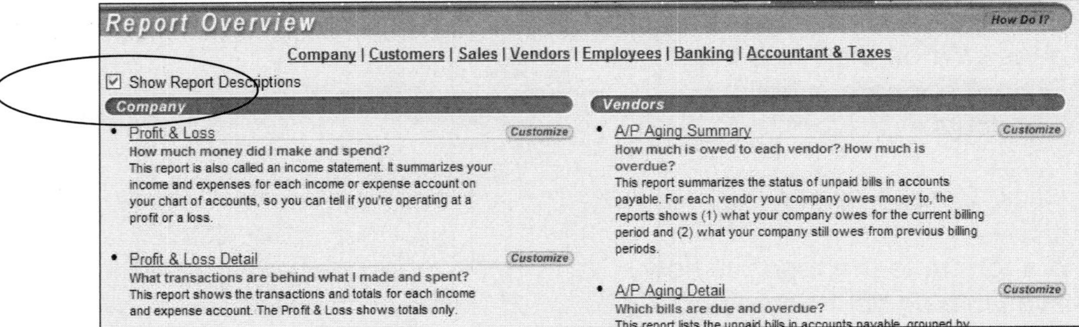

3. Scroll down the screen to read about each report.

4. When you have finished, click again on the check mark in the "Show Report Descriptions" box to hide the brief descriptions of each report.

5. Click on home to return to your home page.

Customizing Options: Display and Date

In Chapters 1-5 of *Computer Accounting Essentials Using QuickBooks Online Edition*, you customized reports by selecting display and date options. To review how to use these options, follow the following steps:

1. Click your home page's memorized link to the January 1, 20XX Balance Sheet.

2. When the balance sheet displays on your screen, click Customize.

3. A "Customize Report-Web Page Dialog" box pops up asking about display and date options.

4. For "Transaction Date" select "All Dates" (leave "From" and "To" blank), select "Accrual" for the "Accounting Method," and for "Columns" select "Total Only."

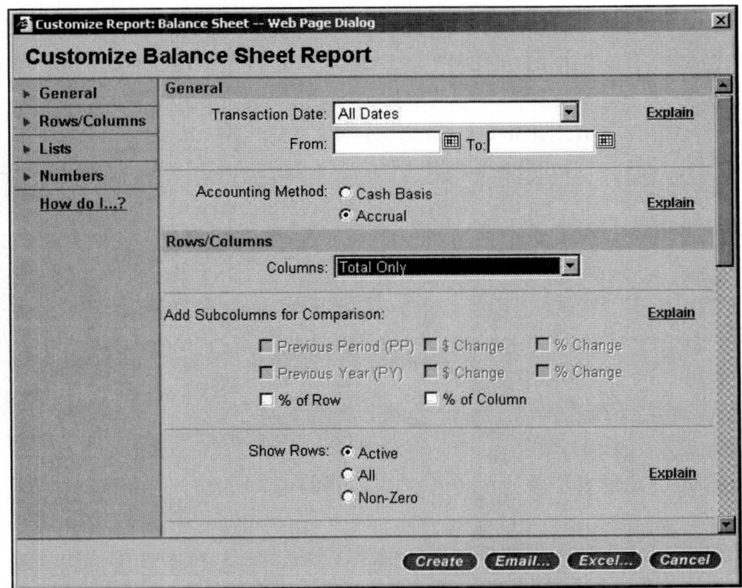

5. Click on Create.

6. A partial view of the customized report is shown below.

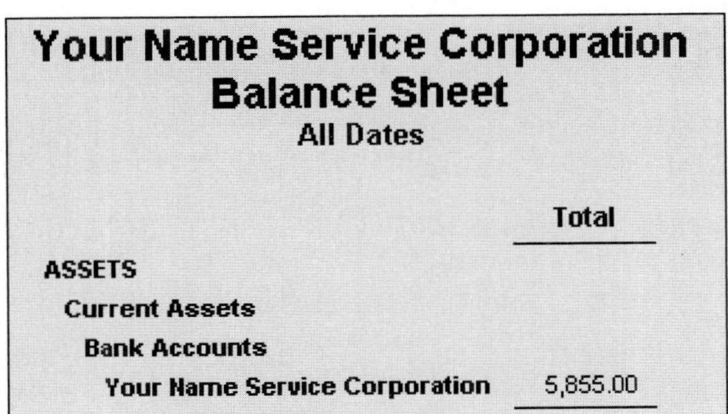

Your Name Service Corporation
Balance Sheet
All Dates

	Total
ASSETS	
Current Assets	
Bank Accounts	
Your Name Service Corporation	5,855.00

Scroll down the screen to see the rest of this customized balance sheet.

Customizing Options: Filters

Follow these steps to filter report information.

1. Move your mouse over "Reports" on the QuickBooks Online Edition menu bar. When the drop-down menu appears, click on All Reports (Report Overview).

2. Click on Transaction List by Customer.

3. When the "Transaction List by Customer" report appears, click on the "Customize" button.

4. A "Customize Report: Transaction List by Customer—Web page Dialog" box appears asking for general, rows/columns, and date filter options.

5. In the "Transaction Date," select "All Dates."

6. Leave "From" and "To" date boxes blank.

7. For "Group By," select "Customer."

8. Compare your Web Page Dialog box to the one shown.

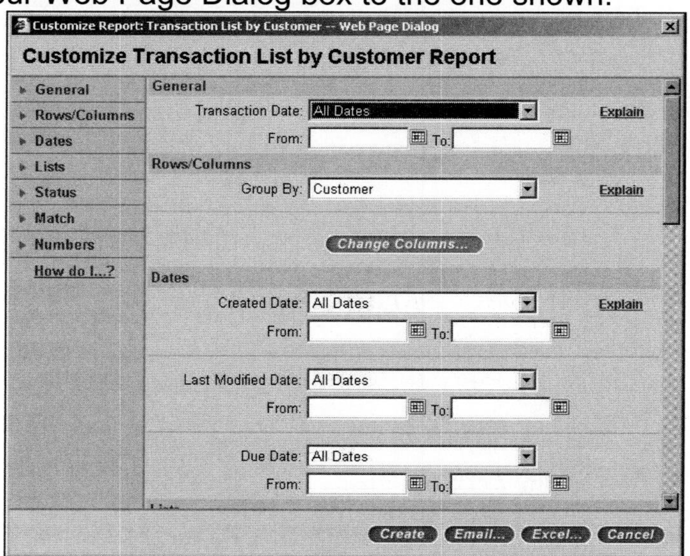

9. Click on the "Create" button.

10. A partial report is shown below. To see the rest of the report, scroll down the screen or print it. Your dates may differ.

Your Name Service Corporation
Transaction List by Customer
All Dates

Date	Type	Num	Memo/Description	Account	Amount
Cash Sales					
10/20/2007	Sales Receipt	1009		Your Name Service Corporation	2,150.00
11/21/2007	Sales Receipt	1012		Your Name Service Corporation	2,300.00
12/24/2007	Sales Receipt	1017		Your Name Service Corporation	2,200.00
01/24/2008	Sales Receipt	1020		Your Name Service Corporation	680.00
Cyberconnect Cafe					
10/01/2007	Invoice	1002	Opening Balance	Accounts Receivable	280.00
10/10/2007	Invoice	1006	Invoice No. 1006	Accounts Receivable	780.00
10/16/2007	Payment	4522		Your Name Service Corporation	280.00
10/19/2007	Payment	5001	Oct. 10	Your Name Service Corporation	780.00
11/08/2007	Invoice	1011		Accounts Receivable	1,560.00
11/17/2007	Payment	5110		Your Name Service Corporation	1,560.00
12/08/2007	Invoice	1014		Accounts Receivable	970.00
12/17/2007	Payment	5225		Your Name Service Corporation	970.00
01/08/2008	Invoice	1019		Accounts Receivable	1,560.00
01/17/2008	Payment	5510		Your Name Service Corporation	1,560.00
NFP Access					
10/01/2007	Invoice	1003	Opening Balance	Accounts Receivable	295.00
10/09/2007	Invoice	1005	Invoice No. 1005	Accounts Receivable	300.00
10/16/2007	Payment	816	opening balance	Your Name Service Corporation	295.00

11. Return to the “All Reports (Report Overview)” screen.

COPY REPORT TEXT TO A SPREADSHEET PROGRAM

You can copy the text of a report to any spreadsheet or word processing program. Start with the "All Reports (Report Overview)" screen displayed on your screen.

1. Link to the Expenses by Vendor Summary by clicking on it.
2. Customize the report. Select “All Dates” for “Dates,” and leave blank the “From” and “To.” For the “Accounting Method”, select “Accrual” and for “Columns” select “Total Only.” Click on Create.

3. When the report displays on your screen, click **Excel...** to view the report in an excel spreadsheet.

4. Compare your spreadsheet to the one shown.

	A	B
1	**Your Name Service Corporation**	
2	**Expenses by Vendor Summary**	
3	**All Dates**	
4		
5		**Total**
6	**Big Bytes Supplies**	7,640.00
7	**Comtel**	1,121.00
8	**Jonathan Brent**	215.00
9	**Regional Utilities**	807.00
10	**Sales Products Supply**	2,480.00
11	**Santa Fe Rentals**	457.00
12	**Sun News**	270.00
13	**TOTAL**	**$ 12,990.00**
14		

CUSTOMIZING GRAPHS

You can also display your report as a graph using your spreadsheet program's "Chart Wizard." Follow these steps to display your expense by vendor report as a graph.

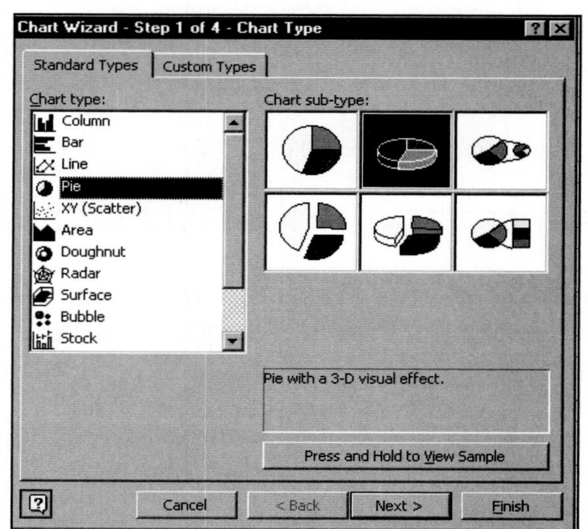

1. With your mouse highlight the vendor names and amounts and click on the Chart Wizard icon on your toolbar in excel. *(Hint: See highlighted area in the previous screenshot.)*

2. A series of "Chart Wizard" screens step you through the process of customizing your graph. In Step 1, select the chart type. Click on "Pie" and the "Pie with a 3-D visual effect" box. Click on "Next>."

3. In Step 2, accept the "Data range" and "Series in columns." Click on "Next>."

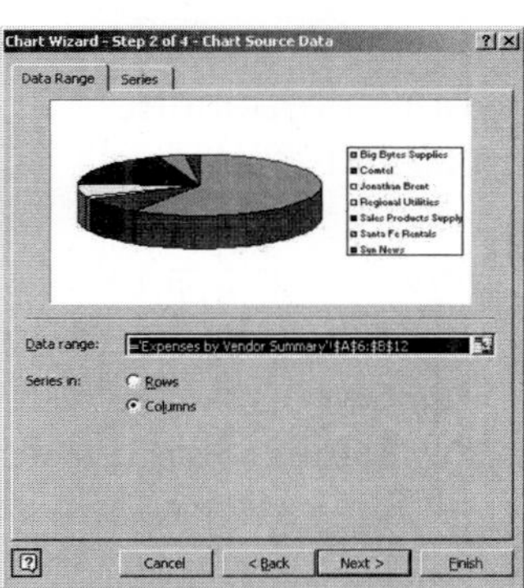

4. In Step 3 set the title, legends and data labels. Click on the "Titles" tab. In the "Chart title" field, type: **Your Name Service Corporation Expenses by Vendor October-January.**

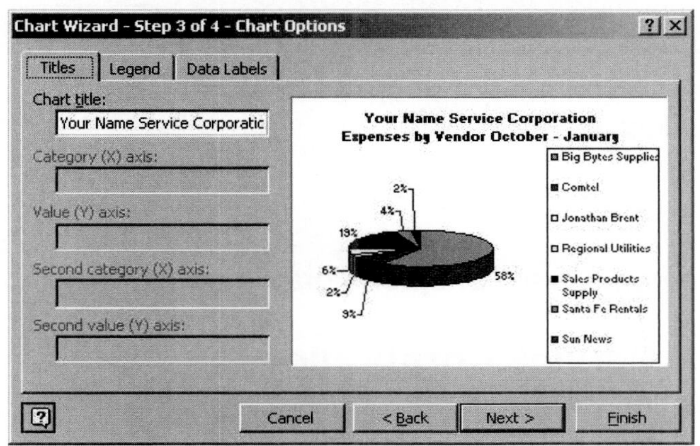

5. Click on the "Legend" tab. Make sure the "Show legend" box is checked and that the "Placement" radio button for "right" is selected.

6. Click on the "Data Labels" tab. In this last tab of Step 3, select the data labels for your graph. Select "Show percent" for the "Data labels" and also check the "Show leader lines" box. Observe that each vendor is shown as a percentage Click on "Next>."

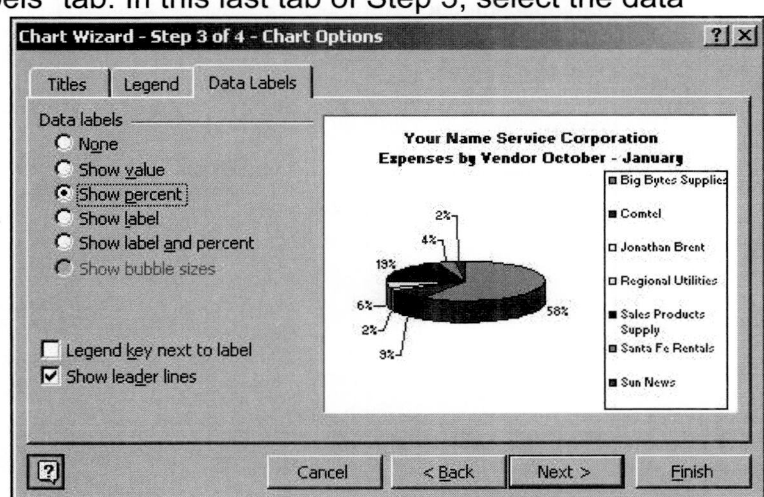

7. In Step 4 of the "Chart Wizard" place the graph "As object in:" your spreadsheet. Click "Finish."

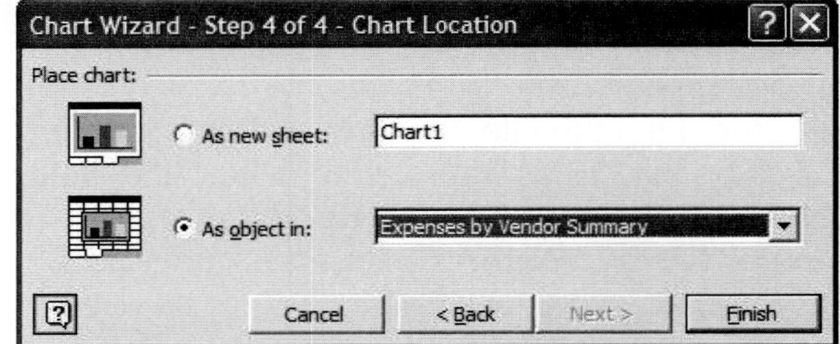

8. Move your graph around your spreadsheet until you are satisfied with its placement. Compare your spreadsheet and graph results to the report shown below.

9. Print your report and graph.

10. Save your report. For the file name, use "Chapter 6 graph."

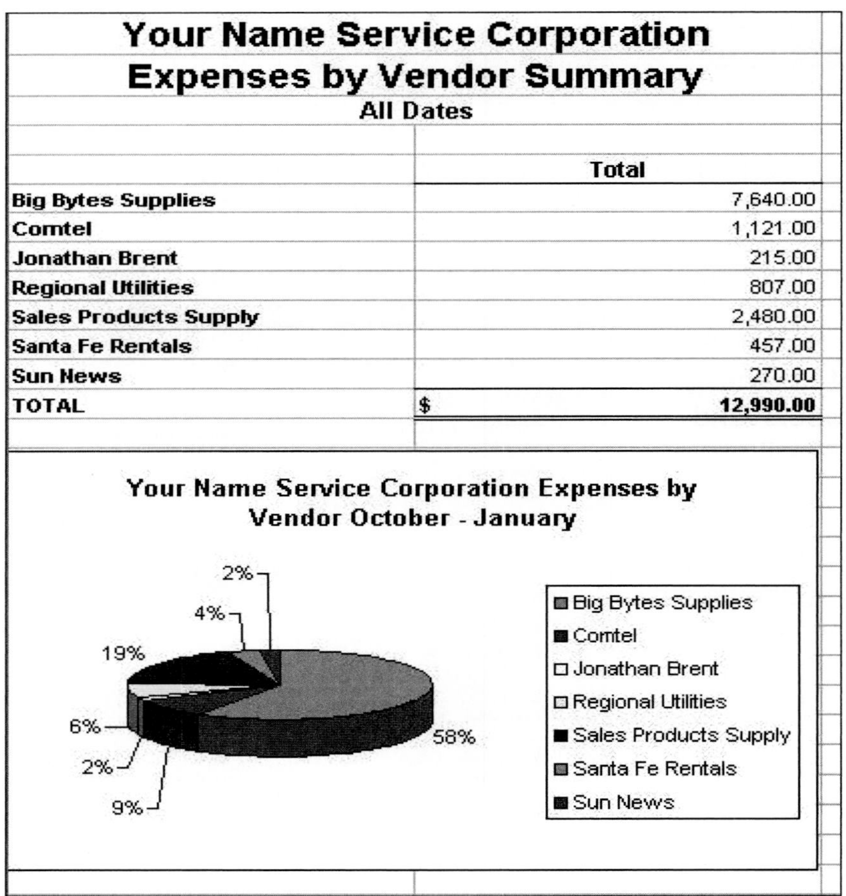

Your Name Service Corporation
Expenses by Vendor Summary
All Dates

	Total
Big Bytes Supplies	7,640.00
Comtel	1,121.00
Jonathan Brent	215.00
Regional Utilities	807.00
Sales Products Supply	2,480.00
Santa Fe Rentals	457.00
Sun News	270.00
TOTAL	$ **12,990.00**

CUSTOMIZATION

On the "Report Overview All Reports" screen, there many different types of reports to customize. You may want to select one or two of them to experiment with customization. For example, click on the Profit & Loss Detail report and customize it by selecting various display, date, and filter options. Remember, by accessing "Help," you can obtain specific information about a QuickBooks Online Edition feature.

ACTIVITY LOG

QuickBooks Online Edition keeps a log of your activities while using the software. To access your "Activity Log," complete the following steps:

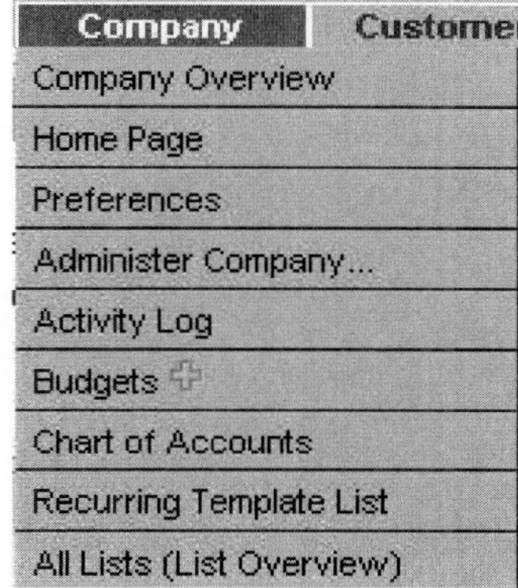

1. Move your mouse over "Company" on the QuickBooks Online Edition menu bar. When the drop-down menu appears, click on Activity Log.

2. When the activity log appears, notice it displays the date and time of your most recent visits first. The log also displays the user and the activities engaged in while on your company site. A partial example of an Activity Log is shown below.

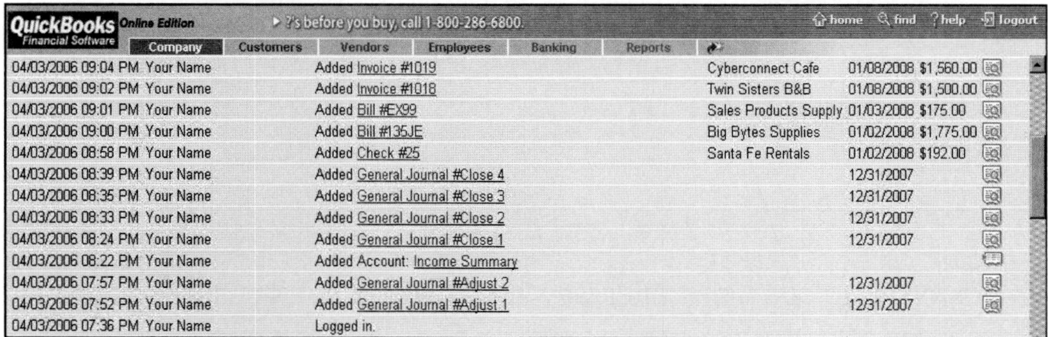

3. Click on the "Customize" button to see how the log can be customized.

4. Print your "Activity Log."

5. Log out or continue with the Check Your Progress activities.

CHECK YOUR PROGRESS

Flashcard Review

1. Memorize reports.
2. Customize reports.
3. Create graphs using excel.
4. Access activity log.

Internet Homework

Start QuickBooks Online Edition. Before logging in to your account, click on "See the video" to view the QuickBooks Online Edition videos and "Product Info" to compare the various QuickBooks products.

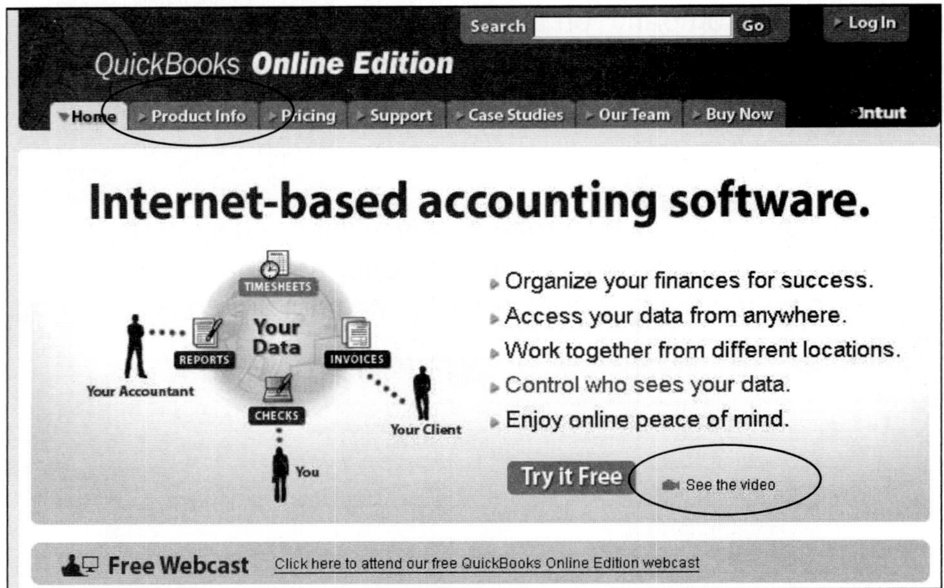

Complete the following questions after viewing a comparison of QuickBooks products.

1. What products is QuickBooks selling? How much does each product cost?

____

____

2. Describe the types of free or risk free trial options each product offers.

____

____

3. Which product has the most features? Which one has the least?

____

____

4. What features does QuickBooks Online Edition have that the other CD-based products lack?

____

____

5. List some features that would cause a company to switch from QuickBooks Online Edition to another QuickBooks software product.

____

____

6. Which feature would be most helpful to your situation?

____

Multiple-Choice. In the space provided, write the letter that best answers each question.

_____1. To customize reports, you start by selecting which of the following QuickBooks Online Edition drop-down menus?

a. Company.
b. Vendors.
c. Banking.
d. Reports.
e. None of the above.

_____2. The Computer Accounting Essentials website is used to:

a. Log in to QuickBooks Online Edition.
b. Check software and book updates.
c. Complete Chapter 5, End-of-Year & Beginning-of-Year transactions.
d. All of the above.
e. None of the above.

_____3. Why should you customize reports?

a. To display the income statement and balance sheet on your screen.
b. To display only the balance sheet on your screen.
c. To give you the flexibility to create the reports you need.
d. To change account balances on your reports.
e. All of the above.

_____4. You can customize reports in what ways:

a. Change general options.
b. Choose row/column options.
c. Select list options.
d. Select number options.
e. All of the above.

_____5. Which of the following is the date default when you display reports?

a. Current date.
b. Date of last transaction.
c. All dates.
d. Last day of the period.
e. None of the above.

_____6. On the January 1, 20XX balance sheet, "Total Bank Accounts" is:

a. $8,485.00.
b $6,662.00.
c. $6,932.00.
d. $9,725.00.
e. None of the above.

_____7. You link to the Sales by Product/Service Summary from the following report list:

a. Sales.
b. Customers.
c. Vendors.
d. Company.
e. None of the above.

_____8. You can display the balance sheet by which of the following date criteria?

a. Fiscal year.
b. Last fiscal quarter to date.
c. This month to date.
d. Last fiscal quarter.
e. All of the above.

______9. Your Activity Log displays by the following date criteria.

a. Fiscal year.
b. Most recent activity first.
c. This month to date.
d. Calendar year.
e. None of the above.

_____10. In Chapter 6, Advanced Features, you made the selections for which of the following type of graph?

a. Bar chart.
b. Income summary.
c. Expenses only graph.
d. Pie chart.
e. None of the above.

True/False. Write T for True or F for false in the space provided.

____11. You must complete Chapters 1 - 5 before doing the work in Chapter 6.

____12. You use buttons in the upper part of your report screen to customize reports.

____13. You can copy the text of a report to any word processing program.

____14. The percentage of expense purchases from Big Bytes Supplies from October - January was 57%.

____15. The percentage of expense purchases from Regional Utilities from October - January was 20%.

____16. If you customize a memorized report, you need to click on "Memorize" to save the changes.

____17. The partial balance sheet created on page 162 is the same as the balance sheet on page 146.

____18. QuickBooks Online Edition contains a graph feature.

____19. Check the www.mhhe.com/yachtessentials3e website regularly for software or book updates.

____20. The work in Chapters 1-6 is cumulative.

Exercise 6-1. Using the reports that you printed in Chapter 6, Advanced Features, answer the following questions.

1. On your expense by vendor graph, the percentage of Comtel is? ____________
2. On your expense by vendor graph, the percentage of Sun News is ____________
3. On your expense by vendor graph, the percentage of Jonathan Brent is: ____________
4. On your expense by vendor graph, the percentage of Santa Fe Rentals is: ____________

Exercise 6-2. Complete the following.

1. Print an “Expense by Vendor” graph pie chart for January 1 - 31, 20XX.
2. Print an “Expense by Vendor” graph pie chart for October 1 - 31, 20XX.
3. Print an “Expense by Vendor” graph pie chart for November 1 - 30, 20XX.
4. Print an “Expense by Vendor” graph pie chart for December 1 - 31, 20XX.

Exercise 6-3. Complete the chart that is shown below.

1.

	October	November	December
Comtel	__________	__________	__________
Sun News	__________	__________	__________
Big Bytes Supplies	__________	__________	__________
Jonathan Brent	__________	__________	__________
Regional Utilities	__________	__________	__________
Sales Products Supply	__________	__________	__________
Santa Fe Rentals	__________	__________	__________

2. Explain why November does not show a percentage for the vendor, Jonathan Brent.

____

____

____

____

____

____

CHAPTER 6 INDEX

Activity log 171
Check your progress 172
Computer accounting essentials website 161
Copy report text to a spreadsheet program 167
Customization 171
Customizing graphs 168
Customizing options: Display and date 165
Customizing options: Filters 166
Customizing reports 164
Exercises 178, 179
Getting started 162
Internet homework 172
Memorizing reports 163
Multiple-choice 174
Reports 162, 164
Software objectives 161
True/False 177
Web objectives 161

Case Problem 1

In Case Problem 1, you complete two months of transactions for your business: February and March 20XX. You *must* complete Chapters 1 - 6, pages 3 - 179, before starting Case Problem 1. The exercises at the end of each Chapter must be completed, too.

In Case Problem 1, you will record transactions for the months of February and March; complete bank reconciliation for each month; and print financial statements.

In Case Problem 2, you will complete the adjusting entries for the first quarter and print end-of-quarter reports. Case Problem 2 culminates the recordkeeping activities for your business.

Case Problem 3 is a student-designed project. You are instructed to write transactions for the next month (April 20XX) and complete the accounting cycle showing a net loss for your business.

Before you start entering transactions for February 20XX, let's look at the January 31, 20XX balance sheet. Make the appropriate selections to print your balance sheet for January 31, 20XX, and then compare it with the one shown in Chapter 5 on page 154.

FEBRUARY TRANSACTIONS

Date	*Transactions*
2/02/20XX	Issued hand-written Check No. 31 to Santa Fe Rentals for equipment rental, $200.
2/02/20XX	Received Invoice 145JE and a shipment of computer supplies from Big Bytes Supplies, Net 30, $1,725.

2/03/20XX	Received Invoice EX133 and shipment from Sales Products Supply for the purchase of office supplies, Net 30, $245.
2/08/20XX	Sold 50 hours of maintenance services on account to Twin Sisters B & B, Invoice Net 30, $1,500.
2/08/20XX	Sold 52 hours of maintenance services on account to Cyberconnect Cafe, Invoice Net 30, $1,560.
2/11/20XX	Paid Big Bytes Supplies, Invoice 145JE, for the February 2 purchase, hand-written Check No. 32.
2/11/20XX	Paid Sales Products Supply, Invoice EX133, for the February 3 purchase, hand-written Check No. 33.
2/17/20XX	Received a check from Cyberconnect Cafe in payment of Invoice dated 2/08/20XX; Check No. 6201, $1,560.
2/17/20XX	Received a check from Twin Sisters B & B in payment of Invoice dated 2/08/20XX; Check No. 450, $1,500.
2/24/20XX	Entered sales receipt for cash sales $2,420, received check No. 805 for 46 hours of repair services and 4 hours of maintenance services.
2/28/20XX	Write Check No. 34 to Comtel for monthly telephone and Internet service, $236.
2/28/20XX	Write Check No. 35 to Jonathan Brent for repairs, $220.
2/28/20XX	Write Check No. 36 to Regional Utilities for monthly utilities bill, $235.
2/28/20XX	Write Check No. 37 from checking account to pay dividends to you, the sole stockholder, $1,500.

RECONCILE THE BANK STATEMENT: FEBRUARY

Your business receives a bank statement every month for your regular checking account. The bank statement shows that checks and deposits have cleared the bank. Use the bank statement below to complete account reconciliation for February.

REGULAR CHECKING ACCOUNT February 1 - 28, 20XX			
Previous Balance		$8,335.00	
3 Deposits (+)		5,480.00	
6 Checks (-)		4,650.00	
Service Charges (-)	2/28/XX	25.00	
Ending Balance	2/28/XX	**$9,140.00**	
DEPOSITS			
	2/20	1,560.00	
	2/20	1,500.00	
	2/27	2,420.00	
CHECKS (Asterisk * indicates break in check number sequence)			
2/1	28	279.00	
2/1	29	201.00	
2/5	30	2,000.00	
2/5	31	200.00	
2/15	32	1,725.00	
2/15	33	245.00	

From the "Banking" drop-down menu, go to the link for Reconcile. Complete the steps for reconciling your February bank statement.

PRINT FEBRUARY REPORTS

Print the following reports for February 20XX.

1. Print February's reconciliation summary.
2. Print February's transaction list by date report.
3. Print February's trial balance.
4. Print February's balance sheet.
5. Print February's income statement.
6. Print January 1, 20XX-February 28, 20XX income statement.

MARCH TRANSACTIONS

Date	*Transactions*
3/02/20XX	Write Check No. 38 to the Pro Insurance in payment of next quarter's insurance premiums, $210.
3/02/20XX	Received Invoice 190JE and shipment from Big Bytes Supplies for the purchase of computer supplies, Net 30, $1350.
3/03/20XX	Received Invoice EX203 and shipment from Sales Products Supply for the purchase of office supplies, Net 30, $195.
3/11/20XX	Paid Big Bytes Supplies, Invoice 190JE, for the March 2 purchase, Check No. 39.
3/11/20XX	Paid Sales Products Supply, Invoice EX203, for the March 3 purchase, Check No. 40.
3/24/20XX	Cash sales $3,280, received check No. 806 for 62 hours of repair services and 6 hours of maintenance services.
3/30/20XX	Write Check No. 41 to Comtel for monthly telephone and Internet service, $280.
3/30/20XX	Write Check No. 42 to Sun News for advertising, $80.
3/30/20XX	Write Check No. 43 to Regional Utilities for monthly utilities bill, $287.
3/30/20XX	Write Check No. 44 from checking account to pay dividends, $1,500.
3/30/20XX	Write check No. 45 to Jonathan Brent for repairs, $105.

RECONCILE THE BANK STATEMENT: MARCH

Your business receives a bank statement every month for your regular checking account. The bank statement shows that checks and deposits have cleared the bank. Use the bank statement below to complete account reconciliation for March.

REGULAR CHECKING ACCOUNT March 1 - 31, 20XX			
Previous Balance		$9,140.00	
1 Deposits (+)		3,280.00	
7 Checks (-)		3,946.00	
Service Charges (-)	3/31/XX	25.00	
Ending Balance	3/31/XX	**$8,449.00**	
DEPOSITS			
	3/25	3,280.00	
CHECKS (Asterisk * indicates break in check number sequence)			
3/5	34	236.00	
3/5	35	220.00	
3/5	36	235.00	
3/9	37	1,500.00	
3/9	38	210.00	
3/21	39	1,350.00	
3/29	40	195.00	

From the "Banking" drop-down menu, go to the link for Reconcile. Complete the steps for reconciling your March bank statement.

PRINT MARCH REPORTS

Print the following reports for March 20XX.

1. Print March's reconciliation summary.

2. Print March's transaction detail report.

3. Print the March 31, 20XX unadjusted trial balance.

4. Print the March balance sheet.

5. Print the March income statement.

6. Print January 1, 20XX to March 31, 20XX income statement.

Checklist of Printouts Case Problem 1	
	February reconciliation summary
	February transaction list
	February trial balance
	February balance sheet
	February income statement
	March reconciliation summary
	March transaction list
	Unadjusted trial balance
	March balance sheet
	March income statement
	Activity log

Name_______________________________________ **Date**____________

CHECK YOUR PROGRESS, CASE PROBLEM 1

1. On January 31, 20XX, what are your total assets? ____________
2. How much is owed to vendors on February 28? ____________
3. How much do customers owe on February 28? ____________
4. What is the balance in your checking account on February 28 after doing the bank reconciliation? ____________
5. Does the February 28 income statement show a net income or a net loss? ____________
6. Does the March 31 income statement show a net income or a net loss? ____________
7. How much is owed to the Pro Insurance on March 31? ____________
8. What is the balance in the dividends account on March 31? ____________
9. What is the balance in your checking account on March 31? ____________
10. What are the cost of computer supplies on March 31? ____________
11. What is the amount of bank service charges for the first quarter of the year? ____________
12. Was any accounts payable incurred during the month of March? (Circle your answer.) YES NO

Case Problem 2

In Case Problem 2, you complete first quarter adjusting entries and print end-of-quarter reports. Case Problem 2 culminates the recordkeeping activities for your corporation.

If your instructor assigns Case Problem 3, the Student-Designed Project, you will have an opportunity to write transactions for the next month and complete the accounting cycle showing a net loss for your corporation.

END-OF-QUARTER ADJUSTING ENTRIES

Record the following adjusting entries in the general journal (*Hint: "Make Journal Entry" under Banking.).*

Date	*Adjusting Entries*
3/31/20XX	Depreciation on computer equipment, $300.00. (Adjust 1)
3/31/20XX	Insurance expired $210.00. (Adjust 2)

PRINT END-OF-QUARTER REPORTS

1. Print the March 31, 20XX transaction list with splits report.

2. Print the March 31, 20XX adjusted trial balance.

3. Print March's income statement.

4. Print a January 1 through March 31, 20XX income statement.

5. Print March's balance sheet.

6. Print the January 1 through March 31, 20XX general ledger.

7. Print your Activity log.

Checklist of Printouts Case Problem 2	
	March 31, 20XX transaction list by day report
	Adjusted trial balance for March 31, 20XX
	March 1 - 31, 20XX income statement
	January 1 - March 31, 20XX income statement
	March 1 - 31, 20XX balance sheet
	January 1 through March 1 - 31, 20XX general ledger
	Activity log

Name____________________________________ **Date**___________

CHECK YOUR PROGRESS, CASE PROBLEM 2

1. On March 31, 20XX, what is the balance in
2. prepaid insurance? ____________

3. How much is owed to vendors on March 31? ____________

4. How much do customers owe on March 31? ____________

5. What is the balance in your checking account on March 31? ____________

5. Does the March 1 - 31, 20XX income statement show a net income or a net loss? ____________

6. Does the end-of-quarter income statement show a net income or a net loss? ____________

7. At the end of the quarter, what is the total amount of depreciation accumulated on your business' equipment? ____________

8. At the end of the quarter, what is the total amount of repairs? ____________

9. At the end of the quarter, what is the total amount of advertising? ____________

10. What is the total amount of fixed assets on March 31? ____________

11. At the end of the quarter, what is the total amount of net income? ____________

12. At the end of the quarter, what is the total amount of utilities expense? ____________

Case Problem 3

You have completed the recordkeeping for a service business in Chapters 1 through 6 and Case Problems 1 and 2. It is the purpose of Case Problem 3, to have you write the next month's transactions for your business. Your transactions should be written so that your business shows a net loss. Include a bank statement at the end of the month so that you can complete reconciliation.

The chart that follows shows the printouts that you should have after your have completed recording transactions for one month.

Checklist of Printouts Case Problem 3	
	April reconciliation summary
	April transaction list
	April trial balance
	April income statement
	April balance sheet
	April general ledger
	Activity log

Good luck! It is your turn to create the transactions for another month and complete the accounting cycle using QuickBooks Online Edition.

Glossary

Accounts payable	Money the business owes suppliers or vendors. (p. 61)
Accounts payable transactions	Purchases of assets or expenses incurred on credit from vendors. (p. 61)
Accounts receivable	Money owed by customers to the business. (p. 53)
Accounts receivable transactions	Credit transactions from customers. (p. 53)
Balance sheet	A balance sheet is a list of assets, liabilities, and capital of a business as of a specific date. (p. 37)
Browser	The software used on a computer to connect and display information from a website called a server. (p.1)
Chart of accounts	A list of all the accounts used by a company. (p. 28)
Closing entries	The purpose of closing entries is to reset revenue, expense, and dividend account balances to zero. When you record and post closing entries, you are transferring the end-of-year (or end-of-period) balances for the

	revenue, expense, and dividend accounts to retained earnings account. (p. 143)
General journal	The general journal shows the debits and credits of transactions and can be used to record any type of transaction. For purposes of this book, you use the general journal to record adjusting and closing entries. (p. 137)
Income statement	An income statement is where a business reports its revenues and expenses and determines its net income or loss for the period. QuickBooks Online Edition refers to the income statement as the "Profit & Loss" statement. (p. 116)
Integrated Services Digital Network (ISDN)	Faster connections to the Internet are possible using an ISDN line. An ISDN line is a digital network that provides faster transmission of voice, video, and text. (p. 2)
Internet	The worldwide electronic communication network that allows for the sharing of information. The Internet is also called the World Wide Web (WWW) or Web. (p. 1)
Internet Service Provider (ISP)	ISPs can be companies such as America OnLine (AOL), CompuServe, Earthlink, or local providers. Usually for a monthly charge, these companies provide a connection to the email and the Internet. (p. 1)
Modem	An abbreviation of MOdulator/DEModulator. A device that translates the digital signals from your computer into analog signals that can travel over telephone lines. (p. 1)

Vendors	This term refers to businesses that offer credit for assets purchased or expenses incurred. (p. 61)

INDEX

Accounts payable 64, 67
Accounts payable transactions 64, 67
Accounts receivable 53, 67
Accounts receivable transactions 53
Activity log 171
Adding an account 33
Balance sheet 38, 40, 41, 42, 43, 44, 48, 49, 142, 146, 154
Bank type of account 30
Beginning-of-year transactions 146
browser 1
Cash payments: write checks 98
Cash sales: enter sales receipts 96
Cash transactions 96
Changing an account name 36
Chart of accounts 21, 28, 30, 31, 32, 33, 36, 37, 39, 49
Check your progress 14, 45, 67, 127, 155, 172
Closing entries 143, 144
Computer accounting essentials website 5, 21, 51, 75, 135, 161
Copy report text to a spreadsheet program 167
Copying report data to excel 42
Customer information 56, 57,58,59
Customer list 58
Customer overview 53, 55, 56, 59, 67
Customer transactions: create invoice 86
Customization 171
Customizing graphs 168
Customizing options: Display and date 165
Customizing options: Filters 166
Customizing reports 164
December transactions 118
Defaults 51, 52
Deleting an account 31
Displaying the accounts receivable register 92
Displaying the balance sheet 40, 65
End-of-year adjusting entries 137
End-of-year closing entries 143
Editing trial balance 106
Enter bills 78
Exercise 1-1 18
Exercise 2-1 49
Exercise 2-2 49

Exercise 3-1 71
Exercise 3-2 71
Exercise 3-3 71
Exercise 3-4 72
Exercise 4-1 132
Exercise 4-2 132
Exercise 5-1 159
Exercise 5-2 159
Exercise 6-1 178
Exercise 6-2 178
Exercise 6-3 179
Flashcard review 14, 45, 67, 127, 155, 172
Getting started.......... 6, 24, 52, 76, 136, 162
Help screens 40
Home page.......... 52
Income statement.......... 141, 153
Integrated Services Digital Network 2
Internet.......... 1, 2
Internet homework.......... 15, 45, 67, 127, 155, 172
Internet Service Provider.......... 1
Log in 12, 13
Log out 12
Mini interview –web page dialog 29
Memorizing reports.......... 163
modem 1, 2
Multiple-choice 15, 46, 68,128, 156, 174
November transactions 110
oe.quickbooks.com.......... 5
opening balance.......... 21, 29, 35, 38, 39, 41, 44, 47, 48
Preferences.......... 51
Post-closing trial balance 145
Printing end-of-year financial statements 141
Printing December reports 122
Printing January reports 150
Printing November reports 113
Printing October's balance sheet.......... 108
Printing October's income statement.......... 107
Printing October's reconciliation report.......... 103
Printing October's trial balance.......... 105
Printing the adjusted trial balance 140
Printing transaction listing by day: October 103

Purchase returns: enter vendor credits 81
QuickBooks online edition toolbar 28, 30, 31, 40, 41
Receive customer payments 93
Reconcile the bank statement: December 120
Reconcile the bank statement: January 148
Reconcile the bank statement: November 111
Reconcile the bank statement: October 100
Reports 162, 164
Revising the chart of accounts 31
Sales returns and allowances: give credit or refund 90
Setting up the cash account 28
Set preferences for customer statements 55
Set preferences for entering transactions 55, 62
Set up customers 56
Set up products and services 59
Set up tasks 53, 56, 59, 63
Set up vendors 63
Software objectives 5, 21, 51, 75, 135, 161
Transaction list by day report 139, 144, 151
True/False 17, 48, 70, 131,158, 177
Vendor information 66, 68
Vendor list 68
Vendor overview 61, 62, 63, 64, 65, 67
Vendor payments: pay bills 83
Vendor transactions: Enter bills 77
Vendors 61, 67
Web objectives 5, 21, 51, 75, 135, 161